Sociology and Social Justice

SAGE STUDIES IN
INTERNATIONAL SOCIOLOGY

Series Editor Chaime Marcuello Servós (2016–ongoing)
Editor, Department of Psychology and Sociology,
Zaragoza University, Spain

Sociology and Social Justice

Edited by **Margaret Abraham**

SSIS SERIES SAGE STUDIES IN INTERNATIONAL SOCIOLOGY: 65

Los Angeles | London | New Delhi
Singapore | Washington DC | Melbourne

Los Angeles | London | New Delhi
Singapore | Washington DC | Melbourne

SAGE Publications Ltd
1 Oliver's Yard
55 City Road
London EC1Y 1SP

SAGE Publications Inc.
2455 Teller Road
Thousand Oaks, California 91320

SAGE Publications India Pvt Ltd
B 1/I 1 Mohan Cooperative Industrial Area
Mathura Road
New Delhi 110 044

SAGE Publications Asia-Pacific Pte Ltd
3 Church Street
#10-04 Samsung Hub
Singapore 049483

Editor: Natalie Aguilera
Editorial assistant: Eve Williams
Production editor: Katherine Haw
Copyeditor: Chris Bitten
Proofreader: Neil Dowden
Indexer: Charmian Parkin
Marketing manager: Susheel Gokarakonda
Cover design: Wendy Scott
Typeset by: C&M Digitals (P) Ltd, Chennai, India

Introduction © Margaret Abraham 2019
Chapter 1 © Michael Burawoy 2019
Chapter 2 © Edgardo Lander 2019
Chapter 3 © Vishal Jadhav 2019
Chapter 4 © Nira Yuval-Davis 2019
Chapter 5 © Bandana Purkayastha 2019
Chapter 6 © Tina Uys 2019
Chapter 7 © Raewyn Connell 2019
Chapter 8 © Ngai Pun, Jenny Chan and
       Mark Selden 2019
Chapter 9 © Margaret Abraham and
       Mathew John 2019
Chapter 10 © Marta Soler-Gallart 2019
Chapter 11 © Evangelia Tastsoglou and
       Maria Kontos 2019
Chapter 12 © Mikhail F. Chernysh 2019
Chapter 13 © Brigitte Aulenbacher and
       Birgit Riegraf 2019

First published 2019

Library of Congress Control Number: 2018939424

British Library Cataloguing in Publication data

A catalogue record for this book is available from
the British Library

ISBN 978-1-5264-6401-9
ISBN 978-1-5264-6402-6 (pbk)

Contents

About the Editor

Margaret Abraham (Editor) is Professor of Sociology at Hofstra University and President of the International Sociological Association (ISA), 2014–2018. Her teaching and research interests include gender, globalization, immigration and domestic violence. She has published in various journals. Her books and special volumes include *Speaking the Unspeakable: Marital Violence Among South Asian Immigrants in the United States* (Rutgers University Press, 2000); *Contours of Citizenship: Women, Diversity and the Practices of Citizenship* (Ashgate, 2010); *Making a Difference: Linking Research and Action* (*Current Sociology*, April 2012); *Interrogating Gender, Violence, and the State in National and Transnational Contexts* (*Current Sociology*, July 2016). She has been engaged in research and activism for more than 25 years.

About the Contributors

Brigitte Aulenbacher is Professor of Sociology, Chair of the Department for the Theory of Society and Social Analyses at the Johannes Kepler University of Linz, Austria, and co-editor (with Klaus Dörre) of *Global Dialogue*. Her research includes contemporary capitalisms; inequality and gender; labour, care and science. Her current project is 'Decent Care Work? Transnational Home Care Arrangements', co-chaired with Helma Lutz and Karin Schwiter, 2017–2020. Recent publications include: *Öffentliche Soziologie, Wissenschaft im Dialog mit der Gesellschaft*, co-edited with Michael Burawoy, Klaus Dörre and Johanna Sittel (Campus, 2017); *Care and Care Work – A Question of Economy, Justice and Democracy*, co-edited with Birgit Riegraf (Special issue, *Equality, Diversity and Inclusion*, Emerald Publishing, 2018).

Michael Burawoy teaches sociology at the University of California, Berkeley. He has been an ethnographer of industry in Zambia, US, Hungary and Russia. He developed the ideas in this chapter while travelling to many countries during his term as President of the ISA, 2010–2014.

Jenny Chan is Assistant Professor of Sociology in the Department of Applied Social Sciences at the Hong Kong Polytechnic University. Prior to joining the university, she was a Lecturer of Sociology and Contemporary China Studies at the School of Interdisciplinary Area Studies, and a Junior Research Fellow of Kellogg College, University of Oxford. She serves as an elected Board Member of the International Sociological Association's Research Committee on Labor Movements (2014–present), an Editor of the *Global Labour Journal* (2015–2018) and a Contributing Editor of the *Asia-Pacific Journal* (2015–present). She has recently received the Early Career Scheme grant from the Research Grants Council of Hong Kong and the John Fell Oxford University Press Research Fund.

Mikhail F. Chernysh, born in 1955, graduated from Moscow Linguistic University in 1977. In 1981 he enrolled in the graduate course of the

Institute of Sociological Studies (now Federal Center of Theoretical and Applied Sociology). In 2005 he defended a doctoral thesis entitled 'Institutions and Social Mobility'. He currently holds the position of the First Deputy Director for Research and Education at the Federal Center of Theoretical and Applied Sociology of the Russian Academy of Sciences. He was elected First Vice-President of the Russian Society of Sociologists and is an author of two monographs and over 130 articles in peer-reviewed journals.

Raewyn Connell is Professor Emerita, University of Sydney, and Life Member of the National Tertiary Education Union. She has taught at Macquarie University, Flinders University and elsewhere. Recent books are *Southern Theory* (2007) about social thought in the postcolonial world; *Confronting Equality* (2011) about social science and politics; *Gender: In World Perspective* (3rd edn, with Rebecca Pearse, 2015); and *El género en serio* [Gender for Real] (2015). Other works include *Schools & Social Justice*, *Ruling Class Ruling Culture*, *Gender & Power, Masculinities* and *Making the Difference*. Her work has been translated into 19 languages. Details at www.raewynconnell.net and Twitter @raewynconnell.

Vishal Jadhav has been teaching sociology for the last 15 years and is presently attached to Tilak Maharashtra Vidyapeeth, Pune. He also taught at the Department of Sociology, University of Mumbai for a short period. He has had several research articles published in national and international journals. He was the co-recipient of the Dudley Seers Memorial award of 2006.

Mathew John (PhD) is a civil servant by profession, but sought to escape the routine of the bureaucrat's life by taking a sabbatical to study the history as well as the sociological and political impact of the Indian railways on life in India. His interest in rural India was sparked during his tenure as a member of a government claims tribunal which decides claims of monetary compensation for citizens killed or injured in incidents due to the railways' negligence. During his term, he heard chilling tales about the travails in rural India that made him delve further into rural angst. He is currently associated with an educational institution that specializes in training elementary school teachers.

Maria Kontos is a Senior Research Fellow at the Institute of Social Research at Goethe University, Frankfurt/Main. She has coordinated several EU projects on gender and migration; among others the 6th FP project

'Integration of Female Immigrants in Labour Market and Society. Policy Assessment and Policy Recommendations'. She has published on biographical methods, integration policies and integration discourses, migration and gender, welfare policy and care, ethnic entrepreneurship and family businesses. Among her recent publications are the co-edited volumes, *Paradoxes of Integration: Female Migrants in Europe* (Springer, 2012) and *Migrant Domestic Workers and Family Life: International Perspectives* (Palgrave Macmillan, 2015).

Edgardo Lander is a sociologist. He is Professor at the Universidad Central de Venezuela (Caracas) and a Visiting Professor at the Universidad Andina Simón Bolívar (Quito). He is a Fellow of the Transnational Institute (Amsterdam) where he currently participates in the New Politics Project. He is part of the Permanent Working Group on Alternatives to Development as well as the Global Working Group on Alternatives to Development (Rosa Luxemburg Foundation). He is an active participant in the World Social Forum process. He has been a left-wing political activist for many decades.

Ngai Pun is Professor of Sociology at University of Hong Kong. She is the author of *Made in China: Women Factory Workers in a Global Workplace* (2005), for which she won the C.W. Mills Award. This book was translated into French, German, Italian, Polish and Chinese. Her latest publication is *Migrant Labor in China: Post-Socialist Transformations* (2016). She has written numerous articles in *Modern China, China Journal, China Quarterly, China Perspectives, Global Labour Journal, Cultural Anthropology, Positions, Feminist Economics, Current Sociology, Inter-Asia Cultural Studies, The South Atlantic Quarterly, The Third World Quarterly*, and *Work, Employment and Society*, among others.

Bandana Purkayastha is Professor of Sociology & Asian American Studies, University of Connecticut. She has published over 60 books, peer-reviewed articles and chapters on intersectionality, migration, transnationalism, violence, peace, religion and human rights, including the recent monographs *Migration, Migrants, and Human Security* and *Human Rights in Our Backyard: Injustice and Resistence in the US* (which was awarded the Gordon Hirabayashi book award by the American Sociological Association (ASA) human rights section). She recently completed a Fulbright–Nehru fellowship to India on water, inequalities and rights. She has been recognized for her research and teaching through multiple national awards, including a 2016 ASA section's career award. She has served in many elected, invited and appointed positions including President, Sociologists for Women in Society; ASA representative to ISA; expert consultant to WHO (on female migrants and health). https:sociology.uconn.edu/Purkayastha.html.

Birgit Riegraf is Professor of Sociology and President of the Paderborn University, Germany. Research fields include feminist theories, theories of social justice, sciences, higher education and organizational sociology. Her current projects are and 'Social Conditions of the Development of Technologies' (2015–2020) and 'Theory in Gender Studies' (with Barbara Rendtorff, Paderborn University, 2016–2020). Recent publications include *Sorge: Arbeit, Verhältnisse, Regime* [Care: Work, Relations, Regimes], Soziale Welt 2, with Brigitte Aulenbacher and Hildegard Theobald (2014); 'Gender in/and the Neoliberal University', *Gender and Research*, with Kadri Aavik and Blanka Nyklová (2017); *Leistung und Gerechtigkeit*, with Brigitte Aulenbacher, Maria Dammayr, Klaus Dörre, Wolfgang Menz and Harald Wolf (2017).

Mark Selden is Senior Research Associate in the East Asia Program at Cornell University, a Research Fellow at the Asian/Pacific/American Institute at New York University and an Editor of the *Asia-Pacific Journal*. He researches the modern and contemporary geopolitics, political economy and history of China, Japan and the Asia Pacific. His work ranges broadly across themes of war and revolution, inequality, development, regional and world social change, social movements and historical memory. His books include: *China in Revolution: The Yenan Way Revisited*; *The Political Economy of Chinese Development*; *Chinese Village, Socialist State*; *Chinese Society: Change, Conflict and Resistance*; *The Resurgence of East Asia: 500, 150 and 50 Year Perspectives*; and *The Cambridge History of Communism*.

Marta Soler-Gallart, Harvard PhD, is Professor of Sociology at the University of Barcelona and Director of the research community CREA. She is President of the Catalan Sociological Association, Vice-president of the European Sociological Association and serves on the Governing Board of the European Alliance for the Social Sciences and Humanities. She is the main researcher of the H2020 European Union funded research SOLIDUS, on solidarity in Europe in times of crisis. Her most recent publication is *Achieving Social Impact: Sociology in the Public Sphere* (Springer, 2017). She is Editor of the ISA journal *International Sociology*.

Evangelia Tastsoglou LLM, PhD, is Professor of Sociology, Coordinator of the International Development Studies Program at Saint Mary's University, Halifax, Canada, and a member of the ISA Research Council and EC. Her research engages feminist and intersectional perspectives on women, gender and various aspects of international migration, Canadian immigration, violence, citizenship and diasporas. Recent publications include: *Interrogating Gender, Violence, and the State in National and Transnational Contexts* (Current Sociology Monographs, Sage, July 2016); *The Warmth of the Welcome: Is Atlantic Canada a Home away from Home for Immigrants?* (Cape Breton University Press, 2015); *Contours of Citizenship: Women, Diversity and the Practice of Citizenship* (Ashgate, 2010); and *Women, Gender and Diasporic Lives* (Lexington Books, 2009).

Tina Uys is Professor of Sociology and Head of Department at the University of Johannesburg. She was Vice-President (National Associations) of the International Sociological Association (2010–2014) and is the current President of Research Committee 46 (Clinical Sociology) for the term 2014–2018. During 2013 she was a Fulbright Visiting Scholar at George Washington University in Washington, DC and at the University of Cincinnati, Ohio. She is rated as an Internationally Acclaimed Researcher by the South African National Research Foundation. She specializes in clinical sociology with a particular focus on advancing the sociological understanding of whistleblowing. She is currently working on a book titled *Whistleblowing and the Sociological Imagination*.

Nira Yuval-Davis is Emeritus Professor and an Honorary Director of the Centre for Research on Migration, Refugees and Belonging (CMRB) at the University of East London and an editor of the book series 'The Politics of Intersectionality' (Palgrave Macmillan). She has written extensively on theoretical and empirical aspects of intersected nationalisms, racisms, fundamentalisms, citizenships, identities, belonging/s and gender relations in Britain and Europe, Israel and other settler societies. Her work has been translated into more than ten languages. Among her written and edited books are *Woman-Nation-State* (1989); *Racialized Boundaries* (1992); *Unsettling Settler Societies* (1995); *Gender and Nation* (1997); *Warning Signs of Fundamentalisms* (2004); *The Politics of Belonging: Intersectional Contestations* (2011); and *Bordering* (forthcoming).

Introduction

Sociology and Social Justice

Margaret Abraham

The concept of social justice has garnered the attention of the world, from academics and activists, to government organizations and international communities. It has captured the emotions of people and nations; it has empowered individuals and groups, and formed movements for social change. While an exact definition is elusive, the notion of social justice is integral to the discourse and practices of equality, liberty, rights, fairness, freedom, and justice. It is a key component in identifying and addressing the changes that are needed across the globe, looking at social structures and processes, at the relations and dynamics that shape society. Social justice, as a concept, draws our attention to embedded issues of wealth and resource distribution, oppression, representation, recognition, access, and safety (see Fraser, 2003; Harvey, 1973; Lister, 2007; Nussbaum, 2006; Okin, 1994; Rawls, 1979; Sen, 2009; UN, 2007; Young, 1990).

Sociologists around the world have a long history of generating research that can affect social change. Building on a spectrum of thinkers, today's sociologists expand both the conceptual and empirical work that continues to enrich our understanding of these issues. We recognize the real transformations that can be brought about by groups of sociologists working together and by engaging with publics (Burawoy, 2005). Feminist sociologists, and postcolonial and critical race theorists have, in highlighting a spectrum of inequalities and injustices, already provided important theoretical frameworks, methodologies, and practices to proactively address the need for social change (see Abraham, 2002; Abraham and Purkayastha, 2012; Abraham and Tastsoglou, 2016; Alatas and Sinha, 2017; Aulenbacher et al., 2014; Bhambra, 2007; Collins, 1990; Connell, 2011; de Sousa Santos, 2015; Kannabiran, 2012; Mies, 1986; Patel, 2010; Richie, 2012; Romero and Stewart, 1999; Tastsoglou and Dobrowolsky, 2006; Yuval-Davis and Werbner, 1999).

Likewise, recent sociologists have documented social movements in different parts of the globe that have challenged dominant structures and various types of systemic discrimination (Bringel and Domingues, 2015; Garita, 2016; Maney and Abraham, 2008/2009; Porta et al., 2006).

Society in the 21st century continues to evolve, with both old and new issues and dilemmas; particularly those connected to globalization and unfettered neoliberal capitalism. Addressing this requires a global community and the development of a *contextual global sociology*, which recognizes that issues are often global but require understanding within specific contexts. Inequalities, violence, authoritarianism, xenophobia, discrimination, and injustices across the world require our analysis and intervention. Through community and collaboration, as sociologists, we strengthen our voice as societal stakeholders, and strengthen our commitment toward building a more just society.

The world is waking up to these issues faster than books can be written or published; however, we owe it to that world to offer our academic rigor as a foundation for greater awareness and deeper understanding. This book aims to contribute in such a way, presenting various concepts and practices of social justice from diverse contexts. Its genesis can be traced back to the 2nd ISA Forum in Buenos Aires, in 2012, with the theme of 'Social Justice and Democratization'. The stories of despair and resistance against injustice, corruption, and state oppression, raised at that time, resonated with the participants. This collection brings together scholars who describe, analyze, and illustrate the various facets of social justice that are found in their worlds and specializations. It also includes some revised plenary presentations from the 2nd ISA Forum. The authors contextualize social justice at particular points in time, and in various parts of the world, and in this way we can find an array of insights suggesting the many ways forward.

In this introduction, I identify some of the major fault lines impacting social justice in our time. Next, the contributions of the authors in this volume are outlined. I conclude by emphasizing the need for sociologists to use their teaching, research, and actions to envision and forge pathways forward, and to mobilize civil society, governments, and institutions. Despite the challenges and complexities of these issues, collaboratively we can take action and build a more just world.

Understanding Social Justice through Injustice

Social justice has been at times dismissed as an amorphous ethical concept lacking the precision needed to integrate into a coherent strategy for meaningful action (Hayek, 1976). Although premised on the principle that all human beings are of consequence and worthy of consideration, the definition of what exactly is just or unjust remains contentious and unresolved. Nevertheless, the term social justice is increasingly used, often as a catchall or node around which the need for systemic change toward greater awareness and social decency aggregate. John Rawls writes, 'Justice is the first virtue of social institutions, as truth is of systems of thought' (1979, p. 3). For Rawls, it is about assuring the protection of equal access to liberties, rights, and opportunities. Defining exactly what constitutes justice is subject to debate and diverse perspectives (see Azmanova, 2011; Bankston, 2010; Feagin, 2001; McGary, 1999; Niedt, 2013; North, 2006). It is ever changing, contested and contextual. Justice is also a process, the principles of which no single theory can delineate.

In the same way, social justice means different things to different people. There are those who believe that the ends of social justice are met only if equality is absolute in every circumstance, and others who believe that social justice is debased if it does not factor in the needs of the disadvantaged. Libertarian and meritocratic theories of social justice accord pre-eminence to individual freedom and choice, and affirm that an unfettered market is socially desirable. There are many other perspectives that emerge from an argument that uncontrolled markets are exploitative and uncaring about the needs and interests of any but the very rich. There are many meanings, approaches, and opinions about social justice, and a comprehensive coverage is beyond the scope of this introduction.

John Rawls is often invoked as a reference point for theories of social justice. He represents the humanistic, egalitarian view of justice, as he writes, 'In justice as fairness, society is represented as a cooperative venture for mutual advantage' (Rawls, 1979, p. 84). Rawls recognizes the utility of market efficiency, and the protection it offers to freedom of choice; the fact that 'a system of markets decentralizes the exercise of economic power' (1979, p. 272). As the market is not suited to answer the claims of need, however, Rawls advocates for the setting up of an institutional framework that provides safeguards against the formation of unreasonable market power, writing that 'inequalities of wealth and authority are just only if they result in compensating benefits for everyone, and in particular the least advantaged members of society' (1979, p. 14). Rawls puts forward a liberal theory of social justice that underscores both individual liberty and egalitarian democracy. The egalitarian view of justice is carried on by Amartya Sen; however, Sen moves away from Rawls, arguing that practical reasoning should explore how to reduce injustice and advance justice rather than aim at characterizing the perfectly just institution (Sen, 2009).

Iris Marion Young situates her theory of social justice in relation to multiple forms of oppression: exploitation, marginalization, powerlessness, cultural imperialism, and violence. She defines oppression as, 'the institutional constraint on self-development, and domination, the institutional constraint on self-determination' (1990, p. 37). For Young, empowerment is primary in the conceptualization of social justice. Meanwhile, Nancy Fraser draws attention to the increasing importance of 'politics of recognition' (1997, p. 3). Her theoretical framework focuses on issues of 'redistribution' and 'recognition' as being the 'co-fundamental and mutually irreducible dimension of justice' (Fraser and Honneth, 2003, p. 3).

The fault lines of social justice move and shift beneath our feet, while always addressing questions of structure and agency, building theory upon social conditions, relations, and processes. These include topics such as: feminism and gender, cultural studies, critical race theory, ableism, indigenous and postcolonial theories, and many more (see Abraham et al., 2010; Abraham and Purkayastha, 2012; Abraham and Tastsoglou, 2016; Bhambra, 2007; Collins, 1990; Connell, 2011; Crenshaw, 1991; Garita, 2016; Mies, 1986; Mohanty, 2004; Purkayastha, 2012; Rege, 2006; Richie, 2012; Tastsoglou and Dobrowolsky, 2006; Yuval-Davis and Werbner, 1999). Many of these emphasize the politics of recognition and representation, and address the importance of intersectionality, citizenship, and community. The needs of inclusion and belonging also play as great a role in conceptualizations of social justice, as access to resources.

An Unequal World

The emergence of the information and high-tech economy has redefined notions of time, space, distance, boundaries, and borders. By altering the social and natural environments, these developments have also changed patterns of global interaction. States have increasingly enabled and accommodated the economic forces of the global market economy – often in the interests of global/transnational elites – but with few opportunities or protections for the poor, marginalized, and dispossessed. Deep social inequalities exist not only across economic regions, but also within societies, including some of the wealthiest economies. In the United States, the top 1% controls 40% of the total wealth and almost a quarter of the country's total income. Millions remain uninsured or with inadequate health coverage, and even as this is written the situation becomes ever more precarious.

In 2016, an Oxfam study indicated that the wealth of the 62 richest people in the world was equal to the wealth of the poorest 50% (3.5 billion people), but in 2017 that disparity had increased to where the 8 wealthiest individuals now own assets equal to the world's most impoverished 50% (Oxfam, 2017). The wealthiest 1% own 48% of the world's wealth, and 20% of the world's population owns a staggering 94.5% of the world's wealth. The Multidimensional Poverty Index (MDI) points to 1.6 billion living in acute poverty, and this number is increasing every day.

Although these statistics are troubling, not everyone agrees that the unequal distribution of wealth is an injustice. The libertarian free-market philosophy accords predominance to individual freedom and choice, and affirms that an unfettered market is socially desirable as it increases productivity by encouraging people to work hard. These statistics, and the realities of inequality in wealth distribution are, however, both a result and indication of how prevalent this perspective has been and is at the present juncture in history. The champions of the free market have held sway for a long time, but there are signs of growing resistance, at least to the systemic aspects within neoliberal capitalism that have exacerbated inequality through structures of injustice and exploitation.

Neoliberalism – the Ideology of Market Power

The dispossessed are everywhere; however, from a global perspective the exploitations of capitalism have landed primarily in the Global South. Tellingly, this comprises the erstwhile-colonized dominions, reinforcing a pattern of exchange whereby those who historically exploited the colonies continue to be beneficiaries in the present global order. The profit- and market-oriented neoliberal construct of free trade, privatization, and corporate globalization has contributed to an entrenchment of economic inequalities and exclusions, and has reinforced the hegemony of a class of governing elites. The glaring disparities have laid bare the dark underbelly of what Jacques Derrida calls 'liberal hegemony' (Derrida, 1994).

While neoliberal globalization has increased productivity, consumer choice, and has removed some barriers to global interactions, it has also exposed its grave limitations in delivering social justice. Profit, not people, is at the heart of the neoliberal agenda. The tyranny of the market has spawned asymmetry and discord in global and human relations. Modern day slavery continues through the use of children in sweatshops, who toil for global brands. Behind the appearance of all nations belonging to the same international community, as neighbors in a global village, is the bleak reality that neoliberalism has created a great wealth disparity among states and people. It has fostered economic regimes in which the goods are consumed and the benefits enjoyed by small privileged groups, while the crumbs are left for the overwhelming majority. Glaring wealth disparities accentuated by cutbacks on welfare and social provisions, combine with economic fissures and widespread pauperization, to produce a socially divided, unsettled world (Harvey, 2005). In reality, it is a world more governed by corporate elites than it is by elected officials.

Those controlling the levers of power – the transnational corporate apparatus and state complex – set the neoliberal agenda in favor of corporations and financial institutions. In most countries, the state acts as the executive wing of transnational and multinational corporations; and the neoliberal scheme formally sanctions the market control of the state (Rose, 1996). This underscores the importance of sociologists working to ensure that, at least in the domain of universal human rights, there is a coming together and collaboration in order to rally our collective power for change. It is important to find congruence even in the views of disparate ideological adversaries.

A striking example of this is the 1948 Declaration of Human Rights, under the aegis of the United Nations Organization, which was the first definitive enunciation of a global concern for the well-being of all citizens of the world. This work must continue so that every human being is bestowed with basic human rights. This is perhaps the most pressing concern for those striving for a more just world. As Nelson Mandela (1990)[1] pointed out, 'to deny people their human rights is to challenge their very humanity'. The area of human rights and human rights violations is one of the most urgent domains for social justice research.

Human Rights Violations

The 1948 Declaration of Human Rights has continued to develop since its inception through multiple resolutions recognizing the need to further consolidate the efforts of the international community, to eradicate poverty, promote full employment and decent work, to promote gender equality and access to social well-being, and to secure justice for all (UN,

2006). Even the most remarkable and forward-thinking laws, statutes, charters, policies, and institutions, however, will not bring about true social justice and change, until there is a societal and cultural shift in orientation, away from the interests of the individual and toward a consideration of others. There can be little progress in enhancing social justice without both individual freedom and a genuine concern for the common good.

The espousal of human rights is about all of us, as global citizens, demonstrating a sincere concern for our fellow human beings, but our scorecard is evidence of an abject failure to match action to sentiment. Integral to the debate around issues of social justice, human rights are based on the doctrine that 'all human beings are born free and equal in dignity and rights' (UDHR, 1948). Human rights go beyond individual rights and parochial concerns, to embrace a universal notion of equal, social, economic, and cultural rights and entitlements. The notion of human rights 'recognizes the inherent dignity and the equal and inalienable rights of all members of the human family' (UDHR, 1948), and this is a formidable challenge in the search for a just society.

Violence Against Women

Violence against women and gender-based violence is another area of social justice that requires the continued attention of sociologists. While there have been strides made in women's legal rights, vast numbers of women continue to be denied control over their own bodies, are excluded from decision making, and denied protection from violence. Millions of women still live in places where domestic violence is not considered a crime, and, even where there has been some progress made in the legal frameworks, millions of women report experiencing violence in their lifetimes and usually at the hands of an intimate partner (Abraham and Tastsoglou, 2016). The systematic targeting of women for brutal sexual violence is also characteristic of modern-day warfare and conflict zones. Human rights and human security still seem to be out of reach for large numbers of women.

The consequences of poverty and lack of opportunity can also be particularly severe for LGBTQ, ethnic, and religious minorities. On 9 March 2015, UN Secretary General Ban Ki-moon presented to the General Assembly a report on Violence Against Women (UNITE, 2015), pointing to its persistence 'at alarmingly high levels' in all countries. The report also noted that a rise in 'extremism and conservatism' has contributed to the further degradation of human rights for women. Although it is normalized in many societies, violence against women is a major infringement of a woman's human rights, which are supposed to be protected by international, regional, and national human rights law. This violence perpetuates unequal opportunity, inequality at a fundamental level, and diminished economic, political, and social 'citizenship' rights for women and girls.

The State as Oppressor

Our world is a cauldron of wars, conflicts, and injustices. Corruption and coercion are routinely used to protect the hegemony of the power elite across nations, and to maintain the status quo. The ability to brand groups, nations, and individuals as terrorists is the prerogative of the wealthiest states. The powerful get to decide who is right and who is wrong, in a world that has situated itself 'post-truth'.

Ours is a deeply divided world where even peaceful dissent is viewed with suspicion. Conflicts and the 'war on terror' provide the perfect alibi for curtailing individual freedoms and rights. Under the guise of national security, stringent anti-terror laws abridging liberties and democratic freedom are enacted to selectively target disruptive elements in society upon suspicion alone. Through rhetoric and media, state surveillance has been sold to the public and normalized. Ethnic, religious, and racial profiling is used to identify 'troublemakers'. The war on terror, like the war on drugs, becomes a veil used to justify the oppression of states against their own people (Loo, 2011). There is a terrifying increase in hyper nationalism, and social phobias and discriminations. The precarious nature of life that has arisen from the predatory economics of globalization and neoliberalism has produced divided societies prone to fear, desperation, and violence. Egalitarian ideals have been transformed into Orwellian instruments to serve the purposes of the powerful. At the very heart of social justice is the issue of power being used by the oligarchic plutocracies to expand and reinforce their dominion, with little concern for those who are harmed in the process.

Mobilization and Mass Movements

The many abuses of power and the disregard for the most vulnerable in society has inspired a wide array of protests and social movements

(Maier and Lebon, 2010; Moghadam, 2012; Robbins and Jamal, 2016; Thörn, 2007). Many movements are working to achieve a social justice wherein all members of society have basic human rights and equal access to the benefits of their society, especially within the context of their everyday lives. Mass protest movements over the last few years have revolved around opposition to tyranny, and the chasm between the privileged and the rest. Rising unemployment rates, gendered violence, and other injustices have struck a chord. The trajectories and outcomes of protests and movements, however, are not uni-linear or immediate. The Occupy Wall Street (OWS) movement, for example, drew attention to issues of inequalities and injustices but did not transform society or impact growing social and economic structures as profoundly as it had hoped to. The Arab Spring protests were largely successful in drawing attention to a call for social justice, and dismantling repressive elitist regimes; however, in the post-revolution period, the historical socio-cultural tensions – including gender discrimination, inter-religious conflict, and religious fundamentalism – have reasserted themselves in many places.

Yet there is hope for contemporary movements to build upon the momentum and consolidate further change. These movements continue to challenge dominant structures and various types of systemic discrimination, including protests led by 'indignados' in Portugal and Spain, indigenous movements around the world, Black Lives Matter, #SayHerName, Ni Una Menos, and the #metoo movement. Stark inequalities and injustices have led to growing unrest across the world and particularly among those who face the brunt of economic exploitation, violence, social exclusion, and political repression. Issues of social justice are being pushed to the forefront of almost every agenda. Across the globe people are mobilizing and challenging oppressive social, political, and economic regimes with indomitable courage. These protests and movements are witnessing the use of new social media, as well as the growth and proliferation of horizontal and transnational networks of individuals and NGOs. In some societies the struggle to achieve social justice has involved efforts to dismantle the existing state apparatus, and to either establish or reform electoral systems and systems of governance so that they are more representative and accountable to different groups. In other societies, movements have increased public participation in state policy formation and implementation. Still others have highlighted and sought to end entrenched systems of violence and discrimination.

The Chapters

Just as the public gathers to form mass movements, so too must sociologists gather, to pool our knowledge and resources, and to offer a movement of our own. It is essential to consider diverse perspectives and practices around social justice, from different contexts around the globe. Only in this way can we gain a greater understanding of what is needed to create a more just world. The contributing authors of this volume raise important considerations for *conceptualizing*, *connecting*, and *contextualizing* social justice and its corresponding discourse.

Conceptualizing social justice is complex and defies reduction or universal definitions. Rather, the challenge and appeal of the concept of social justice is in its very ability to encompass the diversity of perspectives, pragmatics, and possibilities for what it takes to create a just world. In exploring this, the authors draw upon existing frameworks, but also extend and rethink what it takes to address issues of access, redistribution, recognition, representation, empowerment, and citizenship.

Likewise, *connecting* concepts and practices of social justice requires a critical understanding of the divisive dynamics of contemporary globalization, including multiple forms of exclusion, subordination, and disempowerment. The authors highlight larger systemic patterns of injustices often associated with neoliberal globalization, as they describe specific ways in which these are experienced. Theoretically, they frame and document social injustices connecting human rights violations and forms of political and economic inequality at the local, national, and global level. A common thread among many of the chapters is the persistence of gender inequalities and injustices, and the challenges met in addressing them. This is just one of the many connections that can be made between chapters and perspectives, offering bridges to greater collaboration.

Finally, *contextualizing* social justice enables us to see the historical, geographical, economic, political, and cultural influences that shape social justice perceptions and practices throughout time and space. Contextualizing topics and sites – such as social movements, education, human rights, democratization, labor, organizations, suicides, care work, and cyber space – provides specific insights into the various causes, conditions, structures, relations, processes, and manifestations of social justice. It can also help us to (re)conceptualize the dimensions of social justice discourse, allowing us to find areas where we can offer each other greater support and understanding.

The authors in this volume demonstrate the relevance and necessity for sociologists to become influential in shaping the 21st century. The chapters are deliberately left to stand on their own, rather than be divided into sections. This is out of recognition for the variety of intersecting topics and issues that are addressed by many of the authors, and also to show the breadth of what is understood by social justice. Through these chapters, the questions that are posed and the theoretical frameworks that are used compel us to consider the challenges confronting society from a number of different perspectives, with a diverse array of sites where social justice issues occur. There are similarities and differences in the goals, processes, and outcomes associated with each of the chapters, and this allows us an opportunity to rethink, reappraise, and refocus our own sociologist/scholar/activist commitments to advancing social justice in the 21st century.

In Chapter 1, Michael Burawoy, a key proponent of public sociology, emphasizes the important role that sociology needs to play in these times when third-wave marketization has damaged the conditions of work and is destroying society(s). He advocates for a sociology *of* movements, that can offer a unifying vision *for* movements in their relentless struggle to counter market injustice with new forms of participatory democracy. In seeking to understand and explain the connection between social movements and unregulated marketization Burawoy looks to the work of Karl Polanyi.

Edgardo Lander in Chapter 2, contends that the era in which democracy was compatible with capitalism is coming to an end. He explains how a set of exceptional historical conditions made the golden era of liberal democracy possible, an era in which capitalist democracy achieved social justice, democratization, and legitimation, but ultimately led to its demise. Lander argues that the logic of democracy and human rights, as well as the cultural transformations of the counterculture, led to systematic retaliation from neoconservatives and neoliberals who saw the 'excesses' of democracy as severe threats to the capitalist regime. For Lander, financial capital expansion today is based on an increasing appropriation and concentration of global wealth, resulting in growing global inequality and the destruction of democracy.

Chapter 3 by Vishal Jadhav examines the assumptions and historical necessities that led to the framing of a discourse around social justice in the post-independence period in India, whereby equality could be achieved through the elimination of poverty, and as a pathway for development.

He examines the implications of this discourse on social justice in the context of the implementation of the Mahatma Gandhi National Rural Employment Guarantee Act (MGNREGA). He explores the sociological imagination that was incorporated into the Act, around the lives of the poor, their social and political resources, and social capital. Jadhav contends that the present discourse on social justice and right to employment is implicit in MGNREGA, and discusses its implications.

Nira Yuval-Davis, in Chapter 4, views social justice in transversal terms, emphasizing the importance of an intersectional and situated sociological analysis. She highlights critical issues in the relationship between human rights and gender relations. Her chapter focuses on these issues within the context of global feminist politics; however, she also notes the relevance of more generic problems related to the notion of human rights, and its links to democracy and social justice. She addresses the constructed contestations that take place between human rights, women's rights, and cultural rights, raising reservations around the notion of rights as bearers of emancipatory struggles, and the problematics of human rights and human rights organizations as a mode, or tool, of global governance.

Chapter 5 by Bandana Purkayastha directs our attention to the social justice principle in the Universal Declaration of Human Rights, based on the notion of human dignity, and relates it to the notion of human security. Addressing impediments to human security, both latent and manifest, she argues that although charters and conventions create the 'lattice-work for claiming and protecting human rights', human rights must be understood using a framework that extends beyond charters and conventions. To exemplify, Purkayastha draws on lessons from movements that challenge routine violence and work toward building and sustaining peace. The focus of attention, she argues, should be on the conditions that enable people to build secure lives, and which reflect their dignity within contexts of freedom and social justice.

Tina Uys in Chapter 6 looks at whistleblowing within an organization as an issue of rights and social justice. She considers what factors encourage organizational members to take a stand against the abuse of power, thereby ensuring organizational justice for all within the organization. Exploring the connections between belief systems and whistleblowing intentions, she explores the influence of culture on whistleblowing, in particular the African philosophy of *ubuntu* and its emphasis on restorative justice. She explains how the act of whistleblowing contributes to restoring organizational justice in the workplace by strengthening its ethical foundation.

Whistleblowing is thus viewed as an attempt to pursue social justice by rectifying possible wrongs, helping to ensure fairness of processes and outcomes.

Social justice within the sphere of education is examined by Raewyn Connell in Chapter 7. She provides a critical lens on the postcolonial era school system, with its expansionist approach, where neoliberal politics are forcefully transforming education systems along market lines, and are accompanied by new divisions, controls, and a spectrum of new problems. Reminding us of times when sociology engaged with mass education, specifically sociology's influential role in compensatory education, 'war on poverty', development education, gender equity, and multicultural education, Connell points to the growing irrelevance of sociological theories pertinent to wealthy, conservative countries in Europe trying to tackle the main problems of social justice in education today. To address sociology for social justice, she then asks us to consider what resources would sociology need to effectively engage with the world of hungry markets, and schools struggling for equality.

In Chapter 8, Ngai Pun, Jenny Chan, and Mark Selden draw our attention to the realm of labor exploitation, oppression, and a search for social justice. They use the example of Foxconn production facilities in China to illustrate the global factory regime characterized by new forms of labor use and the labor control of a new generation of Chinese workers that have led to multiple suicides. They argue that the use of rural migrant labor is enabled by a state–capital alliance at Foxconn workplaces, which conceals the new political technology of labor use and its consequences on the lives of workers. They describe the despair, grievances, and tragic acts of defiance that arise within these global sweatshops.

Margaret Abraham and Mathew John, in Chapter 9, focus on suicides in India that resonate beyond the personal and draw attention to larger issues of social injustice and inequality. They look at the historical, structural, and political conditions and social relations that contribute to inequalities. They specifically focus on the social, cultural, and political significance of protest suicides that have raised public consciousness regarding iniquities. This includes farmer suicides by individuals facing mounting debts, the inability to get credit from banks, and the failures of their cash crops – all factors associated with neoliberal policies. Also discussed is the role of public sociologists in deconstructing the dynamics of such suicides and their societal implications, as well as helping to bring about transformative change in collaboration with civil society.

In the following chapter, Chapter 10, Marta Soler-Gallart discusses the role of public sociology in reducing inequalities and injustice by engaging with the narratives of individuals and groups who have historically experienced disenfranchisement, marginalization, and 'othering'. Drawing examples from women constructed as the 'other', she demonstrates how these 'other women' contribute important insights toward overcoming gender violence and inequality, and participate in shaping feminist theory, promoting more egalitarian relationships with the researchers and scholars who work with them for social change. Hence, she asserts that rigorous and reliable dialogue between social science researchers and social actors can contribute to better social policies for social justice, and for the betterment of society.

In Chapter 11, Evangelia Tastsoglou and Maria Kontos use cyberspace as the site to consider issues of social justice. Drawing on dimensions of social justice discussed in the literature, they analyze how a newspaper electronic discussion forum in the context of the economic crisis in Greece illustrates claims for redistribution, recognition, and representation within the framework of struggles for social justice. Their particular lens offers a look into the micro-level experience of the crisis, by individuals expressing their perspectives, frustrations, visions, and strategies for themselves and the nation through electronic technology and cyberspace. Tastsoglou and Kontos assert that despite citizenship practice being limited by the online forum, it is still significant in illustrating the spontaneous, 'information', conversational constructions of the crisis, and a spectrum of strategies (including 'exit' strategies) and options that can potentially strengthen citizens' voices to mobilize for social change.

Mikhail F. Chernysh, in Chapter 12, provides a window into social justice perceptions in the contemporary Russian context. He notes that in Russia, the debate around social justice tends to be reduced to a discussion of Russian culture that 'ostensibly preserves traditions of egalitarian distribution'. Drawing on data from an all-Russian survey, Chernysh argues against a cultural interpretation of social justice. Rather, he notes that the survey data point to a spectrum of social justice interpretations based on the notion of justice as being direct action to rectify injustice, with justice understood as proceeding from law. One of the major challenges for Russian society is then the gap between formal and informal institutions, which guarantees fair distribution of goods and services. He further points to the inadequacy in enforcing formal distribution by key social agents, and the existence of informal alternatives whereby high resource groups hold the advantage.

In the final chapter, Chapter 13, Brigitte Aulenbacher and Birgit Riegraf point to the resurgence of interest in the justice theme that is prompted by an increase in experiences of injustice. This is seen as arising from changes in working and living conditions, which entail social vulnerabilities and existential insecurities. In their chapter, they consider whether increased sociological attention to justice issues requires that it be contextualized in terms of the developments in contemporary capitalism. This is discussed with reference to sociological studies on Europe. Aulenbacher and Riegraf use the field of care and care work to illustrate this, citing examples from Austria and Germany. They end by discussing how societal developments require us to reflect on the connections between a critique of daily life, a societal critique, and the relationship between local and global perspectives in sociology.

Together, these authors illuminate the complexity of social justice as a concept. Through their various frameworks, perspectives and rich empirical examples, taken from around the world, we see the strength that lies in a plurality of perspectives and practices. The three underlying themes in this book are: *social justice and democratization*; *social justice and human rights*; and *social justice and economic inequalities*. All of these are currently of interest and are being debated and discussed among sociologists and other academics, activists, and the public, around the world. Through the authors' insightful writings, this book will hopefully stimulate the sociological imagination to challenge and continue these discussions further. By shedding light and awareness upon the ongoing social inequalities that exist, we expand our possibilities for achieving social justice.

The Way Forward

Ours is a world that is increasingly under siege. The best ideals of humanity have yet to be fully realized. Neither the predominance of the state nor the unbridled power of the market has been successful in creating a better world. Social movements have had some success, but greed and ignorance are endlessly creative, giving rise to new forms of injustice and global problems. With the institutions ordained to protect our freedoms – the judiciary, the media – all too often compromised, there is a growing sense that the glimmer of hope remaining is in the third estate: the people. The building of an equal and just society is not possible without the active participation of the main stakeholder, civil society. Though the obstacles are formidable, the silent majority will need to step forward if democracy is to achieve its egalitarian essence. In these difficult times we need to dream big, and, as sociologists, provide the insights and solutions that make a difference for positive change.

As sociologists we have an ethical and professional responsibility to use our sociological imagination, the array of professional tools at our disposal, and to partner in addressing the many obstacles that challenge our world. In this aspiration, the sociological perspective, which is sensitive to all voices, is critical for deepening our understanding of the complicated social, economic and political challenges of our times. There still exists a gap between the sociological imagination and an actual transformation in society. While there are many good theories, the task that remains is to harness our knowledge and collaborate with those who are outside the privileged sphere of academe. To affect change we must offer what we have, and also learn from those who meet and know the challenges of turning theory into practice, or those who live the hard realities that we only study. What is most essential is a proactive, action-oriented, co-ordination with fellow citizens to enable a positive change in the current 'hegemony' in global society.

In the 21st century, public sociologists can contribute to changing society for the better only through 'knowledge mobilization', and organizations such as the International Sociological Association can play a key role in facilitating this. As the global association for sociologists, ISA should help knit together sociologists across the world in a joint endeavor of mutual cooperation and collaboration. We have a responsibility to translate our specialized knowledge in ways that the broader public can access, relate to, and be inspired by. The times we live in need, more than anything else, a sense of connection and community support. We must offer what we know, but we must also offer an example, building equitable, collaborative relationships between colleagues and larger publics. The diversity of our sociological research and perspectives can and should effectively provide a deeper understanding of the current conditions of inequality and offer paths forward toward a more just world.

Note

1   Nelson Mandela in his address to the Joint Session of the House of Congress, Washington, DC, 26 June 1990.

Acknowledgements

This book is dedicated to Mary Abraham, my Amma, and to all those committed to social justice. I am grateful to the many people who made this book happen. Various unanticipated factors delayed its completion, but even so, in the end we were able to move forward and bring it to fruition. My thanks to the contributing authors and to the anonymous reviewers. Special thanks to SSIS Series Editor Chaime Marcuello Servós, for his encouragement and insights; to Vineeta Sinha, ISA Vice President Publications; to Robert Rojek, SAGE Senior Publisher and the SAGE team; Katherine Haw, Senior Production Editor; Chris Bitten, copyeditor; Eve Williams, editorial assistant; and, to all involved in the book production. Sujata Patel reviewed and accepted the monograph proposal as then SSIS Series editor. A very special thanks to Amanda Hester for her invaluable input and meticulous copy editing; and, to Taisha Abraham for her incisive comments. Most importantly, thanks to my life partner, Pradeep Singh, for his support in all ways, including reading the manuscript, offering constructive critique, and assisting with the final formatting!

References

Abraham, M. and Purkayastha, B. (2012) Making a difference: Linking research and action in practice, pedagogy, and policy for social justice. *Current Sociology, 60*, 1–19.

Abraham, M. and Tastsoglou, E. (2016) Interrogating gender, violence, and the state in national and transnational contexts: Framing the issues. *Current Sociology Monograph, 64*(4), 517–553.

Abraham, M., Ngan-ling Chow, E., Maratou-Alipranti, L., and Tastsoglou, E. (eds) (2010) *Contours of Citizenship: Women, Diversity and Practices of Citizenship.* Farnham: Ashgate.

Abraham, T. (2002) *Women and the Politics of Violence.* New Delhi: Har-Anand Publications.

Alatas, S.F. and Sinha, V. (2017) *Sociological Theory Beyond the Canon.* London: Palgrave MacMillan.

Aulenbacher, B., Riegraf, B., and Theobald, H. (eds) (2014) *Sorge: Arbeit, verhältnisse, regime* [Care: Work, Relations, Regimes], Soziale Welt, Sonderband 20. Baden-Baden: Nomos.

Azmanova, A. (2011) De-gendering social justice in the 21st century: An immanent critique of neoliberal capitalism. *European Journal of Social Theory, 15*(2), 143–156.

Bankston, C. (2010) Social justice: Cultural origins of a perspective and a theory. *The Independent Review, 15*(2), 165–178.

Bhambra, G. (2007) *Rethinking Modernity: Postcolonialism and the Sociological Imagination.* New York, NY: Palgrave Macmillan.

Bringel, B.M. and Domingues, J.M. (eds) (2015) *Global Modernity and Social Contestation*. London: Sage.

Burawoy, M. (2005) 2004 American Sociological Association Presidential Address: For public sociology. *American Sociological Review, 70* (February), 4–28.

Collins, P.H. (1990) *Black Feminist Thought*. New York, NY: Routledge.

Connell, R. (2011) Gender and social justice: Southern perspectives. *South African Review of Sociology, 42*(3), 103–115.

Crenshaw, K. (1991) Mapping the margins: Intersectionality, identity politics, and violence against women of color. *Stanford Law Review, 43*(6), 1241–1299.

De Sousa Santos, B. (2015) *If God were a Human Rights Activist*. Stanford, CA: Stanford University Press.

Derrida, J. (1994) *Specters of Marx: The State of the Debt, the Work of Mourning, and the New International* (P. Kamuf, trans.). London: Routledge.

Feagin, J. (2001) Social justice and sociology: Agendas for the 21st century. *American Sociological Review, 66*, 1–20.

Fraser, N. (1997) *Justice Interruptus: Critical Reflections on the 'Postsocialist' Condition*. New York, NY: Routledge.

Fraser, N. (2003) Social justice in the age of identity politics: Redistribution, recognition, and participation. In: N. Fraser and A. Honneth (eds), *Redistribution or Recognition? A Political–Philosophical Exchange* (pp. 7–109). London: Verso.

Fraser, N. and Honneth, A. (eds) (2003) *Redistribution or Recognition? A Political–Philosophical Exchange*. London: Verso.

Garita, N. (2016) *Pueblos in Movement: Feminist and Indigenous Perspectives*. Available at: https://isaconf.confex.com/isaconf/forum2016/webprogram/Paper83737.html (accessed 12 April 2018).

Harvey, D. (1973) *Social Justice and the City*. Athens, GA: University of Georgia Press.

Harvey, D. (2005) *A Brief History of Neoliberalism*. Oxford: Oxford University Press.

Hayek, F. (1976) *Law Legislation and Liberty Volume 2: The Mirage of Social Justice*. Chicago: University of Chicago Press.

Kannabiran, K. (2012) *Tools of Justice: Non-discrimination and the Indian Constitution*. New Delhi: Routledge.

Lister, R. (2007) Social justice: Meanings and politics. *Benefits, 15*(2), 113–125.

Loo, D. (2011) *Globalization and the Demolition of Society*. Glendale, CA: Larkmead Press.

Maier, E. and Lebon, N. (2010) *Women's Activism in Latin America and the Caribbean: Engendering Social Justice, Democratizing Citizenship*. New Brunswick, NJ: Rutgers University Press.

Maney, G.M. and Abraham, M. (2008/2009) Whose backyard? Boundary making in NIMBY opposition to immigrant services. *Social Justice, 35*(4), 67–81.

McGary, H. (1999) *Race and Social Justice*. Cambridge: Wiley-Blackwell.

Mies, M. (1986) *Patriarchy and Accumulation on a World Scale*. London: Zed Books.

Moghadam, V. (2012). *Globalization and Social Movements: Islamism, Feminism, and the Global Justice Movement*. Lanham, MD: Rowman & Littlefield.

Mohanty, C.T. (2004) *Feminism Without Borders: Decolonizing Theory, Practicing Solidarity*. Durham, NC: Duke University Press.

Niedt, C. (2013) *Social Justice in Diverse Suburbs: History, Politics, and Prospects*. Philadelphia, PA: Temple University Press.

North, C.E. (2006) More than words? Delving into the substantive meaning(s) of 'Social Justice' in education. *Review of Educational Research*, *76*(4), 507–535.

Nussbaum, M. (2006) *Frontiers of Justice: Disabilities, Nationalities, Species Membership*. Cambridge, MA: Belknap Press.

Okin, S.M. (1994) Gender inequality and cultural differences. *Political Theory*, *22*(1), 5–24.

Oxfam (2017) *An Economy for the 99%*. Available at: https://d1tn3vj7xz9fdh.cloudfront. net/s3fs-public/file_attachments/bp-economy-for-99-percent-160117-en.pdf (accessed 12 April 2018).

Patel, S. (2010) *The ISA Handbook of Diverse Sociological Traditions*. London: Sage.

Porta, D., Andretta, M., Mosca, L., and Reiter, H. (2006) *Globalization from Below: Transnational Activists and Protest Networks*. Minneapolis, MN: University of Minnesota Press.

Purkayastha, B. (2012) Human rights, global visions. In: A. Omara-Otunnu, S. Mobilia, and B. Purkayastha (eds), *Human Rights: Voices of World's Young Activists* (pp. 1–9). Kolkata: Frontpage Publications.

Rawls, J. (1979) *A Theory of Justice*. Cambridge, MA: Belknap Press.

Rege, S. (2006). *Writing Caste/Writing Gender: Reading Dalit Women's Testimonios*. New Delhi: Zubaan.

Richie, B. (2012) *Arrested Justice: Black Women, Violence and America's Prison Nation*. New York, NY: New York University Press.

Robbins, M. and Jamal, A. (2016) The state of social justice in the Arab world: The Arab uprisings of 2011 and beyond. *Contemporary Reading in Law and Social Justice*, *8*(1), 127–157.

Romero, M. and Stewart, A.J. (1999) *Women's Untold Stories: Breaking Silence, Talking Back, Voicing Complexity*. New York, NY: Routledge.

Rose, N. (1996) The death of the social? Re-figuring the territory of government. *Economy and Society*, *25*(3), 327–356.

Sen, A. (2009) *The Idea of Justice*. Cambridge, MA: Belknap Press.

Tastsoglou, E. and Dobrowolsky, A. (2006) *Women, Migration and Citizenship: Making Local, National and Transnational Connections*. Farnham: Ashgate.

Thörn, H. (2007) Social movements, the media and the emergence of a global public sphere: From anti-apartheid to global justice. *Current Sociology*, *55*, 896–918.

UDHR (1948) *Universal Declaration of Human Rights*. Available at: www.ohchr.org/EN/ UDHR/Documents/UDHR_Translations/eng.pdf (accessed 12 April 2018).

UNITE (2015) *UN Secretary General's Campaign to End Violence Against Women*. Available at: www.un.org/en/women/endviolence/situation.shtml (accessed 14 October 2015).

UN (2006) *The International Forum for Social Development Social Justice in an Open World; The Role of the United Nations*. Available at: www.un.org/esa/socdev/documents/ ifsd/SocialJustice.pdf (accessed 12 April 2018).

UN (2007) Resolution adopted by the General Assembly, 26 November.

Yuval-Davis, N. and Werbner, P. (1999) *Women, Citizenship and Difference*. London: Zed Books.

Young, I.M. (1990) *Justice and the Politics of Difference*. Princeton, NJ: Princeton University Press.

1

A New Sociology for Social Justice Movements

Michael Burawoy[1]

Max Weber was clear that the rise of formal rationality, whether in the form of bureaucracy, law, or mass democracy, does not compensate subject populations for their economic and social oppression. Rather, formal rationality that extends equal rights to all perpetuates the injustices they experience. Weber argued that the only way this might be challenged was through informal means, what he sometimes called 'Kadi-justice' (Weber, 1946, p. 221). These informal means, however, whether they are public opinion or communal action, are often manipulated and staged from above. Weber was very suspicious of what today we call social movements, which he saw as arising from an 'incoherent mass' driven by 'irrational sentiments' (Weber, 1946, p. 221). His theory of collective action belongs to the first wave of social movement theory that stretches from Durkheim and Weber, to Smelser and Parsons for whom collective action was an irrational response to social change.

The second wave of social movement theory, drawing on Marxism, viewed social movements as rational in their pursuit of interests outside parliamentary politics, and they were successful insofar as they managed to develop resources, including an appropriate strategic framing, to achieve their goals. Here sociologists were in pursuit of a general theory of collective action – a theory true across time and space – that took the social, political, and economic context as a background variable. It was only 'new social movement' theory, associated with such writers as Alain Touraine, that considered the context – in his case postindustrial society or the programmed society – as defining the form of collective action.

Today, we need to move toward a third wave of social movement theory that centers on a new context, namely 'neoliberalism' – a nebulous concept that expresses the invasion of markets into all arenas of social and political life. In order to understand contemporary movements for social and economic justice it is necessary, therefore, to define 'neoliberalism'. Here I will take Karl Polanyi's (2001) *The Great Transformation* as my point of departure. But first let me explore the way marketization propels movements for social justice.

From Marketization to New Social Movements

Social justice and democratization are especially pertinent themes in Latin America, which for many years was ruled by military dictatorships. The transition to democracy, fought for bravely by so many, has been a major and indisputable advance. Democracy has not, however, fulfilled all its promises. Primarily, this is because the fall of political dictatorship has been followed by yet another dictatorship – the dictatorship of the market through structural adjustment. In its wake came wave upon wave of injustice and inequality that have inspired Latin Americans, sociologists among them, to battle for a deeper democracy. We see this, for example, in the schemes of participatory budgeting in Brazil, in the Piquetero Movement and factory occupations in Argentina, in the ethnic democracy of Bolivia, and in the student movement of Chile. There has been a relentless struggle to counter market fundamentalism with new forms of participatory democracy.

This Latin American history of the last 30 years is now being replayed across the world. Responding to the silent encroachment of markets, not least in the Arab world, where the self-immolation of Mohamed Bouazizi in Tunisia on 17 December 2010, sparked uprisings across the region in Tunisia, Egypt, Yemen, Libya, Syria, and Bahrain. Calling for 'bread, freedom and social justice' these uprisings may have been revolutionary in their demands but they have not delivered the outcomes they sought. All eyes were fixed on Egypt, where national rebellion gave rise to a frail democracy that was then hijacked by the military. Difficult though it has been to overthrow dictatorships, the real problems only begin after their overthrow, problems that Latin America has been wrestling with for more than three decades.

Partially inspired by these movements, the Indignados of Southern Europe have stood up to the regimes of austerity, imposed by ruling parties aided and abetted by regional and international financial agencies. In 2011 and 2012 we witnessed a wave of remarkable protests that might be allied to trade unions in Portugal, to more anarchist politics in Spain, to Grillo populism in Italy, and to a massive general strike in Greece. There has also been the rise of a neo-fascist Golden Dawn. All of these, however, can be seen as different responses to economic insecurity, unemployment, debt, and dispossession.

The Occupy Movement that began in 2011 made explicit this connection between poverty, capitalism, and the need for protest. Lodged in public spaces, it targeted the 1% that runs the world economy. The movement started in Zuccotti Park, targeting Wall Street, the home of finance capital, and spread across the US, travelled to Europe, Latin America, and Asia. In India, for example, peasantries fought against their dispossession by collusive arrangements between finance capital and the Indian state to form Special Economic Zones, many of which now lie moribund. In China today the engine of growth is no longer the flood of cheap migrant labor to the towns but land appropriation and real estate speculation for the urbanization of rural areas. Again protests, perhaps less known, are spreading across rural China even if they have not been very effective in arresting the formation of a rentier class. Similar struggles are familiar in Latin America, where the expansion of international mining has not only displaced populations but also polluted water and air.

Finally, we must pay attention to the student movement, most spectacularly emanating from Chile, that has been struggling against the marketization of education at all levels. Here, in this most unequal of societies, students are the vanguard of a society throttled by accumulating private debt. We see similar struggles in England, where students have faced soaring fees, also spreading across Europe as financialization and regulation begin to corrode what were once strongholds of public education. In Argentina, the heartland of the public university, the legacy of the Cordoba Revolution of 1918, which opened public education to all – open admissions, no fees, and democratic election of administrators – still holds strong. Elsewhere, in Latin America, however, student movements have had to grow and contest the degradation of higher education.

Should these and other contemporary movements be considered in isolation, perhaps reflective of local or national context, or can we say they all share something to make them global in character? Do they share common features that would justify considering them an expression of a particular historical epoch? In this chapter I answer both questions in the affirmative. Therefore, the first task is to identify a common set of repertoires that define a singular wave of protest that spans the globe.

Common Political Repertoires

These new social movements of the 21st century are responses to various social injustices, stemming from the different forms and dimensions of marketization, but they gain expression and consciousness, not in the economic but in the political arena. The pursuit of political goals, however, is driven by economic deprivation and dispossession. Let us consider some of the features they share.

First, they have in common what differentiates them. They all have a national specificity, whether it be a struggle against dictatorship, against austerity or against the privatization of education. They are framed by their national, political terrains, which exhibit regional patterns – Southern Europe, Middle East, Latin America, South-East Asia, etc. Yet, at the same time, these movements are also globally connected through social media and even traveling ambassadors. Movements have become an inspiration to each other even if their frame of reference is usually national.

Second, they derive from a common inspiration, the idea that electoral democracy has been hijacked by capitalism, and more specifically by finance capital. Governments are beholden to finance capital, which effectively paralyzes electoral democracy – capitalist in content and democratic in form. In Zygmunt Bauman's (2000) terms, there is a separation of power and politics, so that power is concentrated in the hands of the capital–state nexus, while electoral politics is reduced to an ineffectual ritual.

Third, the movements reject formal democracy to adopt direct democracy, sometimes called pre-figurative politics that involve horizontal connections as much as vertical struggles. The General Assemblies of participatory democracy have been the cellular foundation of many of these movements. The challenge, then, is to bring unity and a broader vision to these autonomous, and often separatist struggles. They have had varying success in connecting themselves to wider publics and even when they do accomplish this it is only for short periods.

Fourth, while much has been made of virtual connections, these make concrete real space more rather than less necessary. To be effective, virtual communications requires its complement – the assembly points of public space, Zuccotti Park in New York, Catalunya Square in Barcelona, Tahrir Square in Cairo, Taksim Square in Ankara, and others. These assembly points were crucial to establish dense and creative communities, and the planning of new and novel actions. Social media becomes an auxiliary if essential tool of communication.

Fifth and finally, the occupation of public space has made these social movements vulnerable to a severe and repressive backlash from police, often backed by the military. This repression is consistent with the more general destruction of the public and valorization of the private, but it has prompted a continuing cat and mouse game between movements and police. These movements, however, will not go away. They are a form of 'liquid protest' that disappears here only to reappear elsewhere. We have to look at them as part of a connected global movement, connected by social media that provide the vehicle for continual reorganization and flexibility. The fear of coercion has been replaced by despair and anger.

The conjecture of this chapter is that these social movements can, and indeed must, be understood in terms of their differentiated responses to the marketization that has become a defining feature of our era. This requires a *new sociology of movements* that attends not only to the political repertoires they deploy but also to the pressures of marketization to which they are a response. Such a sociology should advance a unifying vision for these movements, a vision they so badly need, and one that knits them together in a common project – *a new sociology for social movements*. Moreover, the very context and practice of sociology now finds itself subject to pressures of commodification. Sociologists can no longer pretend that we are objective observers, outside society. We are part of the world we study and, therefore, we cannot avoid becoming an interested party, taking sides in social conflict even as we study it. If not, sociology will become irrelevant and disappear. Marketization is undermining the conditions of our own existence just as it is destroying society, and we need to connect the two before it is too late – *sociology itself becomes a social movement*. We take up each of these challenges in turn.

A New Sociology of Social Movements

To better understand this connection between today's social movements and unregulated marketization, I turn to Karl Polanyi's *The Great Transformation*. Written in 1944, explaining the continued existence of capitalism but without denying its problematic character, *The Great Transformation* can be considered a revision of Marx's *Communist Manifesto*, written a century earlier. Polanyi argues that the experience of commodification is more profound and immediate than the experience of exploitation, which, as Marx himself argued, was hidden from those who were supposed to rebel against it. In effect Polanyi takes Marx's theory of commodity fetishism, namely that market exchange obscures its ties to production, more seriously than Marx who thought such illusions would eventually dissolve in the class struggle. For Polanyi, the source of destruction lies with the market rather than with production. The expansion of the unregulated market threatens to destroy society, which then reacts in self-defense. This is what Polanyi (2001, Chapter 12) calls the 'double-movement', and what I will refer to simply as the 'counter-movement' against the market.

One of the virtues of Polanyi's theory, like Marx's, is that it ties the micro-experience of people to world systemic movements of capitalism. The lynchpin of the connection lies in the idea of the fictitious commodity (Polanyi, 2001, Chapter 6) – a factor of production, which when subject to unregulated exchange loses its use value. For Polanyi labor is but one such fictitious commodity; the others are land and money. Today these factors of production are subject to an unprecedented commodification that even Polanyi could not anticipate.

When labor is subject to unregulated exchange, i.e. when it is commodified, when it is hired and fired at will with no protection, when the wage falls below the cost of the reproduction of labor power and when the laborer cannot develop the tacit skills necessary for any production, so the use value of labor also falls. Polanyi writes:

> For the alleged commodity 'labor power' cannot be shoved about, used indis-criminately, or even left unused, without affecting also the human individual who happens to be the bearer of this peculiar commodity. In disposing of a man's labor power the system would, incidentally, dispose of the physical, psychological, and moral entity 'man' attached to that tag. Robbed of the pro-tective covering of cultural institutions, human beings would perish from the effects of social exposure; they would die as the victims of acute social dis-location through vice, perversion, crime, and starvation. (2001, p. 76)

The issue, therefore, is not exploitation but commodification. Indeed, as Guy Standing (2011) has eloquently demonstrated, the problem today is the disappearance of guaranteed exploitation, and in its place the rise of precarity, not just within the proletariat but climbing up the skill hier-archy. Precarity is part of the lived experience behind all contemporary movements – from the Arab Uprisings to the Indignados, from the Occupy Movement to student movements.

One of the conditions for the commodification of labor power is dis-possession from access to alternative means of subsistence, that is to the elimination of all social supports – including minimum wage legislation, unemployment compensation, and pensions but also access to land. The separation of labor from land provides for the commodification of both labor and land, which according to Polanyi threatens the viability of the human species. 'Nature would be reduced to its elements, neighborhoods and landscapes defiled, rivers polluted, military safety jeopardized, the power to produce food and raw materials destroyed' (Polanyi, 2001, p. 76). But, actually, Polanyi is also sensitive to problems resulting from the absence of markets.

> The economic argument could be easily expanded so as to include the conditions of safety and security attached to the integrity of the soil and its resources – such as the vigor and stamina of the population, the abundance of food supplies, the amount and character of defence materials, even the climate of the country which might suffer from the denudation of forests, from erosions and dust bowls, all of which, ultimately, depend upon the factor land, yet none of which respond to the supply-and-demand mechanism of the market. (Polanyi, 2001, p. 193)

These prescient comments point to the inability of markets to defend the integrity of nature, which accords well with recent arguments that climate change represents one of the biggest market failures of our time.

When it comes to the plunder of nature, the destructiveness of markets has led to a host of struggles, especially in the Global South, from land-less movements in Latin America to popular insurgency against Special Economic Zones in India, and protests against land speculation and expro-priation in China. Throughout the world the mining of natural resources has generated militant opposition from communities whose lives and live-lihoods are being threatened. It takes place within cities, too, against such processes as gentrification and the attempt to build global cities, both of which involve the expulsion of the marginal from their homes. We have to extend the commodification of land to the commodification of nature more broadly, including the commodification of water that generated water wars in countries as far apart as South Africa and Bolivia, protest against market solutions to climate change, so-called carbon trading, and most recently against fossil fuel extraction through fracking.

Polanyi regarded money as a third fictitious commodity. For Polanyi money is what makes market exchange possible, but when it itself becomes the object of exchange, when the attempt is to make money from money then its use value as a medium of exchange is undermined. He writes,

'Finally, the market administration of purchasing power would periodically liquidate business enterprise, for shortages and surfeits of money would prove as disastrous to business as floods and droughts in primitive society' (Polanyi, 2001, p. 76). Polanyi was especially concerned that fixed exchange rates between currencies organized through the gold standard would create economic rigidities within national economies while going off the gold standard would create chaos and radical uncertainty. Today, we see how finance capital again becomes a prominent source of profit, making money from money, whether it be through micro-finance, loans to nation states, student loans and mortgages, or credit cards. The extraordinary expansion of debt eventually and inevitably brings about bubbles, which just as inevitably pop. The creation of debt only further intensifies insecurity and immiseration, feeding the protest of the Occupy Movement across the globe.

There is a fourth fictitious commodity – knowledge – that Polanyi did not consider. The theorists of postindustrial society, pre-eminently Daniel Bell (1976), recognized knowledge as an ever-more-important factor of production giving pride and place to the university as its center of production. Bell did not, however, anticipate the way that the production and dissemination of knowledge would be commodified, leading the university to sell its knowledge to the highest bidders, biasing research toward private rather than public interests. Knowledge has become a commodity, and universities now cultivate students as customers who pay ever-increasing fees for instrumental forms of knowledge. The university reorganizes itself as a corporation, which maximizes profit not only through increasing revenues, but through the cheapening and degrading of its manpower, reducing tenured faculty, and increasing the employment of low-paid adjunct faculty (which the university itself produces). Universities also have begun outsourcing services, all the while expanding its managerial and administrative ranks. The protests emanating from the university, from Chile to Quebec – be they from students or faculty – center on its privatization and the distortion of the production and dissemination brought on by commodification.

Contemporary social movements, therefore, can be understood through the lens of these four fictitious commodities, through the creation of the fictitious commodity through different forms of *dispossession*, through the reduction of the fictitious commodity to an *object of exchange* that annihilates its commonly understood purpose, and through the new forms of *inequality* commodification produces. Any given movement may organize itself in the political realm, but its driving force lies in the experience of commodification. But commodification is not a singular phenomenon, it is made up of the combination or articulation of the ways land, labor, money, and knowledge are commodified. There is no one-to-one relation between social movement and a given fictitious commodity, but each movement is the product of the relation among fictitious commodification. For the last 40 years we have been experiencing intensified commodification extended ever more deeply into human life. The wave of protests that have arisen to challenge this round of marketization, however, do not yet add up to a Polanyian counter-movement that would contain or reverse marketization. For that, there needs to be a far greater self-consciousness and vision among the participants, calling for a sociology for social movements.

A New Sociology for Social Movements

Touraine's (1988) theory of social movements was also a theory for social movements. At the center of his recast sociological theory were social movements, making history themselves, what he called 'historicity'. The sociologist was no longer outside society, studying its inherent laws of change, but inside society heightening the self-consciousness of movements in the fashioning of history. This reflected a period – postindustrialism – in which there was confidence in human agency to direct history through the state or civil society. There was an underlying optimism that the galloping wild horse of capitalism could somehow be tamed and directed to human ends. That has all disappeared. We are now living in an era in which markets run amok, devastating all that stands in their way. A sociology for social movements must begin by understanding this period of unconstrained marketization.

We need, therefore, to situate Polanyi's fictitious commodities within a wider framework of the history of capitalism. The essence of *The Great Transformation* lies in an argument about the dangers of the expansion of the market, namely that it leads to a reaction from society that can be of a progressive character (social democracy, New Deal) but also of a reactionary character – fascism and Stalinism. Polanyi's history has one long expansion of the market, starting at the end of the 18th century, destroying society along the way, and leading to a defense of society, secured through a counter-movement directed by states that regulate the market, arising in response to the economic crisis of the 1930s – states that include regimes of social democracy and New Deal as well as fascism and Stalinism.

Polanyi couldn't imagine humanity would dare to risk another round of market fundamentalism. Yet, that is just what has happened, starting in the middle 1970s, and developing on a global scale, leaving few spaces of the planet unaffected. The rising concern with globalization expresses the global reach of markets.

It is important, however, to understand that this is not the first wave of marketization. Indeed, examining Polanyi's own history suggests it is not even the second, but rather the third wave. Where Polanyi saw a singular wave spreading over a century and a half, we can now discern two distinct waves. One advances through the first half of the 19th century and was turned back by the labor movement in the second half of that same century, and a second wave that advanced after World War I and was reversed by state regulation in the 1930s extending into the 1970s, which in turn inaugurated a third wave of marketization that has yet to be contained. These waves of marketization become deeper over time as their scale increases, but they also involve different combinations of the fictitious commodities. The counter-movement to first-wave marketization in the 19th century was dominated by the struggle to decommodify labor. In England this assumed the form of the factory movements, cooperatives, Owenism, trade-union formation, and the Labour Party (Polanyi, 2001, Chapter 14). These local struggles spread, melded together, and compelled changes in state policy.

Three Waves of Marketization and their Counter-movements

The success of labor led to a crisis of capitalism, resolved through imperialist strategies and World War I, which was followed by a renewed offensive of capital against labor, leading to the recommodification of labor. The assault of the market spread to the loosening of constraints on international trade through currencies pegged to the gold standard that, in turn, led to uncontrollable inflation and the renewal of class struggles. The upshot was a variety of regimes that sought to regulate markets through the extension of social rights, as well as labor rights.

These regimes, whether social democratic, fascist, or Soviet lasted until the middle 1970s at which time they faced a renewed and mounting assault from capital not only against the protections labor had won for itself but also against state regulation of finance, marked by the end of Bretton Woods. Indeed, we can see how the offensive against labor across the planet, but especially in the North, led to a crisis of

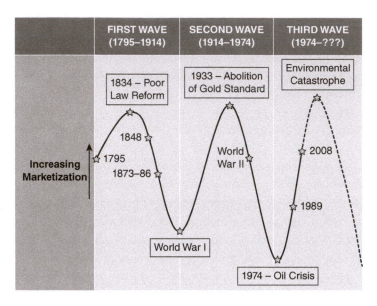

Figure 1.1   Three waves of marketization

overproduction that did not lead to renewed Keynesian politics but to the financialization of the economy via the creation of new moneys that could be extended to individuals in the form of credit (credit cards, student loans, and above all subprime mortgages). This also led to enterprises and countries generating unprecedented levels of debt. The bubble burst when the debtors – whether individuals, enterprises, or countries – could no longer deliver on their interest payments. There were few limits to what finance capital could commodify – from minerals to water, from land to air – creating the environmental catastrophe that the planet now faces. The solution to create new markets in the rights to pollute and destroy the atmosphere – the so-called carbon markets – has not proven to be a solution but a way of making money from the deepening ecological crisis.

Third-wave marketization has gone far deeper than second-wave marketization in the commodification of labor, nature, and money. Moreover, to turn something into a commodity requires first that it be disembedded from its social and political moorings. Labor had to be dispossessed from its supports in the state, peasants had to be dispossessed from access to their land, people had to be dispossessed of access to their own body (so that their organs can be sold). This dispossession requires, in short, the escalation of violence perpetrated by states on behalf of capital, and direct deployment of violence by capital. Violence is at the heart of third-wave marketization in a way that Polanyi never anticipated.

The question now is whether the expansion of the market will generate its own counter-movement. It certainly generates multiple reactive movements, but when and how they will add up to a counter-movement is an entirely different matter. For that we need to develop a sociology that establishes their interconnection – a sociology built on the relation between capitalist accumulation and market expansion. What I have offered here are the building blocks of such a theory – the specificity of third-wave marketization as the underlying cause of social movements, and third-wave marketization understood as the articulation of four fictitious commodities – labor, nature, finance, and knowledge.

Sociology as Social Movement

In underlining the fourth fictitious commodity – knowledge – I am pointing to the transformation of the conditions of knowledge production. What relative autonomy the university possesses is rapidly evaporating in the face of its commercialization. We in the academy can no longer pretend to stand outside society, making it an external object of examination. Academics are irrevocably inside society and we, therefore, have to decide on whose side we are. Those disciplines that are best able to exploit market opportunities are the ones to benefit – the bio-medical sciences, engineering, law, and business schools – and they become the more powerful influences within the university at the potential cost of the social sciences and humanities.

The social sciences, however, do not form a homogeneous block. Ironically, economics has created the ideological justification of market fundamentalism – the very force that is destroying the university as an arena for the independent pursuit of knowledge. Political science, concerned with political order, now aspires to be an extension of economics, reflecting the increasingly collusive relation between markets (and especially finance capital) and nation states. Of course, there are dissidents within both fields, and they play an important role, but the dominant tendency is the endorsement of market fundamentalism through the embrace of utilitarianism. Sociology, too, has not escaped efforts to turn it into a branch of economics, but the anti-utilitarian tradition within sociology from Marx, Weber, and Durkheim all the way to Parsons, Bourdieu, feminism, and postcolonial theory are so well entrenched that economic models have made few inroads.

Sociology was born together with civil society, in an arena of institutions, organizations, and movements, which are neither part of the state nor of the economy. But we should be careful not to romanticize civil society as being some coherent, solidary whole as though it were free of exclusions, dominations, and fragmentations. It is Janus-faced, and can aid in the expansion of the market and state, just as it can also obstruct and even contain that same expansion. This is where sociology is situated – its distinctive standpoint is civil society – examining the economy and state from the perspective of their consequences for civil society, as well as the ways in which civil society supports the economy and the state. Like civil society, sociology looks two ways. On the one side it examines the social conditions of the existence of markets and states. On the other side, along with such neighboring disciplines as anthropology and geography, it can also take a critical stand against the unregulated expansion of the state–market nexus.

In the context of the rationalization and commercialization of the university, sociology is the one discipline whose standpoint viz. civil society behoves it to cultivate a community of critical discourse about the very nature of the modern university, but also conduct a conversation with publics beyond the university, making it accountable to those publics without losing its commitment to its scientific research programs. As the membrane separating the university from society becomes ever thinner, failure to counter-balance the commercialization of the university will end with the destruction of the university as we know it. It is in this sense that we must think of sociology as a social movement as well as scientific discipline, calling for a critical engagement with the world around. To sustain this dual and contradictory role the discipline must develop its own mechanisms for internal dialogue, mechanisms that appear at the local level within the university, at a national level, and most importantly at a global level. Building such a global sociology requires the development of a global infrastructure that fosters dialogue and outreach. In this way we can produce a third-wave sociology to meet the theoretical and practical challenges of third-wave marketization, and to halt the Third World War that is being waged on communities across the planet.

Note

1   This chapter is derived from a talk given at the 2nd Forum for the International Sociological Association in Buenos Aires, 1 August 2012. Many of the ideas in this chapter were developed in dialogue with graduate students in the sociology department at Berkeley – Marcel Paret, Adam Reich, Mike Levien, Julia Chuang, Herbert Docena, Andrew Jaeger, Zach Levenson, Gabe Hetland, and Alex Barnard. They also originate in an imaginary conversation between Gramsci and Polanyi that has stretched over the last decade, conducted most recently with my friends and colleagues in South Africa – especially Jackie Cock, Eddie Webster, and Karl von Holdt.

References

Bauman, Z. (2000) *Liquid Modernity*. Cambridge: Polity Press.

Bell, D. (1976) *The Coming of the Post-industrial Society*. New York, NY: Basic Books.

Polanyi, K. (2001) *The Great Transformation: The Political and Economic Origins of our Time*. Boston, MA: Beacon Press.

Standing, G. (2011) *The Precariat: The New Dangerous Class*. London: Bloomsbury Academic.

Touraine, A. (1988) *Return of the Actor* (Myrna Godzic, trans.). Minneapolis, MN: University of Minnesota Press.

Weber, M. (1946) Bureaucracy. In: Hans Gerth and C. Wright Mills (eds), *From Max Weber* (pp. 196–244). Oxford: Oxford University Press.

2

The End of Liberal Democracy

Inequality in Post-democratic Capitalist Societies

Edgardo Lander

In this chapter I argue two things: first, that the era when liberal democracy was compatible with capitalism is coming to an end, and we are entering a historical period of post-democratic capitalism; second, that we are currently witnessing a perverse feedback mechanism between an increase in inequality and the destruction of liberal democracy – the less democracy there is the more inequality that is created. Growing inequality generates even tighter constraints on capitalist democracy.

In this chapter I address, almost exclusively, issues related to links between democracy and inequality in the United States and the European Union. I will not deal with any of the wide range of vital issues related to the reality or potential for democracy in many existing anti-capitalist struggles and non-capitalist forms of living or with non-liberal modalities of democracy.

A set of highly exceptional historical conditions made the golden age of liberal democracy possible. That was the period in history when capitalist democracy achieved its highest levels of legitimacy, equality, and democratic participation. Those conditions were related to the establishment of the modern colonial world-system, and to the specific circumstances of the bipolar world after World War II.

As regards the long term, I would like to highlight two aspects that were vital for making the social contract of social democracy possible in the central countries of the capitalist system, a social contract that was based on economies of abundance and expectations of uninterrupted growth in the future. These were: the role of the central countries in the capitalist colonial–imperial world-system and the energy base provided by fossil fuels.

The modern colonial and imperial world-system shaped a pattern of global accumulation based on the systematic exploitation of both what is generally called 'nature' and of human labor. An extremely high proportion of the benefits obtained from the use/exploitation of the *commons* all over the world, and of the product of all the diverse modalities of human labor, were expropriated and concentrated within the territory of countries located at the center of the world-system. This enabled historically unprecedented levels of material wealth. This abundance was always unequally distributed yet, to some degree, was shared by wider sections of the population than ever before in the territories at the center of this world-system, namely the developed countries of the western world.

As regards to energy, the massive exploitation of fossil fuels, starting with coal and then shifting to oil and gas, enabled the extraordinary productive and technological leaps of the Industrial Revolution, together with growth rates of both production and population that were unprecedented in human history. Energy that had accumulated for millions of years under the earth's surface was for the first time accessible, cheap, easily transportable, and apparently unlimited. Fossil fuels, as an energy source, have been feeding the productive machine of capitalism for the last two centuries. This made the extraordinary material wealth that characterizes central capitalist countries today. This has contributed to the installation of the idea of progress as common sense, the conviction that sustained and endless economic growth is possible. It was widely assumed that the material living conditions of each new generation would be better than those of previous generations. Furthermore, this conviction fostered the liberal illusion that over time class reconciliation would be possible, that capitalism was not a zero-sum system because there would always be more wealth available for distribution.

To these historical and structural characteristic bases of the global capitalist system over the last five centuries, and to the fossil fuel springboard of the last two centuries, we may yet add another component that arose after WWII: the emergence of the Socialist Bloc and the struggle for dominance in a bipolar world. The issue of global hegemony and the struggle for the legitimacy of liberal capitalist societies became a major concern. The social pact, or contract, of central capitalism through Keynesianism and the welfare state was the answer.

This extraordinary material abundance, on the one hand, and the political demands of the bipolar world, on the other, contributed to create the conditions that made it possible for the protracted struggles of the workers, and in general of the subaltern sectors of society, for better working and living conditions and for the enlargement of democracy, to achieve extraordinary success in the central countries, particularly in Northern and Western Europe. In this golden age, liberal democracy achieved its fullest development.

In this liberal social democratic contract, the state played a key regulatory and redistributive role. These inclusive liberal democracies tended towards lower levels of inequality and an expansion, not only of civil and political rights, but also of the economic rights associated with a social welfare state. This model became, for the majority of the population in these countries, the paradigm of democratic government. It was argued that democracy was only possible in liberal market societies.

Starting in the early 1970s, this expansion of the logic of democracy and social rights, along with the growth of the role of the state, led to a reduction in capital rates of profit. The cultural transformations of the counterculture questioned established authority and were seen as undermining work ethic. All this produced a coordinated, systematic counter-offensive from neoconservative and neoliberal elites. The so-called 'excesses' of democracy and counterculture were seen as representing serious threats to the capitalist regime. The most notable milestones of this counter-offensive, of this *counterrevolution of capital*, were the neoliberal policies of the governments of Margaret Thatcher (1979–1990) and Ronald Reagan (1981–1989). The conservative political/intellectual contributions of *The Crisis of Democracy: Report on the Governability of Democracies for the Trilateral Commission* (Crozier et al., 1975) and Daniel Bell's *The Cultural Contradictions of Capitalism* (1976) were representative of this global ideological offensive.

In Latin America, the beginning of this counterrevolution can be identified with a very specific date: that of the US-backed overthrow of Salvador Allende's government in Chile, on 11 September 1973. Thus begins the systematic processes of reversing liberal democratic achievements worldwide.

Two decades later, with the fall of the Berlin Wall and the collapse of the Socialist Bloc, neoconservatives and neoliberals celebrated what they considered to be their ultimate victory, the end of ideological political options regarding desirable futures for humanity. In this 'end of history' (Fukuyama, 1992), capitalist liberal democracy (purged of its excesses) was conceived of as the only possible point of arrival for all societies.

The paradox is that at the very moment when the final victory of the 'free world' and of liberal democracy was being celebrated, the historical conditions, that had enabled liberal democracy to flourish in the central industrialized countries were also drawing to an end. This turned out to be not the final triumph of liberal democracy at all, but the (temporary) triumph of capital.

Neoliberal globalization and the hegemonic realignments between so-called emerging economies and central countries started to erode the monopoly control that these countries had over the planet's mineral and energy wealth. The physical limits of our planet – especially the end of the era of cheap fossil fuels – undermined the prospect of the continuity of expanded abundance that had provided the material basis for liberal democracy in the West. Climate change, and the general acknowledgment that endless growth is impossible in a finite planet, has led to a questioning of the very foundations of the hegemonic model of civilization from multiple sources. We have entered a new era of post-growth societies.

Today we are in a position to claim that the full potential of liberal democracy was only possible for a brief and very particular historical juncture of capitalist society, and only for a small minority of the world's population. It was based on the deeply unequal appropriation of an ever-expanding material abundance, which ignored the limits of our planet.

Erosion of Liberal Democracy and the Global Increase in Inequality

Over recent decades, two powerful and interrelated trends have been in operation within capitalist centers, especially in the United States and the European Union. These are: steadily growing inequality and a steady cutting back of the scope of liberal democracy. Political systems, states, and political parties in liberal democracies are increasingly controlled by financial capital, and not by the democratic will of the people. This is what Slavoj Žižek (2011) has called the end of the marriage between capitalism and democracy.

In the context of an academic event centered on the issue of inequality, there is no need here for me to elaborate on this issue, given the wealth of information available in these debates and regarding these trends. I would, however, highlight that today's inequality in wealth distribution is unprecedented in the history of humanity. There has been a rapid increase in the concentration of money in the hands of a global oligarchy. Statistical information about this trend is increasingly available. The financial group Credit Suisse has been publishing an annual report analyzing wealth distribution among adults across the globe (including real goods, like homes, as well as financial goods). According to its estimates, the poorest half of the world's adult population owns only 1% of global wealth. A total of 3,051 million adults, representing 67.6% of the world's adult population, own only 3.3% of global wealth. By contrast, the wealthiest 10% owns 84% of global wealth; the wealthiest 1% owns 44%; and the wealthiest 0.5% owns 38.5% (Credit Suisse, 2011).

There are multiple trends and dynamics that illustrate the reduction in the exercise of democracy in central countries. These correlate with the growing power of financial markets in defining key public policies, particularly in the economic sphere.

The Financial Crisis and Liberal Democracy

In Europe's post-2007–2008 debate on how to respond to the financial crisis, democratic claims were on the whole put aside. Market-driven government decision-making openly prevailed. Markets were able to impose their interests upon governments – through the so-called 'Goldman Sachs coups' – that led to drastic cuts in public spending, undermined civil rights, and, in some cases, even imposed constitutional reforms. To pretend that these policies reflect the will of the people, or that these are the result of democratic participation in decision-making with regard to the nation's present and future, is nothing but an act of culpable complicity, particularly in Greece, Italy, Ireland, and Spain, where the dominance of the so-called 'market'-led solutions were dominant, no matter what the social and political consequences.

These governments tend not to make decisions based on the opinions of the people affected, but rather on the evolution of the so-called 'national risk', which is determined by fluctuations in the stock markets and interest rates, the harsh requirements of the so-called *triad* (the European Commission, the European Central Bank, and the IMF), as well as the far from negligible opinion of the German executive.

Latin America has experienced governments, which, after winning elections on the basis of an anti-neoliberal political manifesto, end up doing exactly the opposite as a consequence of the political mechanisms of external debt imposed by the IMF. The imposition of these recessive adjustment policies against the will of the population was hardly democratic. We should stop pretending and call things by their name. If the decision-making processes regarding the most important issues faced by society are not democratic, can these be called democratic societies, even in formal liberal terms?

Electoral Systems are Increasingly Controlled by Money

In the United States, the Supreme Court removed the last obstacle to money gaining full control over the political system in 2010, through the case known as Citizens United versus the Federal Election Commission. The Court held that to establish limits on the expenditure of corporations and unions in electoral processes, insofar as corporations have the same rights as citizens, would constitute a constitutional violation of their freedom of expression, as laid down in the First Amendment to the Constitution. Given the extremely high costs of electoral campaigns in the United States, this decision further increased the power of economic groups to buy legislative and executive election results and decisions to serve their interests. This had obvious impacts on the 2016 presidential campaign.

Surveillance Societies, Turning Orwell's Worst Prophetic Nightmares into Reality

The level of contemporary state surveillance is unprecedented: cameras in public and private places, monitoring of the content of phone conversations, emails, and other electronic means of communication by security agencies, permanent location of citizens through their cell phones, even when switched off, are examples in point. According to research carried out by the *Washington Post*, since the attack of 9/11, a secret security apparatus of huge proportions has been set up in the United States. It is not publicly known how much it costs, how many programs it includes, or how many people are involved. Among its results, the research stresses that the network consists of 1,271 governmental organizations and 1,931 private companies engaged in intelligence and counterterrorism activities, employing 854,000 workers with 'security clearance' status in 10,000 locations across the country and producing some 50,000 intelligence reports each year (Priest and Arkin, 2010).

Right-wing media and politicians infuse the population with fear and insecurity, which reduces resistance to measures that gradually advance towards a full spectrum surveillance society. In this context, huge business opportunities offered by new technologies emerge for the companies involved in what has been referred to as the security-industrial complex. There is broad evidence of the direct participation of companies engaged in these activities and their lobbies in the definition and expansion of policies in the field of security in Europe as well as in the United States (Hayes, 2009).

State of Permanent War

In the United States, a state of permanent war against all imaginable enemies has gradually been normalized. The government enacts undeclared
wars against terrorism, failed states, weapons of mass destruction, pirates,
and drugs. Unlike in the past, war no longer takes place as a succession
of discontinuous events, which have a beginning and an end. It is now a
permanent state of overt or covert fighting on simultaneous fronts: Iraq,
Afghanistan, Libya, Sudan, Somalia, Iran, Syria, and the list goes on. This
logic of permanent war began with the neoconservative policies enacted
under the Bush administration and enjoyed considerable continuity under
the Obama administration.

The United States has approximately 1,000 military bases outside its
own territory; that is 95% of all foreign military bases in the world today.
As historian Chalmers Johnson points out, this is a new form of colonialism, not characterized, as was the European case, by the occupation of
territory but, rather, 'America's version of the colony is the military base'
(Johnson, 2004).

According to the Stockholm International Peace Research Institute
(one of the most reliable centers for the study of military expenditure), in
2010 the United States accounted for 43% of total military expenditures
worldwide, considerably higher than the combined expenditure of the next
nine countries on the list, in order of greatest military expenditure (SIPR,
2010). This military imperialism is in no way compatible with democracy,
either inside or outside that country's borders.

**Political and Legal Constructions of Systematic Segregation
and Social Exclusion**

Until recently, within Europe, universal citizenship was made possible
on the basis of the fact that ethnic and religious 'others' were mainly
elsewhere: in the colonies, and other countries of the Global South. Those
being excluded were not visible. Thus the illusion of an inclusive democracy was possible. This has changed with the mass migration of the last
few decades. The 'others' are not elsewhere anymore; they are a migrant
population living permanently within European territory itself. Here ends
universal citizenship, inclusion, and equality. The illusion that we are all
equal disappears while systematic racism re-emerges with great force,
both in public policies and in the common view of growing sectors of
society. One cannot describe as democratic a society with first-class

citizens who have rights, and second-class citizens – migrants, undocumented workers, Muslims, and foreigners – whose basic rights are denied.

In the United States the marginalized other has always been inside the national territory. Racist mechanisms of exclusion have been reproduced time and again, from slavery right up to the present. As Michelle Alexander (2010) points out in her extraordinary book *The New Jim Crow: Mass Incarceration in the Age of Color Blindness*, in the United States the war on drugs, and the judicial and prison systems combine to ensure that the surplus population – mainly Afro-Americans – remains excluded from society and permanently lose their political rights. Alexander writes:

> Today, due to recent declines, US crime rates have dipped below the international norm. Nevertheless, the United States now boasts an incarceration rate that is six to ten times greater than that of other industrialized nations, a development directly traceable to the drug war. The stark and sobering reality is that, for reasons largely unrelated to actual crime trends, the American penal system has emerged as a system of social control unparalleled in world history. The current system of control permanently locks a huge percentage of the African American community out of the mainstream society and economy. The system operates through our criminal justice institutions, but it functions more like a caste system than a system of crime control. The fact that more than half of the young black men in any large American city are currently under the control of the criminal justice system (or saddled with criminal records) is not – as many argue – just a symptom of poverty or poor choices, but rather evidence of a new racial caste system at work. (2010, p. 7–8)

Under these circumstances, can we really refer to the United States as a liberal democratic society?

Given the implementation of such systematic mechanisms of exclusion, it is no wonder that, on the basis of data from the federal government of the United States, the Pew Research Center states that in 2009 the average wealth of 'white' households was 20 times higher than that of 'black' households, and 18 times higher than that of 'Hispanic households'. This is the largest gap since the government started publishing these statistics, 25 years ago, in a country where the election of its first black president was celebrated as an expression of its overcoming racism (Kochhar et al., 2011).

---

[1]Excerpt from *The New Jim Crow* – Copyright © 2010, 2012 by Michelle Alexander. Reprinted by permission of The New Press. www.thenewpress.com.

A Global Legal System Placing the Rights of Capital Before the Rights of People

One fundamental dimension of the global reconfiguration of the regime of accumulation, of neoliberal globalization in the last decades, has been the implementation of a global legal system, which places the rights of investors before those of citizens. The investment protection treaties and the regime of so-called free trade have established systematic prohibitions concerning public policies that might potentially affect the expected profits of foreign investors. It exists and functions, regardless of both the will of the citizens of the country in question, and of many of the social and environmental goals that in theory guide public policies. The regime of intellectual property rights is at the heart of the new global legal reality, and, in terms of its impact on democracy and inequalities, represents its most perverse component.

The so-called progressive processes of change in Latin America could hardly have happened without the defeat of the imperial project of the Free Trade Agreement of the Americas (FTAA), which sought to constitutionalize the neoliberal precedence of the rights of capital over the rights of people for the whole of the Americas.

The Separation Between Producers and Consumers in Neoliberal Globalization

In the era of Fordism and of the primacy of internal markets, the creation of effective demand for fast-growing industrial production required an expansion of access to consumption, particularly by the working class. Demand for an ever-expanding massive industrial production became highly dependent on workers' income. These were structural conditions that required wage increases, which over time led to a reduction in income inequalities. Neoliberal globalization has produced a growing distance (both social and geographical) between producers and consumers of industrial goods. In these circumstances, industrial corporations rely less on the local consumption capacity of producers (which would operate as an incentive for higher wages) and ever more on their capacity to sell their low-wage products in distant markets. In these new conditions there is no contradiction between low wages and accelerated industrial growth. In the case of China, over the last three decades, its most dynamic markets have been elsewhere. Thus, there is a structural incentive for corporations to keep wages as low as possible in order to compete in the global market. This global race to the bottom has been a key factor in the breaking up of the social democratic contract.

Restriction of States' Regulatory Capacities

Finance capital has gained extraordinary political power as a result of the colossal wealth it controls and the logic of short-term speculation that characterizes it. This has undermined the previous patterns of the extended reproduction of capital, as well as the conditions under which democratic legitimacy had been possible during the golden era of liberal democracy.

One of the main reasons why the current crisis of capitalism is so harsh is the fact that the system has lost most of its regulatory capacity. With neoliberal globalization new conditions have emerged under which capital can freely circulate with few impediments. The regulatory capacity of states, even of the most powerful states, is thus in decline. The realization of the neoliberal long-dreamed 'total market utopia' (Lander, 2002, pp. 51–79) has turned into a nightmare. There are fewer and fewer mechanisms available to moderate its inevitable excesses. Because of this, the short-term interests of speculative capital take precedence over any notion of a general interest in the stability of the system. Once this genie has been set free it is indeed hard to command it to return to the lamp.

Systematic Feedback Between Inequality and Post-Democratic Conditions

In conclusion, I would like to draw attention to the systematic feedback between the processes of democracy rollback and growing inequality. A perverse spiral has emerged wherein the increasing concentration of economic, symbolic, media, and political power of the elites allows them to impose their will on governments, thereby bringing about public policies which increase inequality.

Tax policies in the United States are an illustration of this feedback. Due to the growing political power of corporations, and the neoconservative/neoliberal cultural offensive, in recent decades the US tax structure has been systematically and extraordinarily skewed in favor of corporate interests, and against the majority of wage earners. As a result, tax rates on wages (those paid by the overwhelming majority of the population) are higher than those paid on capital gains, which constitute the main source of income for the extremely wealthy people. This contributes to accelerating the concentration of income and wealth within the hands of this small minority, thus reinforcing their capacity to influence government decisions in accordance with their interests.

In the United States, the average household income of 90% of the population has remained constant over the last 40 years. Since 1970, all the increase in national wealth has fallen into the hands of the richest 10% of the population. There has been a growing concentration of wealth in the hands of ultra-rich oligarchies (Winters, 2011). Between 2002 and 2007, 65% of the increase in the United States national wealth went to the richest 1% of the population (Freeland, 2011). According to the United States Congressional Budget Office, the gap in after-tax income between the richest 1% of the population and the middle and poorest fifths of the country more than tripled between 1979 and 2007, resulting in a greater concentration of income at the top of the income scale than at any time since 1928 (Sherman and Stone, 2010). As the inevitable result of these trends, according to data from the United States Census Bureau (2011), the number of poor in the country increased from 25 million in 1970, to 46.2 million in 2010.

According to a recent study by the Tax Justice Network, even those figures do not fully account for today's extraordinary levels of inequality, or for the capacity of the elite to conceal their fortunes and thereby evade taxes (Henry, 2012). The study shows that a high proportion of global private financial wealth – $21 to $32 trillion, according to conservative estimates – has been sheltered in tax havens where virtually no taxes are paid. These figures only concern financial wealth.

Such growing levels of wealth concentration increase the power of corporations and elites to impose their own agenda on the political system. In the context of the current recession, while millions of families are losing their homes, their jobs and their social security, governments spend billions of dollars to bail out the very financial institutions that caused the crisis.

Calls for tax reductions, and thus further restrictions on the revenue-collecting capacity of the state, not only seek to increase the concentration of wealth in the hands of a small privileged minority. The reduction in the tax burden also serves explicit political ends. It generates fiscal deficits, thus forcing governments to reduce social spending and regulatory policies. In the case of the European Union, the most important political role of fiscal deficit has been that of imposing public policies on governments geared towards generating 'market confidence', this being the condition for providing – at stipulated interest rates – the loans that are required as a result of the deficits.

The post-2007 crisis in the eurozone is illustrative of how the feedback dynamics between inequality and restrictions on democracy operates. This crisis did not start as a fiscal crisis but as a crisis of speculative financial capital. As Paul Krugman (2012) points out, before the crisis Spain had a manageable level of public debt as well as a fiscal surplus. The crisis was a product of financial speculation and the bursting of the housing bubble. It has led to recession, with the subsequent reduction of tax revenue and, with that, to a deficit in public finances. However, under the combined pressure of the 'markets' and the triad arguing that the crisis was the product of excessive and irresponsible spending by the governments of southern Europe, Spanish governments – both of the left-wing PSOE (Spanish Socialist Party) and the right-wing PP (Spanish Conservative Party) – responded with massive transfers of public resources to bail out troubled banks. This created a spiral in which public resources were used to rescue banks, while restrictive policies were enforced, reducing social spending and producing recessionary effects. In this way, a crisis created by financial markets became a unique opportunity for financial elites to achieve several objectives at once, which they could hardly have achieved without the crisis. These objectives are: a massive transfer of resources to finance capital, that is, the bailing out of banks that are 'too big to fail', thus accelerating processes of concentration of wealth; and an abrupt rollback of the historical gains of the welfare state, thus fulfilling one of the basic aspirations of the neoliberal dogma of a total market; and finally, constitutional amendments designed to ensure that these neoliberal reforms cannot be reversed.

For neoconservatives and neoliberals, the expanding logic of democratization, struggles for people's rights, and the claim that profound inequality was not in the 'natural' order of things, as was argued by critical political discourse during the golden age of liberal democracy in the central capitalist countries, was not only seen as a threat to their immediate interests but to capitalism as such. The counterrevolution of capital sought to reverse these menacing trends. This political project has been, overall, extremely successful. Today we live in increasingly unequal post-democratic societies.

Postscript, 2017

The tendencies characterized in this text have continued steadily over the past years. Across the world we are not witnessing short-term disruptions of established political systems, but structural transformations that are re-defining both the practices and the theory of liberal democracy. The main historical achievements of popular struggles in western liberal democracy in terms of solidarity, equality, and inclusiveness have been and continue to be rapidly rolled back. According to Oxfam just eight men own the same wealth as the poorest half of the world (Oxfam, 2017, p. 2).

References

Alexander, M. (2010) *The New Jim Crow: Mass Incarceration in the Age of Color Blindness*. New York, NY: The New Press.

Bell, D. (1976) *The Cultural Contradictions of Capitalism*. New York, NY: Basic Books.

Credit Suisse Research Institute (2011) *Global Wealth Report 2011*. Zurich: Credit Suisse Research Institute.

Crozier, M.J., Huntington, S.P., and Joji Watanuki, T. (1975) *The Crisis of Democracy: Report on the Governability of Democracies for the Trilateral Commission*. New York, NY: New York University Press.

Freeland, C. (2011) The rise of the new global elite. *The Atlantic*, January–February.

Fukuyama, F. (1992) *The End of History and the Last Man*. New York, NY: The Free Press.

Hayes, B. (2009) *NeoConOpticon: The EU Security-Industrial Complex*. Amsterdam: Transnational Institute. Available at: www.tni.org/report/neoconopticon (accessed 13 April 2018).

Henry, J.S. (2012) *The Price of Offshore Revisited*, Tax Justice Network, July.

Johnson, C. (2004) *America's Empire of Bases*, Tomdispatch.com. Available at: www. tomdispatch.com/blog/1181/ (accessed 13 April 2018).

Kochhar, R., Fry, R., and Taylor, P. (2011) *Wealth Gaps Rise to Record Highs between Whites, Blacks, Hispanics*, Pew Research Center, Social and Demographic Trends, 26 July. Available at: www.pewsocialtrends.org/2011/07/26/wealth-gaps-rise-to-record-highs-between-whites-blacks-hispanics/ (accessed 13 April 2018).

Krugman, P. (2012) Europe's great illusion. *The New York Times*, 1 July.

Lander, E. (2002) La utopía del mercado total y poder imperial. *Revista Venezolana de Economía y Ciencias Sociales*, 8(2), pp. 51–79.

Oxfam (2017) *An Economy for the 99%*. Available at: https://d1tn3vj7xz9fdh.cloudfront. net/s3fs-public/file_attachments/bp-economy-for-99-percent-160117-en.pdf (accessed 12 April 2018).

Priest, D. and Arkin, W.M. (2010) Top secret America: A hidden world, growing beyond control. *The Washington Post*, 20 July.

Sherman, A. and Stone, C. (2010) *Income Gaps Between Very Rich and Everyone Else More than Tripled in Last Three Decades, New Data Show*. Washington, DC: Center on Budget and Policy Priorities. Available at: www.cbpp.org/sites/default/files/atoms/files/6-25-10inc.pdf (accessed 13 April 2018).

Stockholm International Peace Research Institute (SIPR) (2010) *Background Paper on SIPRI Military Expenditure Data*. Available at: www.sipri.org.

United States Census Bureau (2011) *Income, Poverty and Health Insurance Coverage in the United States: 2010*. Washington, DC, Chart 4: 14.

Winters, J.A. (2011) Oligarchy and democracy. *The American Interest*, November–December.

Žižek, S. (2011) Now the field is open. *Al Jazeera*, October 29.

3

Social Justice, Inequalities and Democracy in India

Issues and Challenges[1]

Vishal Jadhav

Justice has always evoked ideas of equality, of proportion of compensation. Equity signifies equality. Rules and regulations, right and righteousness are concerned with equality in value. If all men are equal, then all men are of the same essence, and the common essence entitles them of the same fundamental rights and equal liberty. ... In short justice is another name of liberty, equality and fraternity. (BAWS, 3: 25, 2014)[2]

In India, there exists a long history of discussions and debate regarding social justice. One significant line of reasoning has promoted the idea that equality (of opportunity) is possible only when poverty is eliminated. A belief in this perspective led the intellectual and political elite in 1947, when India became independent, to advocate for the planning of poverty-alleviation programmes to ensure economic development with growth. Since 1947, the government of India (GOI) has promoted poverty-alleviation programmes and schemes in order to nurture humane development. The most radical of these schemes was introduced in 2005. This was called the Mahatma Gandhi National Rural Employment Guarantee Act (MGNREGA). It aims to provide social security to about 22%[3] of India's households, who are designated as being below the poverty level (BPL),[4] and who are located in rural India where 70% of the Indian population reside. Through this Act, the State has guaranteed the BPL card holders employment for 100 days a year (Dreze and Khera, 2011).

This radical intervention has received both acclaim and criticism from its supporters and opponents, and an extensive literature is growing around its beneficial impacts and promotion of social justice in India. The supporters of this Act suggest that the MGNREGA gives rights to the poor for the first time. These rights help to slow down the distress sale of land, restrict migration, free bonded labourers from extra-legal relations of patronage, and help empower women (Kannan and Breman, 2013). There are, however, an equal number of opponents to this Act, who suggest that it promotes corruption and leakages due to political and administrative inefficiencies, and leads to an increase in costs rather than benefits. Many critics suggest the repealing of this Act.[5]

The argument against the Act is based on government data that indicates the scheme's outreach is limited – less than 50% of the poor have been able to access and benefit from the Act.[6] The data also suggests that a large variation exists even among those who are able to gain access. In some regions only 15–20% of the poor have benefitted from the scheme, while in others the number is as high as 60–70%. Often the explanations for these variations are given in terms of the play of local and regional issues. For instance, research on the Employment Guarantee Scheme in Maharashtra by Moore and Jadhav (2006) amply demonstrates the effectiveness of the patronage networks that the landed Maratha caste members organise in order to draw benefits for their constituency. It has been suggested that the success or failure of this legislation is related to the support that it receives from the party in power in the various states or provinces of India. Commentators highlight how local-level leadership can effectively implement the legislation (given India's federal system) while, alternatively, others have highlighted how the localised networks of caste and community, which are intertwined with political parties, have worked to siphon off and transfer the benefits of the Act to the non-poor. Some studies have faulted the lack of social capital possessed by the poor, and have blamed trade unions and NGOs for not intervening on their behalf and ensuring a level playing field for these vulnerable groups. In addition, literature has highlighted the ambiguous role played by the local bureaucracy which has generally followed the dictates of their social and political bosses in order to divert these funds to those whom their superiors favour.[7] In these circumstances, the question is: how do we evaluate the credibility of social justice policies by the State in India?

This chapter moves away from a discussion of the implementation problems and its focus on political institutions, to an analysis of the conceptual map of the legislation. This is not to suggest that an analysis of power, caste, and community networks, and the role played by the local bureaucracy is not significant. These factors are related, however, to the discursive aspects of the legislation, and cannot be attributed merely to actors such as local bureaucrats and interest groups without taking into account how their mental make-up and their social imagery is shaped by the hegemonic discourses regarding poverty alleviation. This chapter argues that poverty-alleviation programmes (particularly MGNREGA), their rules and regulations, are part of a discourse that can be deconstructed in order to explicate the assumptions that underwrite this Act. There is a long history in India, in the post-independence period of interventions, of non-party political formations and people's movements demanding reduction of poverty, and ensuring that social justice for marginal communities is safeguarded by the State (Joseph, 2006). This chapter contends that the present discourse on social justice and right to employment is implicit in MGNREGA. The chapter examines the assumptions and historical necessities that led to the framing of this discourse of social justice in the post-independence period. It asks what implications this discourse on social justice had on the formulation of the MGNREGA. What was the sociological imagination that was incorporated into the Act, regarding the poor and their lifeworlds, their social and political resources, and their social capital?[8]

This chapter argues that behind legislative interventions lies a sociology of action that directs actors (who implement legislation) to observe, recognise and assess micro practices of social life (such as corruption, clientelism and patronage) or situated practices (such as casteism, patriarchy and religion-based identity politics). If these meanings of social life (interplay of identities and meanings within the larger normative order, e.g. social locations based on caste–class–gender–religion–linguistic identities and their interplay) are not incorporated in the way designs of government programmes are conceptualized, there are no social memories that can aid actors in political intervention.[9] In these circumstances the latter convert themselves into discourses. Thereby, they defeat the very purpose of State involvement in social justice interventions. For instance, women's reservation in political forums is a welcome legislation in terms of a step towards the empowerment of women. The interplay of caste, class, religion and other locational identities within the given structural order, however, organises power relations through which some sections of women remain at the margins. This power relation in turn classifies individuals and communities into pre-imposed administrative categories. This kind of classification can, and does, lead to exclusions and marginalisation of individuals as a by-product of the process of legislation and law. In such a case, wherein a highly rationalised and essentialised citizenship map informed by a colonial episteme is preconceived by the State, it fails to capture with precision the fluidities and infinite possibilities of social reality. This bureaucratic obsession of attempting a superimposition between the State-conceived model on the one hand and the myriad lifeworlds on the other often leads to misconstrued comprehensions of the social. The chapter argues the inevitable incongruence occurs because the State lacks the vocabulary and imagination to address and comprehend issues related to the heterogeneous sociabilities and the infinite permutations that are generated through the interplay between them in the everyday social.

In most legislations, therefore, there is a policy oversight of the Indian State as it fails to identify the uneven nature of livelihoods and infrastructural processes that organise and structure the lifeworlds of the poor. Specifically, the poor, in India, are often small peasants and petty producers; they engage socially, combine, and exchange low-value labour, goods and services, through unorganised rural and urban economies. These unofficial economies reproduce themselves through monetary and non-monetary activities. The poor are also socially organised as micro groups of individuals through households and families, kin and caste affiliations. There are also various groups and affiliations of inequality that run along the lines of gender, age, expression of sexual identities, differential abilities, access to citizenship, and group and community rights.

The MGNREGA legislation has little to no clarity about the variabilities that structure the nature of social exclusions in India, and the moorings of these exclusions in colonial and post-colonial histories.[10] The Act conceives of rights and equalities from the perspective and heritage of colonial liberal philosophy. It is constantly shifting its discourse between a) the theory of individual liberties and rights, and b) community rights, and the particular discrimination faced by deprived and marginalised groups. This constant oscillation between individual and group identity, in understanding social justice, has created two separate registers that each have unique legislations and notions of redressal.

Compounding all of this, the Indian State has used the MGNREG Act to essentially institutionalise an informal structure of distribution of power and resources that works in tandem with the formal structures of bureaucracy and party politics, through the use of the 'middleman' or 'fixer'.[11] The middleman is related (sometimes formally and often times informally) to the State bureaucracy and party machinery, and acts as a mediator and interface. Middlemen in India introduce, interpret, access and ensure (via their networks of social capital) that the Act's outreach to its beneficiaries is accomplished through the commission or payment of rents. Together with the party functionaries and the State bureaucracy, these individuals

use to their advantage the interplay of caste, community and gender affiliations, together with that of geography, to distribute patronage and thereby
influence the distribution of resources allocated under the auspices of multiple programmes, acts and legislations. New legislation in particular must
recognise these practices and nuances of power, in order to ensure that
their outreach makes it to the actual and real beneficiaries.

We begin our discussion by explaining the two main processes by
which the lifeworlds of the poor in India are structured. These are the
economic and the political. The economy organises individuals, families
and households, all social networks via social capital, while the political,
via the State and its actors and institutions, either through its presence or
absence, engages with the social networks of individuals to then organise
the economy. This chapter therefore begins with a discussion of the economy and how it organises the sociabilities that structure the networks of
individuals and households across rural and urban India, to create regional
networked social spaces. The chapter then examines how State and law
are debated in India, and examines the reasons for the intellectual distance
between legal conceptions and micro-practices of discrimination in India.

The underlying question is whether State legislation for social justice
in India is inevitably flawed. In its conclusion, the chapter will explore the
answer to this through a brief case study of similar legislation, which went
through a radical overhaul as a consequence of the involvement of social
movements that mobilised the affected poor to demand work and to ensure
that the State legislation targeted and benefited them and them only. This
happened in the decade of the 1970s, in the case of the Employment
Guarantee Scheme implemented in the State of Maharashtra, at a time
when the State was perceived to be sensitive to the concept and policy of
'development'. This raises the question of whether it would be possible
to repeat the same experiment with MGNREGA. India today has moved
out of the era of a developmentalist State and into that of neoliberalism. In
such an environment can India enlarge its conceptions of social justice in
order to move forward in an effective way?

Petty Production and Uneven Capitalism

Our discussion of India's economy begins with a case study:

> Govind is 55 years old. He is a member of the scheduled caste (SC), formerly
> known as untouchables. At the beginning of the 21st century the SC represent
> about 17% of the Indian population. Govind and his wife Nirmala, who is

50 years old, have a small plot of agricultural land measuring 1.5 acres, which is still registered under his grandfather's name in a village called Nakshet, Taluka Penn, district Raigad, Maharashtra. Govind's mother is 75 years old. She is physically challenged and illiterate, and is dependent on Govind and his wife for survival. This piece of land is tilled by Nirmala who is able to grow enough paddy to feed the family, which includes Govind's mother, Govind, his wife, their son and his wife, plus their five-year-old son, and Govind's unmarried daughter, for nine months at the most. Nirmala has to get potable water from 2 km away, and also do daily chores in the house, along with working the field. During the times of sowing paddy, transplantations and also harvesting, she has to pay to employ extra labour at the rate of 150 rupees a day.

Govind has one son and two daughters. The son and one daughter are married. Govind works as a security guard in a private firm at the Taluka headquarters, which is roughly 40 km from his village. He works on a contract basis and earns 3000 rupees a month. His son is also employed in one of the factories in the Taluka place, and he has rented a room wherein he, his wife and Govind reside. The son also earns 3000 rupees a month, and his wife who works as domestic help in several homes, earns about 1000 rupees a month. They send a part of the money back to Govind's mother, who resides in the village.

Govind pays his son for the monthly food expenses. Govind's brother-in-law stays with his son in the rented room and is also employed on a contract basis. The brother in-law pays Govind's son for this accommodation (monthly on a per-cot basis). Because Govind paid the initial 'pagadi' (a traditional form of deposit) of 1500 rupees, 20 years ago, the rented room is in the name of Govind and therefore he does not pay for his accommodation. Govind is able to send back 2000 rupees every month to his wife and mother. The unmarried daughter is also staying at the rented room to help with the daily chores of the household. Govind has a grandson who needs to be looked after, as all members of the household are busy doing contractual jobs from morning to night and sometimes on different shifts, and so the unmarried daughter also is involved with childcare.

All members of Govind's family, and his son's family, have applied for registration for the MGNREGA scheme. Govind does not have a birth certificate, nor is the land on which he lives in his name, but he has a BPL (Below Poverty Line) card.[12] Govind and his unmarried daughter are unable to get job-cards because they are now urban dwellers (they reside in the rented room year-round).[13] Govind's wife, though residing year-round in the village, is also not registered for a job-card. This is because she stays as a single with her mother-in-law and is thus unable to successfully negotiate with the local authorities. Govind's mother was not provided with a job-card because of her age and physical infirmity. In this context the local Tehsildar (an administrative officer who operates at the intermediate level, i.e. between the district collector and the Talathi or the village land records officer. This officer is well networked within the local patronage system and is influenced by the local political structure) chose to offer Govind's son employment under the scheme, as he considered him an able-bodied young male but did not choose to offer employment to the other members of the family. Govind's son is earning relatively more in his current job than he would get under MGNERGA, and so he did not choose to join the scheme.

This case study highlights the strategies of survival in Govind's household. It highlights how the economy dictates ways through which families reorganise into smaller units, through multiple households. It also highlights the dependence of the poor on the informal sector as their source of livelihood. Additionally, it shows how households like these may consist of individuals who are not all related by blood, as in Govind's family. Survival is difficult as much of the money gathered by the various individuals in the household goes into daily expenses and, as in Govind's case, also medical treatments (of Govind's mother). There is hardly any surplus left to put towards savings. As both Govind and his wife are getting older, and their age is affecting their employability, this lack of savings becomes an ever-greater issue.

The MGNREG Act pays money for manual labour on piece rates, so even if Govind or his wife were to get employed through the scheme, how much would they really be able to earn by working for a minimum of eight hours a day? At times the expenditure of their household exceeds the total income of the family. To ensure that this does not happen, the family lives frugally so that many of their meals consist of non-nutritional food items, leading to a vicious cycle of illness and medical treatment. This also affects their chances of getting hired as agricultural labourers (whose wage rates are higher than the MGNREGA).

The Govind case study highlights certain assumptions that the State and the MGNREGA have taken for granted. One is the misrecognition that the concept of a household is equal to that of a family. As this case study demonstrates, one family can have two or more households, which may be located in the same territorial space or in disparate areas. Therefore, when members of the household apply for work, the administrators disqualify them on the basis of this flawed single household criterion. This is especially true when many households live together as a joint family in rural areas. Similarly, the State is flawed in how it envisions the rights of households headed by single women, and completely fails to address the issues that arise in regard to the rights of aged individuals who are single, or who are differently abled. The Act does not have the requisite imagination to make adequate provisions to address the complex realities of the poor, let alone the rights of these diverse individuals.

The focus of this chapter is to understand the social system that organises petty production wherein most individual's households and families in the country find an economic identity. It is difficult to estimate the number of individuals, households and families that are involved in this production system. Most data we use are related to statistics on the 'informal sector' and the unorganised economy. This is, however, a derivative of the whole. Given that professional knowledge denotes formal economy as being organised around the manufacturing and service industry, the informal sector and economy denotes the economic activities that are not a part of these organised manufacturing and service industries. Trying to understand the informal sector in this way, however, leads to complications as it eliminates a lot of economic activities and does not outline the systemic elements that structure the petty production economy.[14]

In India, approximately 93% of the working population is involved in the informal sector and the largest proportion of this is in the 'self-employed' sector (Sakthivel and Joddar, 2006). Thirty-six percent of this population lives below the poverty line. We call this the system of petty production. This population contains mainly semi-independent peasants who have some land. They may also have small family businesses and small assets, and could be simultaneously considered petty commodity producers and traders. They exploit their own family members and also hire labour. It should be pointed out that this economy is not confined to the urban area and only organised within towns and cities, as is sometimes thought. Wherever urbanisation has been rapid and extensive, it has been concentrated in urban areas. Given the range and scope of the informal economy, however, it is best to describe it as being an economy that not only organises towns and cities, but also connects these up with rural areas into a network of inter-connected nodes.

The informal economic system covers a range of monetised and non-monetised market transactions involving commodities and services, produced, distributed, consumed and reproduced (sometimes through recycling) in Indian society. It includes household labour and other forms of non-capitalist production: market exchanges, including gifts (through weddings and festivals); barter; and various transactions relating to the cultural system of clientele and patronage. It also includes the manufacturing and service industries where it is often difficult to distinguish at what point work is organised, and when and where it is not. The informal economy also includes the market transaction of firms and units not registered for direct taxation and licensing.

The informal economic system is highly flexible, extremely diverse and simultaneously segmented. Flexibility is achieved by capital through casualisation of labour through physical movement. This flexibility combines time, economic sectors, strata and regional clusters in differential combinations. The cycles of organising these economies are highly competitive, mobile and driven by short-term profits. Since colonial times, this economy has organised various kinds of technologies and relations of production, together with the control and discipline of labour (from unfree/bondage/slave labour to free and self-employed). The sites of the informal economy – households, sweatshops, small-scale industrial units and agricultural land – differ in distinct ways at different times and places. The work in this economy, however, is always low-skilled or unskilled labour. In this context enumeration of these sites and workforce within the received and preconceived template of labour classification, as employed by the State, becomes a difficult task. No wonder some of these sections of society remain outside the ambit of the programmes and enactments of the Welfare State.

Classic concepts of political economy do not give us the frame to understand this economy. In this economy we cannot identify the bourgeoisie and the working classes nor do the latter 'form' themselves in contestation with the capitalist class. Thus it is impossible to find a workforce engaged with struggle against capital. Rather the workers are engaged in struggles between themselves for work.

This economy has articulated pre-modern sociabilities (locations based on caste, tribe and religion) and identities to organise labourers into households which are knitted together as families and kin groups. Its members participate in a combination of work activities, simultaneously and over time, with extremely low wages. One example of this is the workers in manufacturing where there are no boundaries between organised and unorganised work. Thus a household or family may have members doing agriculture work, home-based labour production, work in sweatshops, and also be involved in retail across time and territories. As short-term and long-term migration to and from urban and rural communities increases, some families might fragment into two to three households and regroup with other labourers into new households or new families.

In these situations, it is difficult to distinguish when the household and the family are separate or together. Wages remain low and are segmented in terms of gender and caste, or ethnicity. As a result of this, competitive wages and long-term work are never continuously available to all labourers. The system works off the absolute poverty of the workers. This affects the long-term stability of households and of the continuity of settlements, and, in turn, investments in housing. These households generally live in temporary shelters and barracks built with recycled material pieces of wood and cardboard, tarpaulin and corrugated sheets. These are then termed slum settlements.

A combination of intermediate classes control this economy in a maze of outsourcing processes that organise production, distribution, consumption and reproduction of commodities and services, together with the reproduction of households and families. The flexibility of the system demands that work is intermittent, leading to high levels of job insecurity with wages almost never providing real-food equivalence. This most negatively affects the more vulnerable strata of the populations: women, children, the old, transgender and the SC/dalit,[15] 'Other Backward Classes' (OBC),[16] Muslim,[17] Scheduled tribe[18] and Adivasi[19] groups.

It is this vulnerability that allows the system to be controlled by competitive fractional intermediate class and caste groups, including the middleman/fixer who controls the market of labour, commodities and capital, as well as the political system. These middlemen control labour through a patronage system that combines class subordination with pre-modern ideologies of class, caste, ethnicity, religious identity, gender and sexuality. In this process, the labourers become segmented. Because of this segmentation, in this system, one rarely finds the classic Marxist capital versus labour conflict. Rather, in most instances, the struggle over resources is organised in terms of caste and ethnic or religious confrontations. The distinctiveness of this new economy is in the way it organises these ideologies of pre-modern sociabilities, in order to structure, in uneven and diverse ways, the processes and sites of production, distribution, consumption and reproduction. As a result, it creates islands of culturally distinct systems of organisation, integrated with each other and yet dispersed across the country. It is important that one recognises this unique process, in order to understand how to create a system that can counter its complexities in order to reach the beneficiaries of the poverty alleviations Act.

Understanding the State, Law and Rights in India

This section elaborates the philosophical foundations of law and social justice in India and indicates how its discourse remains intellectually distant from the lifeworlds structured by the capitalist economy. The chapter deliberates on the paradoxes that interface law, rights and power in the country.

Post-independence, the principle of law making in India embodies the philosophy of liberalism, which was inherited as part of the nationalist engagement with the colonial experience. Liberalism makes individuals the basis of law and society. It also advocates that society and its institutions exist to further the ends of individuals, without showing favour to one group or another. It is based on the belief that individuals know best what their needs are and seek State support in fulfilling their aspirations. In this context, the law needs to guarantee liberty and equality to all individual citizens. Of prime importance, in liberalism, are the individual legal rights to freedom of opinion, expression, association and movement; the use of one's property and labour as one pleases; and the right to freely practise one's religion. Political rights and constitutional procedures, such as the independence of the judiciary, the separation of legislative and executive power, freedom of the press and electoral accountability, are designed to enhance and enable these individual rights and freedoms, and to place limits upon government power. Within all of this it is assumed, however, that the liberal individual is a human being not otherwise differentiated by status, class, caste, ethnicity, religion or gender.

In India, however, there is another template upon which laws and rights have been framed, and upon which social justice has been advanced. This version has defined social justice as being linked to the caste system and was articulated in the late 19th and early 20th centuries by the *Satyashodhak Samaj* (Truth seeking society) and the Justice Party, in western and southern India respectively. They argued that social justice implies emancipation from the discriminatory and hierarchical caste system and demanded that redress be given against past stigma and discrimination. One of their many demands was for opportunities to be given to the discriminated, through affirmative action and the introduction of quotas for these disadvantaged groups in local and provincial governments (Omvedt, 1994).[20]

The colonial State accepted this latter demand for quotas, called reservation in India. The introduction of this policy for social justice suggested that caste discrimination could be successfully addressed through quotas and reservation. It introduced a special category called 'Depressed Classes' and enumerated them in order to make policies on quotas. In the 1931 census, the colonial administrators took into account various cultural criteria such as measures of impurity (access to wells, schools and temples for instance), and rechristened the 'Depressed Classes' as 'Scheduled Castes'. The government then gave these groups, together with the Muslims and scheduled tribes, a statutory status that paved the way for group-based quotas. The continuation of this policy was adopted by the newly formed independent Indian State, which created a nodal Ministry of Welfare in 1950, to organise policies to address demands from marginalised groups. Since the 1970s, the Indian State has had to engage with further demands from groups that claim discrimination, such as women, other backward classes, children and the old, the mentally and physically disabled, and transgender, by creating various programmes and policies within its welfare ministries. The ministry's role is to protect and safeguard the interests of these disadvantaged groups, economically, socially and culturally (Omvedt, 1994).

The constitution of India thus recognises a differentiated citizenship. While the law makes the individual the bearer of rights, the constitution recognises the 'community' as being a collective unit of social and political life across the nation. Roy (2010) suggests that the State recognises citizenship through two prisms, i.e. through individual rights and identities and also through the identity of belonging to a collective/community (2010, pp. 18–19). The early part of the post-independence debates in India demanded and obtained proportionate political constituencies for SC and ST representatives, and for public sector employment and public education institutions. Community rights most often are not enforceable by courts but were reminders to the State to usher in egalitarian conditions. The Directive Principles envisage an active role for the State in providing a range of welfare rights, from ensuring livelihoods, equal work for equal pay, healthcare for workers, a living wage, and provisions for just and humane work conditions, to the right to work, education, public assistance, equal justice and access to adequate nutrition.

The discourse on 'community rights' has remained embedded in its liberal formulations (Bajpai, 2011). Over the years there has been the development of ideas that have introduced new laws and legislations regarding these rights. What is interesting to note is that community and individual rights do not intersect in policy interventions; these are always seen as different and distinct. Law, in India, including the present social security laws, remains caught in the discourse of individual rights, while the discourse around 'community rights' has shifted to bring onto one united platform issues relating to religious minorities, deprived castes and tribes, and women.

Today, we can identify two templates upon which issues of social justice are being discussed by the Indian State: the material and the cultural. The present reality of both of these has been inherited from the colonial State. The material bases itself on an assessment of individual income, consumption and nutrition levels, and uses the offices of economists and statisticians to comprehend poverty levels and compute the number of poor. The MGNREGA resides in this stable. The cultural bases itself upon ethnographic studies, done by social anthropologists and sociologists whose fieldwork to understand group-based cultural and social discrimination is seen as being a legacy from the colonial era. The material framework identifies individuals who are below the poverty line (BPL) in order to give them access to schemes that might alleviate their poverty. The cultural framework uses qualitative methodologies to examine cultural attributes of discrimination between castes and caste-like groups, in order to identify such groups and allocate proportionate seats to them within education institutions, public sector employment and in political constituencies.

Ideally there would be a way to reorganise these two frameworks to allow them to intersect, so that access to schemes like the MGNREGA legislation would be made more available to those who most need its help. Below is an example of a movement that took place in the State of Maharashtra to implement a precursor scheme of MGNREGA, the Employment Guarantee Project (EGS), introduced in 1972.

Social Justice Through Social Movements

The Employment Guarantee Project (EGS) was formally inaugurated in India in 1972. The origin of its central idea, of guaranteed employment, can be traced back to discussions among socialist ideologues in the 1940s in western India.[21] Its introduction in India was also a consequence of the pressure put upon the government by activists, who had earlier intervened to provide drought relief to the poor in 1972 (Joseph, 2006). The lack of consistent and efficient response from the State to ensure drought relief led these activists to frame a law to guarantee employment to the poor, providing them with the right to demand work from the State and be paid for it. Once EGS was introduced as a scheme, the activists organised the people to demand appropriate and timely implementation and expansion to ensure proper working conditions for the rural poor. They considered the poor to be workers and wanted the State to legislate and implement all the appropriate rights related to a strong workforce, such as minimum wages, regular payment schedules, eight-hour-shift work days, yearly holidays and accessible work sites around a radius of 5 km.

In addition, these activists raised issues regarding the nature of work and services needed in work sites where a large number of women and scheduled castes were present. They wanted the government to ensure equality of opportunity for work and equal wages between women and men, and between castes. They also wanted equal access to be provided for dearness allowance, crèche, potable water, shelter, maternity relief and identity cards. In their work, however, they also highlighted systemic issues of discrimination occurring on the basis of sex, sexuality and castes, in the accessibility and nature of the work being allocated. The main focus was on the sexual division of labour in government work. Eventually, as work was outsourced through contractors, it demanded that the State abolish this system, providing permanent employment to muster clerks (those who keep and maintain employment registers) and extending the Employment Guarantee Scheme to forest work, and demanded wages in kind through the use of food coupons. In order to make the EGS administrative mechanism transparent, and not dependent on existing local caste power structures or middle men/fixers, the activists demanded political representation at the village and block level. As a consequence, the EGS has always been represented in government and academic literature as the most successful anti-poverty programme of the Indian State (Moore and Jadhav, 2006).

It is because of these sorts of activist interventions that there exists extensive discussion around theories of social exclusions and their relationship to social justice. The literature on social justice recognises that in India inequalities based on social exclusions have had a long history and have been part of the historical processes of colonialism, which continues to manifest itself within the capitalist economy, social processes and institutions.[22] A significant section of this literature focuses on exclusions, and discriminatory practices experienced by four major groups in India: the Scheduled Caste, the Scheduled Tribe, Muslims and women. Studies have argued that the Scheduled Castes have continuously faced discrimination in the labour market in spite of having access to education.

Though formally freed from traditional bondage systems and extra legal social relationships, they continue to face wage and occupational discrimination in both rural and urban areas (World Bank, 2011).

In the case of Muslims in India, the GOI's Sachar Commission (Government of India, 2006) has suggested that nearly 40–60% of Muslims in India are artisans. Often they are settled in urban areas and have poor access to formal employment, literacy and modern skills. In addition, they face discrimination based upon communal, religious and sectarian ideologies, which legitimate that discrimination.

Tribal groups, on the other hand, have distinct lifeworlds. They tend to be small and marginal communities of farmers, as well as stakeholders in forest, mineral and water resources. They live in isolated areas in central and north-east India. Not only do they not have access to services available in various parts of 'developed' India, but they have also had to face displacement from their land and assets. This practice of displacement happens on a continuous basis as new 'development' projects are introduced in these geographically isolated areas.

Within each of these groups, women face additional discrimination, leading to differential survival and health problems due to the sexual division of labour. Women carry double and triple the burdens of men, legitimised through a patriarchal ideology that controls biological reproduction with unequal access to consumption of products within the household. While women face domestic violence within the household they, together with other members of these excluded groups, face both symbolic and physical violence in the public domain as well.

As a consequence, commentators such as Corbridge et al. (2005) and Bajpai (2011), have thus asserted that exclusion concerns itself with relational issues and interfaces the social, cultural and political aspects of inequalities with the economic. This perspective posits that an evaluation of the status of individuals and societies must go beyond income, utility, rights and resources, and into the actual lives of the poor. Simultaneously the literature on social justice also asserts that individual disadvantages need to be located within group disadvantages, which in turn relate to group identity. Group identity in this context is the cultural devaluation of people based on who they are (or rather who they are perceived to be). Exclusions are related to the use of beliefs, norms and values used to disparage and stereotype, invisibilise, ridicule and demean, those that are 'despised' by dominant groups. These beliefs determine access to economic opportunities, incomes, the nature of livelihoods, nature of work, access to basic water and sanitation, society, health and education, and even physical housing services and political citizenship. As a result disadvantaged groups not only face income discrimination but also other disadvantages such as access to potable water, and health and education, which continue over lifetimes and through generations. Social exclusion reflects the multiple and overlapping nature of the disadvantages experienced by groups and categories of the population (Bajpai, 2011).

The State in India has accepted a limited understanding of exclusions. What is needed is a broader and more complex understanding of exclusion which understands exclusion as being part of intersecting structures that combine to form various elements of discrimination. This perspective of intersectionality has emerged to clarify the relationships between varied and seemingly unrelated processes of social and economic exclusions. It draws attention to the way power is practised and assesses the interface this has with social and cultural hierarchies. The theory of intersection reflects the many dimensions and subordinations of the many kinds of marginalised. The focus in the theory of intersectionality is on power; it analyses the social location of the subalterns and those who are discriminated against, in terms of criss-crossing systems of oppressions.[23]

This section began with a description of the EGS, and how the Indian State was forced to make its poverty-alleviation programme accountable and transparent by activist groups who were able to mobilise the poor. Is there such a possibility today in the case of MGNREGA? It doesn't seem likely. There is little involvement or interest being shown by activist groups towards mobilising the poor to support or advocate for their rights in this scheme. In the case of the EGS, these groups were involved from the beginning. Likewise, the country and the State have changed. Politics in India has moved towards the right. The new political regime that captured power in 2014 is a coalition (called the National Democratic Alliance, or NDA) of right-wing parties led by the Bharatiya Janata Party. The NDA was initially reluctant to continue funding MGNREGA. It changed its stance by 2015–16, however, and viewed this scheme as an opportunity to expand its constituency (Sampath and Rukmini, 2015; Damodaran, 2016; Mathew, 2016). It is also observed that the State under the new political regime has also accepted neoliberal policies that have displaced the earlier developmentalist model of the State (Sampath and Rukmini, 2015). If one views examples from other parts of the world, the notion of participation encouraged in the neoliberal era brings forth a new conception of politics, completely different from the earlier one. For example, Leal (2007), on the basis of an analysis of African and Latin American NGOs fighting for the cause of the poor, suggests that these organisations have already been co-opted into the larger marketisation ideology that the State espouses. Their interventions thus remain superficial, never addressing structural issues regarding poverty, social exclusions and social justice.

Notes

1   This chapter is a revised version of a mimeo prepared jointly with Sujata Patel on this theme in 2012 (Patel and Jadhav, 2012). This chapter was submitted to the editor at the end of 2013 and primarily assesses the discourse of social justice and right to work in India in the context of a rights-based piece of legislation called the Mahatma Gandhi National Rural Employment Guarantee Act or MGNREGA that was introduced by the political regime led by the United Progressive Alliance (UPA, which includes the Congress and the left-wing parties). In 2014 a right-wing political coalition replaced the UPA and brought in some changes in the Act. This chapter does not examine this phase, i.e. the post-UPA regime.

2   Ambedkar was impressed by the ideas of Professor Bergbon, a scholar in the field of the philosophy of religion. He was especially inspired by Professor Bergbon's comprehension of the concept of justice. It is in this context that Ambedkar contends that Professor Bergbon's definition of justice was an all-encompassing one. This quote has to be read in this context.

3   According to the census of 2011, there are 1.2 billion Indians. Of these, 22% are poor. The poverty line is calculated at Rs 32 a day (50 US cents according to May 2014 foreign-exchange rates). This announcement inaugurated a major debate regarding the validity and credibility of GOI's computation of the poverty line. On this debate see also Deshpande and Bhattacharya (2013).

4   BPL is an economic benchmark and poverty threshold used by the government of India to identify the poor. The poor are given BPL cards to access poverty alleviation schemes.

5   Dreze and Khera (2011) contend that it was never easy to get such a kind of guarantee from the state and there were many contradictory forces that opposed this idea. They employ Chomsky's concept of 'flak' or the technique that the ruling elite resorts to in order to put down any idea that challenges the entrenched interests of these sections of established power. The anti-NREGA lobby propaganda revolved around issues of corruption, nepotism and even populism. Terms such as 'expensive gravy train', 'costly joke', 'corruption guarantee scheme', 'wonky idea' and 'gargantuan guzzler of taxpayers' money' were employed in this war of ideas and interests (Dreze and Khera, 2011, pp. 14–16). They narrate the story of how the NREGA campaign gradually became more personal in nature and labels such as 'liars', 'poster boy of economic reforms' 'jholawala economists' became the language of the anti-NREGA camp to sabotage this revolutionary idea of the working class (Dreze and Khera, 2011, pp. 12–13).

6   Data presented by the Comptroller and Auditor General (CAG), which surveyed 68 districts and 141 blocks in 26 states. See CAG Audit Report Points to Irregularities in Implementation of MGNREGA. *Times News Service*, 23 April 2013. Available at: http://timesofindia.indiatimes.com/india/CAG-audit-report-points-to-irregularities-in-implementation-of-MGNREGA/articleshow/19692420.cms (accessed 20 May 2014).

7   See Corbridge et al. (2005) who analyse the state to examine and comprehend the bureaucratic filters that ensure that state aid does not reach the poor. See also the recent book of Akhil Gupta titled *Red Tape* (2012) which argues that bureaucratic interventions in India remain structurally arbitrary and invites its actors to be corrupt.

8   According to Habermas (1981), the concept of 'lifeworld' relates to the every-day world that we share with others. This includes all aspects of life barring organised or institution-driven ones. For example, it includes family life, culture and informal social interactions. I have employed the term to mean a social universe in which the actors com-prehend the normative order and have a feel for the way power is organised – in a way very similar to Bourdieu's (1990) concept of practice.

9   Bourdieu (1990) clarifies that the social practices internalized in the body (habi-tus) which then reproduces culture are not, however, objectively determined. Nor are they exclusively the product of free will. They are produced by the interaction of the social context (structure) and the response of the actor (agency). Therefore the actor's practices involve a combination of conscious, intended action and unconscious, unintended action (due to naturalisation of reality, which Bourdieu refers to as 'doxa').

10   We use the concept of exclusions rather than inequalities to indicate that individu-als are not merely economically unequal, they face differential ideological and cultural forms of discrimination that legitimise this inequality. These forms of discrimination affect their entry into employment structures, formal education institutions and access to other services as well as having 'good health' and thus being able-bodied. Differential access to these cultural and ideological attributes or capacities creates constraints to their being healthy, literate, being employed or being empowered.

11   'Fixers' is a term given by James Manor (2000) to political intermediaries who mediate between individuals and groups and powerful politicians, bureaucrats and caste elders, and articulate the interests of the 'silent majority' to ensure a transfer of funds for some if not all of this group. In some places these individuals are called com-mission agents because they take a percentage cut if transfers take place through their initiatives.

12   Below poverty line is the population whose income levels fall below the minimum living income as stipulated by the government of India. This index is calculated by the Indian government each year through an economic survey.

13   Job cards are attendance cards that are issued by the government to prospective labourers. The job card enables an individual to join the workforce.

14   This section draws heavily on Harriss-White and Gooptu's (2001) paper on the unorganised sector and the NCEUS Report.

15   Dalit meaning 'the broken man' is a concept now associated specifically with the SCs. In some discussions it can cover the entire working class and labouring groups of India.

16   Other backward classes (OBC) is a generic term used by the Indian state to clas-sify those groups who are socially and economically disadvantaged but who may not be defined within the purity–pollution scale as the scheduled castes. In 1980 they were sup-posed to be 52% of the population. This figure was scaled down to 41% in 2006–7. If scheduled castes, scheduled tribes and other backward classes are counted as one, that is those who are socially, culturally and thus economically disadvantaged, then they consti-tute a little less than 70% of India's population.

17   The Muslims were part of groups defined as minorities (today these constitute about 20% of the population), which were classified in terms of religious affiliation to non-Hindu faiths. Other than the Muslims (around 13%), these include Christians, Sikhs, Buddhists, Jains and Zoroastrians, among others.

18   The category of tribe was imported from Africa and was used for groups that practised animism and thus could not be placed within the Hindu fold. Two sets of groups were given this status – groups located in central India and those based in the north east. Today these groups constitute around 8% of India's population with about 15% living in the north east and are divided into about 750 tribes, each different from the other in terms of social and cultural traits. After independence GOI also included in this category of the Scheduled Tribe, the groups named as Denotified Tribes. The Denotified Tribes are those communities that were originally listed under the Criminal Tribes Act of 1871 under which the colonial state gave itself powers to arrest them under non-bailable offences. Though this Act was repealed these communities continue to face the stigma of being criminals and the representatives of the state continue to illegally arrest them, torture and abuse them oftentimes without any justification.

19   Adivasi, meaning the original people or the autochthonous, is a concept used by some scheduled tribes of central India to describe themselves and their political movements.

20   Affirmative action in respect of reservations/quotas in government services for the depressed groups was inaugurated in a princely state called Kolhapur as early as the 1890s (O'Hanlon, 1985).

21   This part of the chapter is based on research done in 2003–4. See Patel (2006); Chari (2006); Jadhav (2006); and Joseph (2006).

22   There is extensive literature in this area from a range of perspectives that cover positions as different as the World Bank (2011), Amartya Sen (2000) and left-wing academics (Sengupta et al., 2008).

23   Intersectionality is a feminist sociological theory and is a methodology of studying the relationships among multiple dimensions and modalities of social interactions and subject formations. The theory seeks to examine identities that interact on multiple and often simultaneous levels, contributing to systematic social inequality.

References

Ambedkar Babasaheb Writings and Speeches (BAWS) (2014), Volume 3, Second Edition compiled by Hari Narake. New Delhi, Dr. Ambedkar Foundation, Ministry of Social Justice and Empowerment, Government of India.

Babasaheb Ambedkar Writings and Speeches, 3(25), 2017/BAWS, *3(25)*, 2014.

Bajpai, R. (2011) *Debating Difference: Group Rights and Liberal Democracy in India.* New Delhi: Oxford University Press.

Bourdieu, P. (1990) *The Logic of Practice.* Cambridge: Polity Press.

Chari, A. (2006) Guaranteed employment and gender construction: Women's mobilisation in Maharashtra. *Economic and Political Weekly*, *41*(50), 5141–5148.

Corbridge, S., Williams, G., Srivastava, M. and Vernon, R. (2005) *Seeing the State: Governance and Governmentality in India.* Cambridge: Cambridge University Press.

Damodaran, H. (2016) *MGNREGA 2.0: Modi to Spend a Record Rs 60,000 Crore on what was UPA Flagship Scheme*. Available at: http://indianexpress.com/article/india/india-news-india/mgnrega-nda-government-pm-modi-employment-days-mgnrega-3092201/ (accessed 19 July 2017).

Deshpande, A. and Bhattachrya, P. (2013) *Everything You Wanted to Know about the Poverty Debate*. Available at: www.livemint.com/Politics/vS6ouWt9vWB9Sn t7As7LHI/Everything-you-wanted-to-know-about-the-great-Indian-poverty.html (accessed 14 May 2014).

Dreze, J. and Khera, R. (2011) Employment guarantee and the right to work. In: R. Khera (ed.), *The Battle for Employment Guarantee* (pp. 3–20). New Delhi: Oxford University Press.

Government of India (2006) *Social, Economic and Educational Status of the Muslim Community in India*. Delhi: Cabinet Secretariat.

Gupta, A. (2012) *Red Tape: Bureaucracy, Structural Violence, and Poverty in India*. Delhi: Orient Blackswan.

Habermas, J. (1981) *The Theory of Communicative Action*. Cambridge: Polity Press.

Harriss-White, B and Gooptu, N. (2001) Mapping India's world of unorganized labour. *The Socialist Register*, *37*, 89–118.

Joseph, S. (2006) Power of the people, political mobilisation and guaranteed employment. *Economic and Political Weekly*, *41*(50), 5149–5156.

Kannan, K.P. and Breman J. (eds) (2013) *The Long Road to Social Security: Assessing the Implementation of National Social Security Initiatives for the Working Poor of India*. New Delhi: Oxford University Press.

Leal, P.A. (2007) Participation: The ascendancy of a buzzword in the neo-liberal era. *Development in Practice*, *17*(4/5), 539–548.

Manor, J. (2000) Small time fixers in India's states: 'Towel over the Armpit', *Asian Survey*, *40*(5), 816–835.

Mathew, L. (2016) *Why the BJP Embraced MGNREGA, the 'Living Monument' of the UPA's Failures*. Available at: http://indianexpress.com/article/explained/why-the-bjp-embraced-mgnrega-the-living-monument-of-the-upas-failures/ (accessed 19 July 2017).

Moore, M and Jadhav, V. (2006) The politics and bureaucratics of rural public works: Maharashtra's employment guaranteed scheme. *Journal of Development Studies*, *42*(8), 1271–1300.

O'Hanlon, R. (1985) *Caste, Conflict and Ideology: Mahatma Jotirao Phule and Low Caste Protest in Nineteenth-century Western India*. London: Cambridge University Press.

Omvedt, G. (1994) *Dalits and the Democratic Revolution: Dr. Ambedkar and the Dalit Movement in Colonial India*. New Delhi: Sage Publications.

Patel, S. (2006) Empowerment, co-option, and domination: The politics of employment guarantee scheme of Maharashtra. *Economic and Political Weekly*, *41*(50), 5126–5133.

Patel, S and Jadhav, V. (2012) Intersectional exclusions and poverty and poverty alleviation legislations: A case of the Mahatma Gandhi National Rural Employment Guarantee Scheme (MGNREGA) and the social security act. *HiVOS*, The Hague (mimeo).

Roy, A. (2010) *Mapping Citizenship in India*. New Delhi: Oxford University Press.

Sakthivel, S. and Joddar, P. (2006) Unorganized sector workforce in India: Trends, patterns and social security coverage. *Economic and Political Weekly*, *41*(21), 2107–2114.

Sampath, G. and Rukmini, S. (2015) *Is the MGNREGA Being Set Up for Failure?* Available at: www.thehindu.com/sunday-anchor/is-the-mgnrega-being-set-up-for-fail ure/article7265266.ece (accessed 19 July 2017).

Sen, A. (2000) *Social Exclusions: Concept, Application and Scrutiny*, Social Development Papers No.1. Manila: The Asian Development Bank.

Sengupta, A., Kannan, K.P. and Raveendran, G. (2008) India's common people: Who are they, how many are there, and how do they live? *Economic and Political Weekly*, *43*(11), 49–63.

World Bank (2011) *Poverty and Social Exclusion in India*. New Delhi: Oxford University Press.

4

Gendering Human Rights in the Pursuit of Social Justice

Nira Yuval-Davis

This chapter locates itself within the normative methodological discourse of public sociology, which views social justice in transversal terms, emphasizing the importance of an intersectional and situated sociological analysis. It is within this context that I want to highlight some of the critical issues that concern the relationships between human rights and gender relations. Although most of my chapter focuses on these issues within global feminist politics, they are also relevant when examining some of the more generic problems related to the notion of human rights, and its links to democracy and social justice.[1]

The chapter starts with an examination of the relationships between the notions of women and gender, women and the human, and women and rights. Some of the issues raised in this discussion are then illustrated in a description of the global feminist campaign, which was organized in the 1990s, through several UN conferences: the Vienna conference on human rights; the Cairo conference on population and reproductive rights; and the Beijing conference on women. Of particular importance here are the constructed contestations that have been taking place between human rights, women's rights, and cultural rights.

The next section of the chapter discusses other reservations, which have been raised vis-à-vis the notion of rights as bearers of emancipatory struggles. It is within this context that alternative approaches, such as those of capabilities and human security, are mentioned, as well as some of the problematics of human rights and human rights' organizations as being a mode, or tool, of global governance.

The concluding remarks, at the end of the chapter, point out the centrality of gender rights in the context of the 21st century, and its contradictory and often contested relationship with human rights, democracy, and social justice.

Women and 'Gender'

Gender is a relational concept. Even when discussing women within the context of same-sex relationships, or women's autonomy, the notion of gender, like many social constructs, is intimately linked with that of power.

In this context it is important to reflect on the differentiation between the notions of gender and sex. This has been a debate that started even before the rise of the second wave of feminism (Yuval-Davis, 1997, pp. 5–11). Christine Delphy (1993) outlined the development of the debate around sex and gender as stretching back through the work of Margaret Mead, the Parsonian theories of sex roles, and even the ground-breaking work of Ann Oakley's *Sex, Gender and Society* (1972). There is a progressive denaturalization of the divisions of labour and the psychological differences between men and women, and a stress on cultural variation ('gender'), unlike physiological differences, which are attributed to biology ('sex').

Delphy, however, and in a very different way Judith Butler (1990) point out that gender precedes sex, in both the cultural construction of the social division of labour (Delphy), and its meaning (Butler). Gender is the very means by which sexual differences are constructed (and used) as being both natural and pre-social.

As Hood-Williams (1996) pointed out, any so-called 'objective' scientific project to define who is female or male, either via the presence or absence of a particular chromosome or gene, has a circular logic: the scientist 'must already know what it is to be a man [socially] before they can confirm it genetically' (p. 11). As Foucault (1991) and Laqueur (1990) have pointed out, the mere need to construct every human being as either male or female is historically – and therefore culturally – specific.

Judith Butler concluded from the above that one should not differentiate between gender and sex, as they are both socially constructed discourses. While I agree, I argue that there is yet still a need to differentiate between the gender and sex discourses, as they each have separate agendas. Gender is a mode of discourse, which relates to groups of subjects whose social roles are defined by their sexual and biological difference, as opposed to their economic positions or their membership in ethnic and racial collectivities. Sexual differences are a mode of discourse in which groups of social subjects are defined as having different sexual and biological constitutions.

The insistence on discursive constructions of meaning, and on the non-natural, non-essentialist nature of both sex and gender, has brought about a blurring of the boundaries between the two. Anyone who has taken part in feminist politics in non-English speaking countries, however, will know that one of the first and most urgent tasks of feminist discourse is to either discover or invent a word in the local language for gender. This alone works as a major political lever for change, and for the possibility of envisioning a different social reality. Unless there is a separation between the discourses around sex and gender, biology will be constructed as destiny in the moral and political discourse of the society. This separation of biology and destiny equally applies when discussing emancipatory and social justice issues relating to men, hermaphrodites, or transsexuals (Connell, 2012), as well as when discussing feminist politics focusing on women.

Women and 'the Human'

A common argument among feminist theorists and activists is that all too often the construction of the human has made women invisible, 'hidden from history' (Rowbotham, 1973). It has made women seem inessential (Spellman, 1988), and thus helped to legitimize their construction as inferior, which has further led to their exploitation and exclusion from an equal share in social, economic, and political power and resources. Further along in this chapter I expand on the specific political campaign that aimed at remedying this, calling for the recognition of women's rights as being human rights. First, however, I want to explore the question that Etienne Balibar (1990) called 'the paradoxical nature of the universal', which is at the basis of the UN's Universal Declaration of Human Rights, and which has facilitated such invisibility and exclusion of women from conceptions of the human.

Balibar (1990) argues that the notion of the universal is paradoxical, because when we promote the interests of everyone this generality tends to hide and therefore exclude the concerns of the non-hegemonic, the different, and the marginal, thus resulting in social injustice. Appiah (2006) expressed this paradox somewhat differently when he argued that two different elements are necessary components in a cosmopolitan approach. The first is the idea of universality, that we have commitments towards all other human beings, even those with whom we have no familial or friendship relations, or even that of common citizenship. The second element is that we need to respect not just other human beings in the abstract, but also specific human beings, with specific beliefs and practices that give their lives meaning, without expecting or wishing all peoples and all societies

to become the same. Appiah (2006) further argues that these two cosmopolitan ideals, the universal and the respect for legitimate difference, have
conflicting inner tensions, and therefore cosmopolitanism should not be
seen as the name of the solution but as the name of the challenge.

Appiah's double-edged construction of the cosmopolitan idea reflects
Michel Wieviorka's dilemma: 'Why is it so difficult to be anti-racist?'
(Wieviorka, 1997). Wieviorka argued that, not so long ago, it was not
difficult to differentiate between racists and anti-racists. Increasingly,
however, there are divisions among those who see themselves as being
anti-racist, and those who accuse them of encouraging racism (through
systems, structures, and cultural practices) if not of actually being overtly
racist themselves. The reason for this basic disagreement is that there are
two visions of non-racist, or anti-racist, society. One vision is universalistic – all people need to be treated the same, especially in the public sphere.
The other vision is based on the politics of recognition and claims public
acceptance of multicultural and affirmative action practices as being a pre-
condition for accomplishing a non-racialized society.

The universalistic position views the public acceptance of forms and
difference as being a kind of racialization, through the reification of
boundaries and discrimination. The pluralist position accuses the first
camp of recognizing and legitimizing only majoritarian discourse, which
is usually western-centric, heterosexist, and middle class in nature, and of
rendering as invisible the standpoint and interest of excluded racialized
minorities.

The debate around anti-racism can also be seen as reflecting feminist concerns regarding what constitutes sexual equality. In his article,
Wieviorka (1997) does not really resolve this dilemma except by saying
that neither extreme position is valid. I argue that the dichotomy of univer-
salism and relativism, whether it relates to race or gender, is a false one.
We need to look at the universal in the way that Dipesh Chakrabarty et al.
(2002) does. He writes, 'The universal … can only exist as a placeholder,
its place always usurped by a historical particular seeking to present itself
as the universal' (Chakrabarty, 2002, p. 105). The aim of emancipatory,
anti-racist, and feminist politics is to aspire to establish a universal system
of social justice, which includes many particulars, and which would be as
inclusive as possible, at the same time knowing that this is a process and
not a goal.

This is the most important sociological insight when analysing the relationship between gender and human rights; that is, the role of individual

and collective social agents in constructing the meaning of the human in a non-exclusionary way, which nevertheless recognizes differences. It is from this transversal dialogical epistemology (Cockburn and Hunter, 1999; Yuval-Davis, 1997, 2011), which embodies the construction of socialagents, that we need to examine the particular of women as bearers of rights.

Women's Rights

Citizenship rights and human rights were born at the same time and place: the French Revolution. Historically, however, they developed along different trajectories. As various feminist theorists have pointed out (Pateman, 1988; Vogel, 1991; Yuval-Davis, 1997), it was not only in this moment that women were excluded from becoming formal bearers of rights in the modern liberal state as it emerged, but likewise in what Carol Pateman (1988) has called 'the fraternal sexual contract'. The construction of the entitlement of men to democratic participation conferred citizenship status not upon individual men as such, but in their capacity as representing the familial household. In most countries women have long since won the right to vote (though in Qatar and the United Arab Emirates the right to vote was granted only in 2005–06, in Saudi Arabia women were given the right to vote – but only in municipal elections – in 2015, and in the Vatican women are still absent when new popes are elected). Women's other political, civil, and social rights, however, continue to be subject to struggle and contestation in different ways all over the world. This is in spite of national and international legislation of non-discrimination.[2]

When dealing with women's rights, it is not just a question of women being entitled to have the same rights (and responsibilities) as other citizens. As elaborated elsewhere (Yuval-Davis, 1997), women's membership in various collectivities is virtually always of a double nature. On the one hand, women are members of groups like any other; on the other hand, there are always specific rules and regulations aimed at controlling women and their autonomy. These rules and regulations relate to women's roles as biological, cultural, and symbolic reproducers of national, ethnic, and other collectivities of belonging.

Debates during the 1970s and 1980s, in the UK and elsewhere, challenged the so-called protective legislation, which forbade women, during their reproductive years, from working in particular industries, in military roles, or even on night shifts, thus preventing women from many opportunities for upward mobility and the establishment of a career (Baer, 1978;

Lewis and Davis, 1991). Merely achieving rights equal to those of men is not always enough, nor is it a sufficient solution to the many challenges confronting women. Feminists active in many local contexts, as well as in global campaigns, have focused their attention on what is being called 'sexual rights', or 'human rights of the body'. These encompass the right to contraception, safe abortions, and protection from domestic violence and forced marriage, as well as the freedom of movement and work in the public sphere (Cornwall et al., 2008; Petchesky, 2003). While not all women in all social and geographical locations either have or are denied access to all of these rights, a global transversal solidarity movement has been made possible across these differences, and around the common value of women's – and all human's – rights over their own bodies. The manner in which these rights are claimed and recognized, however, can range from being status quo to being transformational (Miller, 2004).

Pheng Cheah (1997) has argued that we need to reimagine human rights as being simply the rhetorical structure 'given to us' in our present historical condition, for asserting counter-hegemonic statements of justice (1997, p. 235). In this sense, they are a necessary and irrepressible expression of contemporary movements for social change. Attempts to concretize universalist principles by adapting them to particular circumstances of gendered, racialized, and sexualized bodies show us that human rights are always both universal, historical, and individually specific at the same time. Campaigns that are aimed at making abortion safe and legal for women, on the one hand, and those aimed at preventing forced sterilization and the abuse of unsafe contraception devices, on the other hand, vary in different global locations but would pursue similar transversal feminist agendas (Petchesky, 2003).

The common concerns of women precede, but are also being reconfigured by, the field of study, which Ken Plummer (2003) and Sashsa Roseneil (Roseneil et al., 2012) call 'intimate citizenship rights'. This refers to the rights and responsibilities which arise out of the 'moral chaos' (Plummer, 2003) that has been the result of rapid advances in technology, and which create the need for new legislation on a whole range of issues. These issues include using genetic research to create 'designer babies' and cloning, to redesigning adult bodies using radical new techniques of cosmetic surgery for a range of procedures including sex changes and the transplantation of body parts.

Liberal theories of social justice (Rawls, 1971, 2009) have tended to focus on the relationships and tensions between rights for freedom, and rights for equality. As discussed, the debate concerning women's rights, and body rights more generally, cannot be reduced to a simplistic tension between these two. They need to probe more closely into the definition and meaning of equality and freedom in different social, cultural, political, and economic contexts, including not only gender, but also other inter-sectional complexities. It is in this striving for social justice, concerning contestations in relation to gendered human rights, that a global feminist movement has dealt with some crucial struggles.

Women's Rights are Human Rights

In the aftermath of the Second World War, the Universal Declaration of Human Rights was produced by a multi-national, multi-cultural team working under the leadership of Eleanor Roosevelt in the newly estab-lished United Nations. While some would argue that the declaration was in actuality the USA exporting the principles of its own constitution to post-fascist Europe and the rest of the world (Sharma, 2006), for many others, the declaration became important as a secular framework and a yardstick to assess and fight for liberty and social justice all over the globe. It established a baseline of ethical principles, which can be found in many cultures and religions today.

It was not, however, until 1993 that the UN called a special conference in Vienna to discuss the issue of human rights. This was the first of a series of UN conferences during the 1990s, around which an important global feminist movement would develop (one which Niamhe Reilly, in 2008, called 'cosmopolitan feminism'). It was in Vienna that a major slogan of this movement, 'women's rights are human rights', was first widely used.

During that conference the feminist coalition organized various panels and a tribunal in the UN forum for NGOs. These events drew many people and a great deal of attention. A few of the leaders from this coalition were even allowed into the official section of the UN conference to present their arguments to the various government delegates. These presentations were highly influential. The Programme of Action from the 1993 Vienna Human Rights Conference, and the Declaration on the Elimination of Violence against Women, adopted by the General Assembly that same year, expressed the consensus of the world's governments that 'gender-based violence and all forms of sexual harassment and exploitation' constituted violations of human rights. Those achievements, and the estab-lishment of a UN Special Rapporteur on Violence against Women, were the fruit of global organizing by women's NGOs, as was the public tribunal where women from different parts of the world testified about rape in armed conflict zones, forced prostitution, marital rape, and the like. These public actions 'put VAW [violence against women], and in particular sexual violence, on the map as a global human rights problem' (Miller, 2004, p. 25). They also laid the groundwork for the subsequent Hague and Rwanda tribunals, and for the International Criminal Court Statute, which has codified the definition of rape, sexual trafficking and slavery, as well as forced pregnancy and sterilization, in situations of armed conflict, as being war crimes, crimes against humanity, and, in certain circumstances, genocide. This is an improvement upon the Geneva Convention, at which the strongest terminology used for such actions was 'crime against honour' (Copelon, 1995).

Originally the success of this movement in Vienna, and then later in Cairo and Beijing, was a major source of satisfaction, if not euphoria, for many feminists. Part of the strength of this movement has been that it united feminists from all over the world. Often the most organized, innovative, and inspirational feminist leaders for this movement have come from countries in the Global South. The movement provided an excellent space in which to pursue and develop global solidarity around various issues concerning women's sexual rights. It provided a space to examine, in a transversal dialogue, how the differential situated gazes of the different participants were recognized, even as solidarity was built around the shared values of a pursuit of social justice and women's autonomy over their bodies.

During the follow-up meetings after these conferences, however, the mood began to change, as ever more efforts were required just to maintain the partial achievements gained in the resolutions of the previous conferences. Many began to question the extent of the added value of these resolutions beyond rhetoric, given the extreme levels of effort, and other resources, which were required to be invested in these meetings, instead of being directed towards other local and transnational feminist and emancipatory forums (such as AWID[3] and the World Social Forum[4]).

The main reason for this frustration was the growing strength of the conservative and religious global Right, which, while using the discourse of human rights for the pursuit of their own political goals, uses the notion of culture and tradition as a way of opposing the goals of the global feminist movement. The global Right, in the North as well as in the South, constructed individual women's quests for freedom and social justice as subservient to collective cultural rights within the discourse of 'the clash of civilizations' (Huntington, 1996) which are defined in particularistic, homogenized, and mutually exclusive essentialist cultural collectivities.

Women's Rights and the Question of Culture and Tradition

Cultural rights constituted part of the original design for the UN's Declaration of Human Rights, passed in 1948, which was to consolidate the rights listed in the declaration into a single treaty encompassing civil, political, economic, social, and cultural rights. US lobbying resulted in the division of the implementing covenant into an International Covenant on Civil and Political Rights, and one on Economic, Social, and Cultural Rights (16 December 1966). The latter was given a lower status, as being something to be 'achieved progressively' rather than implemented immediately. The situation started to change after the fall of the Soviet Union and the end of the Cold War. At this point it became clear that civil and political rights fitted much more conveniently into the discourse of neoliberal globalization than did social and economic rights.

At the UN conference on human rights in Vienna in 1993, some of the most heated debates were focused on what were called 'Asian values'. Some interpreted the debate as being constructed between individual rights to freedom and collective rights to development (Herman, 2002). These relate to economic and social rights, which have been marginalized in much of the human rights discourse, and which have been slowly reclaimed as part of the human rights discourse in the post-Cold War period. However, it is in this construction of the collective rights of groups, and how they are linked to cultural rights, that much of the debate concerning women's rights has been focused. What – and whose – are these cultural rights?

The notion of cultural rights arises out of a paradoxical contradiction. On the one hand, it arises out of the denaturalization of culture, when the various practices of daily life, life-passage ceremonies, and ways of viewing the world stop having a hegemonic discursive performative authority, and the possibility of diversity is publicly accepted. On the other hand, for any definition of cultural rights, which include a multiplicity of cultures, there is the need to define what cultures are. This involves a construction of homogeneous communities with fixed boundaries, which, more often than not, are defined by particular cultural agents who have been picked by the state as being 'authentic' representatives or leaders of the minority and 'other' cultural collectivities. Very often, the mere act of the state sponsoring particular cultural agents and defining what is the culture and tradition of the 'other' invests these agents with additional powers that help them to dominate within their own communities against contesting agents with contesting versions of those cultures (Anthias and Yuval-Davis, 1992; May, 1999; Rattansi, 2011).

Some feminists, notably Susan Okins (1999), have argued that 'multi-culturalism is bad for women', as they tend to then accept as a given the hegemonic constructions of culture and tradition. Such a position is prob-lematic in at least two ways. Firstly, it excludes hegemonic white western people from having a specific culture, as though, presumably, not having a culture is good for women. In such a construction, culture then becomes a signifier of racialization. Secondly, it colludes with a definition of culture as being fixed, reified, and homogeneous among members of particular communities.

A very different position concerning culture and tradition has been developed among the participants of the global feminist movement, against whom much of the debate around 'Asian values' has been directed. I was part of a group of global feminists who advised Faridah Shaheed, the special Rapporteur on Cultural Rights of the Commission on Human Rights, on a report she has written for the Commission, on the impor-tance of ensuring equal cultural rights for all women and girls (Shaheed, 2012). The position of the report is that it would be a mistake to view the debate on women's rights and cultural rights as being a debate between individual and collective rights. Rather, it is a debate about the notion of culture, power, and the relationships of these to more general issues of social justice.

It is important to recognize that cultural models become resonant with both subjective and collective experiences. They become the intersectional ways in which individuals experience themselves, their collectivities, and the world, and thus often occupy central spaces in identity narratives. There is no human who is not constructed culturally by both self and others. Culture should not, therefore, be understood as having specific, fixed inventories of symbols and ways of behaviour, or artifacts, which coherently constitute cultures of specific national and ethnic collectivities. Cultures are dynamic social processes that use selectively various resources in accumulated inventories, operating in contested terrains in which different voices become more or less hegemonic in their offered interpre-tations of the world. Often cultural discourses resemble a battleground of meanings more than a shared point of departure. Cultural homogeneity is a result of particular power relations, and is always more noticeable at its centre than in the social margins (Bhabha, 1994; Bottomley, 1992; Yuval-Davis, 1997). It is for this reason that, when considering issues of social justice, culture should never be looked at in a way that is isolated from the influence of social and political power.

Culture is not something restricted to only certain areas of life, and, in particular, is not only found in those areas that are unregulated by the State, and of greater relevance in some societies than others. All human activities and institutions are permeated by culture, including the law and legal systems, which still tend to predominantly reflect men's experiences, opinions, and interests. 'Culture' should not be seen as being independent of the actions of people, institutions, rules, and regulations, and encompassing beliefs, attitudes, and practices, all of which are subject to change and contestation. The cultural canvas of every society reflects contestations over meanings and values, customs, and practices, and raises the crucial question of who is accepted as being the legitimate or authentic voice of a community.

Because of this there is the need for greater pluralism in how expressions of cultural practices are accepted, encouraged, and allowed, not just by various governments but by the international community as well. As Faridah Shaheed (2012) emphasizes, the right to be equal and the right to access and participate in cultural practices should be presented not as a conflict of rights but as different dimensions of women's struggles for empowerment. If we view women as being equal bearers of cultural rights to those of men, they must also have the right to change the aspects of their culture that subordinate and disempower.

The rights of women to be equal bearers of cultural rights, however, strongly clashes with the reality of many women's lives in different parts of the globe. It is this dissonance between the formal rhetoric of entitlement to rights, and the everyday experiences of so many women's and men's lives, that has been part of the reason why so many feminists and other emancipatory activists have become disenchanted with the discourse of human rights.

Human Rights and Human Security

When discussing the experience of the Vienna conference many years later with Charlotte Bunch (the Director of the Centre for Global Leadership at

Rutgers University) who was one of the main organizers of the feminist alliance promoting the 'women's rights are human rights' slogan, we both expressed a certain feeling of discomfort regarding the project and the slogan itself, in spite of the large amount of good and important work in all parts of the world that had been accomplished.

Part of the initial reason for inventing this slogan was tactical. It was created to push the feminist agenda into the agenda of the human rights conference in 1994, and to influence specific governments' policies in this area. It was also a part of the agenda of feminist movements all over the world, which has been to expose the gendered aspects of all major social relations and structures and to prevent them from being 'hidden from history' or excluded from the supposedly universal constructions of the human. Yet another reason that feminist goals were presented in terms of 'women's rights are human rights', was that in the post-Cold War period the discourse of emancipation, and the discourse of liberation, became delegitimized to a certain extent with the decline of the Marxist left after the fall of the Soviet Union. The liberal discourse of rights had come to occupy the hegemonic space, which had been left vacant.

It may be that this narrowing down of feminist possibilities and liberation struggles is also partly responsible for our sense of discomfort. The discourse of human rights prioritized certain types of feminist goals, which focused on the rights of individual women. It addressed challenges such as domestic violence, but had no space or creativity to accommodate alternative social and political visions of society as a whole.

This is not to say that the discourse on human rights is not important, or that it has no positive value in and of itself. As Mary Robinson (2005), who used to be the UN Commissionaire of Human Rights, expressed, rights create the conditions that encourage enhanced accountability through higher levels of citizens' empowerment, easier consensus, and increased transparency. This can then complement mainstream development efforts to promote good governance and participation (Robinson, 2005, p. 29). Many successful feminist and anti-racist struggles have been won, throughout the years and in many places on the globe, using this discourse and claiming the various human rights they are entitled to. Many more, however, have found that such victories have often been formalistic, if not ultimately co-opted and turned toward discourses on human security, capabilities, and ethics of care as being more ready alternatives to actual emancipation.

Although the original declaration of Human rights talked about social, economic, and cultural rights, as well as civil and political rights, the latter were separated and were accorded a more inferior status during the period of the Cold War. One of the critiques of the discourse of human rights at the 1994 Vienna conference was that the pursuit of human rights is led by people who take having enough food to eat for granted. Indeed, Michael Ignatieff (2001), when heading the Centre for Human Rights at Harvard University, defined human rights as a specific form of politics with a mini-malist kernel that is aimed at defending people's rights to free agency, the ability to make decisions, and to be protected from abuse and oppression. However, this equation of human rights with negative freedom sounded too extreme and minimalist even to Amy Gutman, the Princeton professor who has written the introduction to Ignatieff's book. She points out that 'the right to subsistence is as necessary for human agency as a right against torture. ... Starving people have no more agency than people subject to cruel and unusual punishment' (Gutman, 2001, p. ix). Ignatieff counter-claimed, however, and argued (what I consider to be debatable) that there has never been mass famine in a democratic society where people could have objected to unreasonable government policies, and therefore he did not feel that Gutman's critique contradicted his overall approach.

As a result of such critiques, international human rights organizations, like Amnesty International, have incorporated various economic, social, and cultural human rights into their original aims.[5] Other organizations, however, including many feminist NGOs, have found the discourse of rights to be too formal and legalistic. They argue that in many concrete situations, especially in the Global South, it becomes almost meaningless. These organizations have instead turned to the notion of 'human security' (Chen, 1995; Timothy, 2004).

The human security approach to development can be seen as a cos-mopolitan, moral, and political project of belonging, in which the actual well-being of humans, as well as their formal rights, is what counts. The 1994 UNDP report stated that human security is 'articulating a preventa-tive "people-centered" approach that focused jointly on "freedom from fear and freedom from want"' (Alkire, 2002, p. 4). It has been heavily influenced by the capabilities approach developed by Amartya Sen (1981, 1992) and later on by Martha Nussbaum (Nussbaum and Sen, 1993; Nussbaum, 1995), which rejects the discourses of rights and entitlements, as well as general measures of opulence, such as GNP, and it instead focuses on the ways people positioned in all groups in society are capable of achieving quality of life through personal achievement and freedom. It argues that resources have no value in themselves, apart from their role in promoting human functioning. Many feminist struggles, even if they describe themselves in terms of human rights struggles, aim at achieving these substantive gains for women – and men's – lives, rather than just achieving formal legal rights that do not always translate into real gains.

The issue of social and economic, and not just civil and political, rights and capabilities are vital when we discuss the issue of gender and human rights. They are even more important when examining the relationships between rights and capabilities, and the question of political power and the political will required to instil durable social change. Feminists like Ros Petchesky (2003), Sonia Correa (Correa et al., 2008), and Andrea Cornwall and Maxine Molineux (2008) have pointed out some of the major dilemmas and tensions that exist in the work of human rights feminists in different parts of the globe.

One of the most common challenges confronted by feminists is the tension that exists between human rights as a legal discourse and human rights as a mode of activism. Within this tension is one's attitude towards the state, which can often be both the source of the human rights violations and the source of the legal authority, or rule of law, which exists to pursue and criminalize those who violate women's sexual and other rights. There is a problematic relationship between the liberal discourse with its politics of rights, and the wider, situated contexts and considerations involved in social justice. There is the need to explore both the conditions under which engagement with the state is possible, as well as the risks involved in doing so; risks that relate particularly to the independence and overall objectives of the feminist agenda. This has become a major source of debate between 'autonomous' and 'entrist' feminists (Yuval-Davis and Vargas, 1998).

A particular challenge related to this has been the notion of 'gender mainstreaming'. While feminists have fought to achieve recognition for gender equality and its inclusion in political and policy agendas, this has often translated into no more than a formalistic rhetoric, which in no way compensates for the loss of resources or the positioning of autonomous feminist watchdogs whose agenda became co-opted along the way.[6]

The dilemmas involved in all of this are not just in determining the right feminist or human rights activist positioning vis-à-vis the state or political authorities. In the next section of the chapter I examine briefly some of the ways that the regime of human rights has been operating as a tool of global governance, and some of the ways constructions of gender relations and of feminism have come to occupy them.

Human Rights and Women's Rights as a Global GovernanceTool

Kate Nash (2012) argues that equating the politics of human rights with the normative goals of emancipatory social movements, let alone of women's social movements, is misleading, given the diversity of organizational forms through which human rights are being defined and the complexity of multi-scalar law through which claims to justice are being made. While the politics of 'women's rights are human rights' constructs human rights as being a tool for claiming rights, largely mobilized from below, it is important to remember that human rights laws are part of national and international governing institutions, and, as such, are part of the inventory of political tools available to be used by hegemonic powers.

Human rights are not just a normative value system adopted by various local, national, regional, and transnational campaigns. Nor are they just a formal international legal convention that has been incorporated into many national and supranational legal systems (like the EU). Human rights have also become the raison d'etre of a number of multi-scale policy organizations, both statutory and voluntary, which are dedicated to facilitating, enabling, and distributing aid and support to various people and groups in societies all over the world; particularly for those who are deprived of exercising their human rights directly.

Given the situated gaze of the international NGOs and other organizations engaged in supplying human rights services, there can easily develop a contestation between them and various activist organizations, which present themselves as representing the local culture and tradition, and who construct the NGOs as agents of the imperialist West. There are also other incongruities between what is conceived by the NGOs as being local needs and those conceived by local people. Nadera Shalhoub-Kevorkian (2012) describes how the human rights organizations that established mobile clinics to serve the needs of Bedouin women in their unrecognized settlements in the Negev were resented by many of these women whose needs the clinics were meant to serve. Before the establishment of these clinics, Bedouin women were allowed, by their husbands, to travel to the city for medical services. Now, however, their husbands use the existence of these clinics to curtail their wives' travelling (Shalhoub-Kevorkian, 2012).

A major political and moral dilemma has arisen around the dislocation of particular groupings and whole populations from their human rights. The lack of comprehensive rights for women especially has become a rhetorical tool of Western governments when seeking to legitimize military interventions in the Middle East and Global South. Women's rights, as well as human rights, have become a tool for both civil and military global governance.

This has particularly become the case since the attacks of 9/11, after which humanitarian intervention became the global discourse framing global governance (Bhatt, 2012). In this context, there is the perceived need to develop global policy related to ungoverned territories in failed and fragile states, as well as the need for state building through the new technologies of warfare. It is within the context of this global governance policy that the gendered character of war – and of human rights – is being configured.

Gender relations and the ideology of feminism have been used in particular ways in this new regime of humanitarian militarism. For many years feminist networks all over the world circulated petitions calling on global powers to put pressure on the Taliban, who were ruling Afghanistan and who had applied the most extreme restrictions on women's lives: forbidding them to have formal education and work outside the home. However, many of these same feminists felt betrayed and manipulated when these calls were used as a moral justification for the war in Afghanistan in 2001. When President George W. Bush justified the invasion of Afghanistan as being in order to rescue Afghan women from the Taliban, he linked, in his speeches before the UN General Assembly, 'sexual slavery of girls and women' to the 'moral' objectives of the 'war against terror' (Miller 2004, p. 17). As Zilla Eisentein (2004) pointed out, emancipatory feminism and imperial feminism are not the same thing.

Feminism should not be homogenized. Liberal feminists, whose only goal is to fight against the glass ceiling which tends to block the power and position of elite women in particular, should not be conflated with emancipatory feminists. Emancipatory feminists approach issues of gender relations and social justice in an intersectional manner and view gender as only one of the axes of discrimination and disadvantage that need to be fought against and which mutually constitute specific women's positions (Abraham, 1995; Brah and Phoenix, 2004; Crenshaw, 1989; Yuval-Davis, 2009).

Because of this, the UN Security Council resolution 1325, about adding women to peace negotiations, is much too simplistic, essentialist, and reductionist. Too many women in power – from Golda Meir to Indira Gandhi, to Margaret Thatcher – to mention just some of the most powerful women in the field of governance of the latter half of the 20th century – can illustrate the point that women are not inherently peace-seekers.

Nominalist rhetoric cannot overcome power politics in the pursuit of social justice.

Even the idea that there is an inherent nature for women has far-reaching implications for the politics of global feminism which have been pursued in the campaigns under the slogan of 'women's rights are human rights'. Ros Petchesky (2009) points to the incident in Abu Ghraib, in which women soldiers in Iraq were shown abusing and sexually torturing Iraqi prisoners. Likewise in the Gujarat, Hindutva women have been active supporters of the extreme atrocities enacted against Muslim men and women. Petchesky (2009) writes:

> The violated male bodies of Abu Ghraib, Guantánamo and Gujarat seem to mock certain of Beijing's most basic premises: that women are primarily the victims rather than the perpetrators of bodily abuses; and that, as such, women are, or should be, the privileged beneficiaries of bodily integrity rights … My purpose is not to repudiate feminist visions but rather to challenge the exclusive privileging of women as the bearers of sexual rights and to open up discussion of new, more inclusive coalitions of diverse social movements for the human rights of the body.

In a similar way, Ratna Kapur (2002) describes how viewing women exclusively as 'victim subjects' combines both gender essentialism and cultural essentialism (2002, p. 6). The portrayal of women in the Third World as victims of their culture reinforces both stereotypes, of women as being victims, and of Asian, African, or Middle Eastern cultures as being inferior. This double move plays into the hands of powerful political forces that seek legitimacy for patrolling borders and waging war under the cover of protecting women. Such politics also obscure the active presence of multiple gendered and sexual subjects on the national and global political stage.

Feminism is not just about women, and it is definitely not just about the oppression of women by men. Any examination of the relationship between gender and human rights, and issues of social justice, cannot remain focused only on women, nor can it homogenize women and men. In specific historical moments, in specific locations, and in relation to specific individuals and groupings, there are situations in which some women oppress other women, some women oppress men, as well as there being men who oppress women and other men. An intersectional analysis must take into account the macro-patriarchal social relations and structures. We must be sensitive to particular configurations of power and how other social divisions of power such as race, ethnicity, class, ability, sexuality, etc. mutually constitute gender, as well as other social divisions. It is important that we not conflate social locations, identifications, and normative political values (Yuval-Davis, 2011).

Concluding Remarks Regarding Human Rights, Democracy, and Social Justice

The issues raised in this chapter are just a few of the many that arise when we examine, analyse, and deconstruct the contested and situated social and political dynamics related to issues of social justice, gender, and human rights. They are, however, central to the situated sociological imagination that needs to be part of any emancipatory public sociological agenda in the quest for social justice. They involve a destabilization of the notions of the human, the universal, the right and just, as well as the categories of women, gender, and feminism.

As a feminist human rights defender from Egypt told me many years ago: 'The litmus case is minorities and women. Tell me how they're treated and I'll tell you how emancipatory the regimes in which they live are. The rest is all pure rhetoric.'

Notes

1   For a more general discussion of these issues please read Chapter 5, 'On the Cosmopolitan Question', in my book *The Politics of Belonging: Intersectional Contestations* (Sage, 2011).

2   While I was writing this chapter, the 15-year-old Malala Yousafzai miraculously survived being assassinated by the Taliban in Pakistan for campaigning for girls' right for education.

3   www.awid.org/.

4   www.ong-ngo.org/en/the-2013-world-social-forum-will-take-place-in-tunis-march-23rd-to-28th/.

5   www.amnesty.org/en/economic-social-and-cultural-rights.

6   http://awid.org/eng=/News-Analysis/Announcements2/Gender-Development-The-Beyond-Gender-Mainstreaming-Learning-Project.

References

Abraham, M. (1995) Ethnicity, gender, and marital violence: South Asian women's organizations in the United States. *Gender & Society*, 9(4), 450–468.

Alkire, S. (2002) *Conceptual Framework for Human Security*. Available at: www.researchgate.net/publication/242201569_A_Conceptual_Framework_for_Human_Security (accessed 16 April 2018).

Anthias, F. and Yuval-Davis, N. (1992) *Racialized Boundaries*. London: Routledge.

Appiah, K.A. (2006) *Cosmopolitanism: Ethics in a World of Strangers*. New York, NY: W.W. Norton.

Baer, J.A. (1978) *The Chains of Protection: The Judicial Response to Women's Labour Legislation*. Westport, CT: Greenwood Press.

Balibar, E. (1990) Paradoxes of universality. In: D.T. Goldberg (ed.), *Anatomy of Racism*. Minneapolis, MN: Minnesota University Press.

Bhabha, H. (1994) *The Location of Culture*. London: Routledge.

Bhatt, C. (2012) Human rights and the transformations of war. In: P. Hynes, M. Lamb, D. Short, and M. Waites (eds), *The Sociology of Human Rights*, special issue of *Sociology*, 46(5), 813–828.

Bottomley, G. (1992) *From Another Place: Migration and the Politics of Culture*. Cambridge: Cambridge University Press.

Brah, A. and Phoenix, A. (2004) Ain't I a woman? Revisiting intersectionality. *Journal of International Women's Studies*, 5(3), 75–86.

Butler, J. (1990) *Gender Trouble: Feminism and the Subversion of Identity*. New York, NY: Routledge.

Chakrabarty, D., Bhabha, H.K., Pollock, S., and Breckenridge, C.A. (eds) (2002) *Cosmopolitanism*. Durham, NC: Duke University Press.

Cheah, P. (1997) Positioning Human Rights in the current global conjuncture. *Public Culture*, 9(2).

Chen, L.C. (1995) Human security: Concepts and approaches. In: T.M.A.L.C. Chen (ed.), *Common Security in Asia: New Concepts of Human Security*. Tokyo: Tokyo University Press.

Cockburn, C. and Hunter, L. (1999) Transversal politics and translating practices. *Soundings*, Special issue on Transversal Politics, 12(Summer).

Connell, R. (2012) Transsexual women and feminist thought: New understandings and new politics. *Signs*, 37(4), 857–881.

Copelon, R. (1995) Gendered war crimes: Reconceptualizing rape in time of war. In: J. Peters and A. Wolper (eds), *Women's Rights/Human Rights*. New York: Routledge.

Cornwall, A., Correa, S., and Susie, J. (2008) *Development with a Body – Sexuality, Human Rights & Development*. London: Zed books.

Cornwall, A. and Molineux, M. (eds) (2008) *The Politics of Rights: Dilemmas for Feminist Praxis*. London: Routledge.

Correa, S., Petchesky, R., and Parker, R. (2008) *Sexuality, Health and Human Rights*. New York, NY: Routledge.

Crenshaw, K. (1989) *Demarginalizing the Intersection of Race and Sex*. Chicago, IL: University of Chicago.

Delphy, C. (1993) Rethinking sex and gender. *Women's Studies International Forum*, 16(1), 1–9.

Eisenstein, Z. (2004) *Against Empire: Feminisms, Racism and 'the' West*. London: Zed Books.

Foucault, M. (1991) *The History of Sexuality, Vols 1, 2, 3: The Use of Pleasure* (Robert Hurly, trans.). London: Penguin.

Gutman, A. (2001) *Human Rights as Politics an Idolatry*. Princeton, NJ: Princeton University Press.

Herman, E.C. (2002) Forward. In: D. Chandler (ed.), *From Kosovo to Kabul: Human Rights and International Intervention*. London: Pluto Press.

Hood-Williams, J. (1996) Goodbye to sex and gender. *Sociological Review*, *44*(1), 1–16.

Huntington, S.P. (1996) *The Clash of Civilizations and the Remaking of World Order*. New Delhi: Penguin Books.

Ignatieff, M. (2001) *Human Rights as Politics and Idolatry*. Princeton, NJ: Princeton University Press.

Kapur, R. (2002) The tragedy of victimization rhetoric: Resurrecting the 'native' subject in international/post-colonial feminist legal politics. *Harvard Human Rights Journal 15*, 1–37.

Laqueur, T. (1990) *Making Sex*. Cambridge, MA: Harvard University Press.

Lewis, J. and Davis, C. (1991) Protective legislation in Britain 1870–1990: Equality and difference and their implications for women. *Policy and Politics*, *19*(1), 13–26.

May, S. (1999) *Critical Multiculturalism*. London: Routledge.

Miller, A.M. (2004) Sexuality, violence against women, and Human Rights: Women make demands and ladies get protection. *Health and Human Rights*, *4*(2), 17–47.

Nash, K. (2012) Human rights, movements and law: On not researching legitimacy. In: P. Hynes, M. Lamb, D. Short, and M. Waites (eds), *The Sociology of Human Rights*, Special issue of *Sociology*, 46(5), 797–812.

Nussbaum, M.C. (1995) Human capabilities: Capable human beings. In: M. Nussbaum and J. Glover (eds), *Women, Culture and Development: A Study of Human Capabilities* (pp. 61–104). Oxford: Clarendon Press.

Nussbaum, M.C. and Sen, A. (1993) *The Quality of Life*. Oxford: Oxford University Press.

Oakley, A. (1985). *Sex, Gender and Society*. London: Temple Smith.

Okins, S.M. (1999) Is multiculturalism bad for women? *Boston Review*. Available at: www.bostonreview.net/BR22.5/okin.html (accessed 16 April 2018).

Pateman, C. (1988) *The Sexual Contract*. Cambridge: Polity Press.

Petchesky, R. (2003) *Global Prescriptions: Gendering Health and Human Rights*. London: Zed Books.

Petchesky, R. (2009) *Rights of the Body and Perversions of War: Sexual Rights and Wrongs Ten Years Past*. Beijing: UNESCO. Available at: www.sxpolitics.org/wp-content/uploads/2009/03/petcheskyissjfinal.pdf (accessed 16 April 2018).

Plummer, K. (2003) *Intimate Citizenship*. Seattle, WA: University of Washington Press.

Rattansi, A. (2011) *Multiculturalism: A Very Short Introduction*. Oxford: Oxford University Press.

Rawls, J. (1971) *A Theory of Justice*. Cambridge, MA: Harvard University Press.

Rawls, J. (2009) *A Theory of Justice*, Revised edition. Cambridge, MA: Harvard University Press.

Reilly, N. (2008) *Women's Human Rights: Seeking Gender Justice in a Globalizing Age*. Cambridge: Polity Press.

Robinson, M. (2005) What rights can add to good development practice. In: A. Alston and M. Robinson (eds), *Human Rights and Development: Towards Mutual Reinforcement*. New York, NY: Oxford University Press.

Roseneil, S., Crowhurst, I., Hellesund, T., Santos, A.C., and Stoilova, M. (2012) Remasking intimate citizenship in multicultural Europe. In: B. Halsaa, S. Roseneil, and S. Sumer (eds), *Remaking Citizenship in Multicultural Europe*. London: Palgrave Macmillan.

Rowbotham, S. (1973) *Hidden from History*. London: Pluto.

Sen, A. (1981) *Poverty and Famines: An Essay on Entitlement and Deprivation*. Oxford: Clarendon Press.

Sen, A. (1992) *Inequality Reexamined*. Cambridge, MA: Harvard University Press.

Shaheed, F. (2012) *Ensuring Equal Cultural Rights for Women and Girls*, Special report submitted to the UN Human Rights Commission.

Shalhoub-Kevorkian, N. (2012) The grammar of rights in colonial contexts: The case of Palestinian women in Israel. *Middle East Law and Governance*, *4*, 106–151.

Sharma, A. (2006) *Are Human Rights Western? A Contribution to the Dialogue of Civilizations*. Oxford: Oxford University Press.

Spellman, E. (1988) *Inessential Woman*. London: The Women's Press.

Timothy, K. (2004) Human security discourse at the United Nations. *Peace Review*, *16*(1), 19–24.

Vogel, U. (1991) Is citizenship gender specific? In: U. Vogel and M. Moran (eds), *The Frontiers of Citizenship* (pp. 58–85). London: Macmillan.

Wieviorka, M. (1997) Is it so difficult to be anti-racist? In: P. Werbner and T. Modood (eds), *Debating Cultural Hybridity*. London: Zed Books.

Yuval-Davis, N. (1997) *Gender and Nation*. London: Sage.

Yuval-Davis, N. (2009) Intersectionality, citizenship and contemporary politics of belonging. *CRISPP (Contemporary Review of International Social and Political Philosophy)*, Special Issue on Contesting Citizenship, *10*(4).

Yuval-Davis, N. (2011) *The Politics of Belonging: Intersectional Contestations*. London: Sage.

Yuval-Davis, N. and Vargas, G. (1998) Latin American feminism in the 90s – A conversation. *International Feminist Journal of Politics*, *1*(2), 299–322.

5

Beyond Charters and Conventions

Human Rights Through the Lens of Social Justice and Peace

Bandana Purkayastha[1]

Introduction

Most scholarly discussions on human rights, human security, and social justice, focus on structures and processes that promote equality, freedom, and the enabling conditions for building lives of human dignity. In practice, however, the focus of human rights has often been on the legal edifices that are associated with the notion of rights. Here, I draw upon the concept of human rights enterprise (see Armaline et al., 2012, 2015) to move the discussion beyond charters, conventions, and states as benefactors of human rights to focus on the terrain of struggles through which human rights are claimed, contested, and achieved.

In order to link human rights and social justice in this way, I offer two related reflections. First, I discuss the making of the human rights charter as being an outcome of a larger social justice struggle to ensure human security. I show that the idea of people's well-being, and their ability to build lives of human dignity, free from want and threats of survival (the central principles of which are embedded in the human rights charter and conventions), has led to the development of ideas about human security. While human rights charters and conventions create the lattice-work for claiming and protecting human rights through institutionalized channels, I show that ideas of human security emerge through people's struggles to attain rights and justice. Second, I turn to contemporary struggles over human rights and security. Drawing upon lessons from struggles that have challenged violence unleashed by a constellation of state and extra-state entities, I argue that we need to pay attention to the ways in which people *redefine* rights in their quest for building secure lives. We need to examine how these definitions reflect a person's inherent dignity within the contexts of freedom, peace, and social justice.

The chapter begins with a brief discussion of the perspective of human rights enterprise. After this, I outline the struggle to access social justice through the development of the human rights charter in the mid-20th century. I then draw upon contemporary examples to discuss struggles over security: national security promulgated by states and dominant groups versus human security advocated by many marginalized groups. I conclude with a general discussion on social justice struggles.

Social Justice and Human Rights

Achieving social justice, that is, achieving the societal conditions in which people can build lives of human dignity, inevitably involves struggles to claim and access rights. Whether these are formal legal rights, which are achieved through large-scale struggles against repressive states (Kumar, 1990; Morris, 1984; Naidoo, 2006), or substantive rights achieved through persistent everyday actions within democracies (Glenn, 2002), social justice is achieved through struggles over power, voice, and access to resources. The development of human rights charters and conventions are arguably a significant part of this ongoing struggle for social justice.

Before delving into the struggles over human rights, it is important to note that the connections between human rights and global social justice struggles are relatively obscured in dominant strands of human rights scholarship and practice. In the Global North, over the years, many dominant voices within human rights scholarship have tended to simplify the history of human rights by drawing a direct line between selected western democratic principles and the Universal Declaration of Human Rights (UDHR). It is entirely possible to read scholarly accounts of human rights as being part of a linear evolution from the Enlightenment and the establishment of modern western democracies, to the passage of the human rights charter and its subsequent enforcement (Donnelly, 1982; Moyn, 2010). In the US, where I am located, in the popular imagination, human rights constitute an American gift, a gift from the western civilization to the world; democratic ideals and the leadership of Eleanor Roosevelt are the main symbols associated with the drafting of the Universal Declaration of Human Rights (UDHR), and its subsequent conventions.

From this vantage point, we rarely hear much about human rights violations within the US, in any sustained way, within the mainstream discourse (for exceptions see Armaline et al., 2012; Peck, 2011). Furthermore, there is scant recognition of the participation of African-American and other marginalized groups who were actively engaged in the struggles, victories, and setbacks that led to the formulation of the Universal Declaration of Human Rights (Andersen, 2003). That many of the earliest claims to women's rights was opposed by the American representatives has been obliterated in contemporary claims about the role of the US in shaping women's rights as human rights (Falcón, 2016). Social justice principles enshrined in cultures in other countries are less visible in the dominant scholarly conversations, as are accounts of the international contributions to human rights and social justice struggles from the Global South (for detailed discussions on these themes see: Falcón, 2016; Ishay, 2008; Lauren, 1998; Pearce, 2001; Purkayastha, 2009a).

Aware of these gaps in our understanding of human rights, and the multi-disciplinary human rights literature's focus on legal edifices, I draw upon the sociological literature, which draws our attention to struggles to acquire and access rights. I use a human rights enterprise approach, which my colleagues William Armaline, Davita Silfen Glasberg, and I developed, to describe human rights, not in terms of nation-states, international charters, and conventions alone, but as a terrain of struggles between groups seeking human rights and states that are reluctant to support these groups' claims (Armaline et al., 2012, 2015).

This approach connects human rights to social justice in two important ways. First, the human rights enterprise approach focuses on the struggles of marginalized groups to claim rights: it draws our attention to social justice movements and organizing their successes and setbacks. Consistent with this approach I show that even though the struggle to fashion human rights was sparked by the repressive actions of many states against their own people, the outcome of the initial struggle was that states recaptured the right to become the arbitrators of these human rights. Second, this approach conceptualizes the state, not only as governments, but also as constellations of political and economic interests, which derive their privileges and power by depriving marginalized groups of their human security. Thus, social justice struggles for human security are directed towards a nexus of political and economic interests that prevent these groups from achieving lives of human dignity. As many groups involved in these struggles have argued, their security as human beings, their very ability to survive and construct lives of dignity, is often jeopardized by the dominant economic and political powers pursuing their own interests and safeguarding their privileges at the expense of the marginalized.

Human Rights and Human Security: The Mid-20th Century Struggles

On 10 December 1948, when the United Nations released the Universal Declaration of Human Rights (UDHR), the document, proclaiming people's rights to political, civil, economic, social, and cultural human rights, reflected the imprint of many people around the world. At that time, the world was haunted by the images of concentration camps and the atrocities committed against Jews in the name of nationalism. Representatives from former and existing colonies described the ways by which colonial powers subjugated societies around the world, in order to create and maintain their own economic prosperity and political power (Purkayastha, 2012). The colonized were tired of the killings, their lack of political liberty, economic repression, and the depletion of their resources to fulfil the needs of colonial powers. They were tired of supporting colonial war efforts yet remaining subjugated. People were tired of wars, of the unprecedented numbers of people who had been killed in the Second World War. People were tired of the suffering caused by economic deprivation, including the deaths resulting from the deadly famines that resulted from procurement of food for the armed forces (Mukherjee, 2011).

A large number of people were tired of racism. Diverse groups spoke out against ideologies and institutions that classified human beings as being less than individuals. Global attention was drawn toward issues of cultural genocide, and to apartheid policies that forced human beings into segregated spatial and social locations, depriving them of the life chances that the otherwise racially privileged enjoyed. Public attention began to focus on internments, and the life-imprisonment of activists who organized for political independence from repressive rulers (Kathrada, 2004). For marginalized groups the incipient human rights charter promised security: security of personhood, security of food, shelter, and the ability to live lives of human dignity. Wanting security from state repression, the colonized around the world organized through international platforms to achieve some of their goals. They networked and helped to keep issues like racism on the UN agenda; they exchanged ideas about successful tactics of protests (for example the Gandhian methods that had been successfully used in India), which they subsequently deployed in their own countries as they struggled to access rights and human security (Andersen, 2003; Chabot, 2002; Horne, 2008).

A careful reading of the histories of these struggles shows that these early claims for rights were never about political and civil rights alone. Since their understanding of human security was based on the understanding of their political, economic, and social marginalization, these groups demanded what Gandhi called *purna swaraj*, that is, equality, political, economic, and social independence, to enable them to build just societies. This also involved weaving a vision of rights and obligations towards other humans, as being one of the core principles of humaneness and justice (Parikh, 2001). The independence movements in India – against British colonialism – included a vision of political independence *and* conditions promoting economic and social self-determination. They demanded rights for the hitherto marginalized: women, lower caste, and tribal groups (Kumar, 1990). Similarly, the struggle for civil rights in America called for political, civil, economic, and social rights (D'Angelo, 2001; Lawson, 1997; Morris, 1984).

The history of racial justice struggles prior to, during, and in the aftermath of the writing of the UDHR shows that different groups (in diverse countries) were aware that political freedom and civil rights would mean little if people died early, or were in constant ill health, or were too poor to travel to voting sites to exercise the political rights promised to them (Andersen, 2003). Thus, activists repeatedly organized to draw attention to the state and to the dominant group-sponsored legal and political edifices, and the violence that severely restricted the life-chances of the marginalized. While many powerful states argued that democratic forms of government would ensure human rights, these groups understood democratization as being just one step in the process of achieving human security with racial justice.

Racial justice was only one strand of the many struggles over human rights. Reflecting the voices of women's movements that existed around the world, women's rights leaders, such as Minerva Bernadino (Dominican Republic) or Hansa Mehta (India), struggled to ensure the UDHR was written in non-gendered language and paid attention to women's rights. A multitude of non-governmental secular and religious organizations joined in the criticisms of the untrammelled power of states. Peace, justice, rule of law, democracy, non-discrimination, right to self-determination of all people including women, indigenous groups and racial minorities, and protection of the vulnerable during times of war, all emerged as crucial demands.

Many indigenous groups demanded their groups' right to practice their cultures, pointing out that their forced assimilation had lead to cultural genocide. The demand for these rights became a cause of concern for many states when they realized that marginalized groups were accessing international platforms in ways that could undermine their entrenched power structures. Countries that were willing to speak about rights in principle, or protest against rights violations in other countries, were extremely reluctant to have their own records subject to similar scrutiny (Purkayastha, 2012).

The history of struggles over the making of the UDHR shows that the recognition of 'the inherent dignity and of the equal and inalienable rights of all members of the human family [as] the foundation of freedom, justice and peace in the world' was bitterly resisted by dominant states, including democratic states (OHCHR.org). These powerful states contested the demands of the UDHR by framing their concerns in the language of national sovereignty and state security. They claimed the power to pick and choose which rights they would uphold or bestow, and whose rights they would ignore. Citizenship, with its embedded hierarchies, remained the preferred vehicle for bestowing stratified rights and for controlling groups that demanded an expanded set of human rights. Thus the final version of the UDHR reflects both the revolutionary idea that humans are invested with rights irrespective of the political system through which they are governed, and also a capitulation to the status quo by making states responsible for those rights.

The 1948 charter declared that all humans are entitled to lives of human dignity, 'without distinction of any kind, such as race, colour, sex, language, religion, political or other opinion, national or social origin, property, birth or other status' (UDHR, 1948). Furthermore, the UDHR insisted that 'no distinction shall be made on the basis of the political, jurisdictional or international status of the country or territory to which a person belongs, whether it be independent, trust, non-self-governing or under any other limitation of sovereignty' (UDHR, 1948). The charter recognized that in recent history a 'disregard and contempt for human rights [has] resulted in barbarous acts which have outraged the conscience of mankind', and it recognized the aspiration for a socially just world 'in which human beings shall enjoy freedom of speech and belief and freedom from fear and want' (UDHR, 1948). The mechanisms developed for enforcing these rights, however, were relegated to states who retained their power to sort and sift their support for human rights. In the years after the writing of UDHR, as conventions and charters codified these rights, many states have signed onto conventions but with formal declarations that they would not be bound by parts of these conventions (Human Rights Bodies, 2016).

Despite ceding power to states, at the international level, the UDHR achieved one other social justice principle. It expanded the rights terrain beyond the political and civil rights associated with democracies. After a successful struggle by the (former) Soviet Union and its allies, the charter raised economic, cultural, and social rights to the level of political and civil rights. By doing so UDHR and its subsequent charters and conventions, such as the International Convention on Political and Civil Rights (ICPCR) and the International Convention on Economic, Social, and Cultural Rights (ICESCR), recognized the indelible links between the two types of rights that were necessary to ensure people could build secure lives of dignity. The issue of fair access to material conditions of life, which are inherent in the discussions of human security and social justice, emanate from these holistic sets of rights. The declaration also made a large number of hitherto vulnerable groups – like indigenous people – visible as rights holders, by declaring their rights, as groups, to practise their own cultures.

Overall, groups seeking rights wanted formal institutional edifices that could be used to exert power over states. They wanted to be freed from the actions of powerful people and entities that, despite charters and conventions, enforced exclusions, often resorting to violence to enforce boundaries in their everyday life. Many of their specific concerns were never wholly addressed. While the ICPCR and ICESCR addressed a gamut of human rights, the specific situation of women or racial (and ethnic) minorities was not formalized until much later. For instance, the International Convention on the Elimination of Racism (ICERD) was open for signature in 1965, while the Convention on the Elimination of Discrimination Against Women (CEDAW) was not formalized till 1979. The mechanisms for the enforcement of these conventions remain weak (Ertürk and Purkayastha, 2012; Purkayastha et al., 2012). Thus, at this level, a key component of the social justice struggle are the mechanisms to ensure protection from states, which remain relatively ineffectual, especially in the case of powerful states that can ignore international criticisms with impunity.

Following the passage of UDHR, a crucial part of the struggle for claiming human rights intensified within states. Two examples showcase how the struggles have proceeded with both victories and defeats through the national terrains. The case of apartheid in South Africa provides a case in point. During the early years of the UN, networks focussing on racial justice had drawn together activist leaders from many countries. Using the emerging political opportunity to proclaim their demands in an international platform, organized groups and prominent individuals had raised social justice questions, which states did not want to answer publicly. Their demands converged with those of the leaders who were drawing attention to the conditions of racial minorities in the United States and South Africa. At a general assembly of the United Nations, Indian representative Vijay Lakshmi Pandit (who was also the first woman president of the general assembly) charged South Africa with racism. General Smuts angrily answered that apartheid was an internal South African matter, not a subject of discussion at the international platform (Kathrada, 2004). But South Africa had been named and shamed internationally. The decades-long, arduous struggle against South African apartheid within the country, which was already in progress, with its toll of deaths, broken lives over generations, and the sacrifices of many, ultimately led to the system's dismantling in 1994. The international processes of 'naming and shaming' tactics, and the divestment movements, also contributed to the prolonged struggle for social justice within that country.

The struggle for racial justice within the US provides another example. The struggle of groups like the National Association for the Advancement of Colored People (NAACP) to claim political, civil, economic, and social rights for all people encountered the reality of the power of racist structures within the US and its post-war politics. During the Cold War the Soviet Union and the US accused each other of failing to ensure economic, social, political, and civil rights for their citizens. Within the United States, several units of the government, as well as political, economic, and social elites, embarked on a highly successful campaign to equate the claims for economic and social rights by marginalized groups to being communist, and, consequently, anti-American. Thus, groups like the NAACP, which had championed these human rights for decades, faced a difficult choice – should they continue to claim the entire gamut of rights and lose the campaign, or to continue with a narrower campaign on political and civil rights only. NAACP chose the latter. Despite the significant victories achieved through the Civil Rights struggle, recent accounts of the US's progress on CERD, via shadow reports filed by non-governmental organizations to the UN, show weak progress on civil, economic, social, and cultural rights in the US (Purkayastha et al., 2012).

The 21st century has seen continuing and sustained structural violence against African-Americans (Black Lives Matter, 2016), with an emphasis on imprisonment (Alexander, 2010), an assault on voting rights (Armaline et al., 2015), and the political discourse of marginalization and bigotry surrounding the 2016 presidential elections (Blow, 2016). All of these illustrate the unfinished nature of this struggle. Thus the assessment of human security of racial minority groups, whether they experience insti- tutionalized violence, unequal chances of survival, or whether they have unequal access to education, health care, housing, and voting rights, remain as an open question in the 21st century, despite international mechanisms to work towards addressing discrimination on the basis of race.

Human Rights and Competing Notions of Security in the 21st Century

Even as the use of human rights charters, conventions, and instruments opened up space for marginalized groups to claim human rights by the late 20th century, the rapid expansion of neoliberal political-economic forces, and the new globalized security 'anti-terror' regimes in the 21st century, shaped new terrains of struggles. Some scholars argued that in the 1990s, 'human rights values and institutions played a greater role in establishing stability in the global order and ensuring more democratic forms of political and economic participation at the local level' (Wilson, 2005, p. 3). Even if we accept this characterization of the global order, and many scholars do not, it is clear that the 'war on terror' ushered in an era where political and civil rights were rapidly undermined, including the introduc- tion of processes that delinked rights from citizenship (Walsh, 2014).

Even more problematic, is how the language of human rights has been co-opted to justify state-sponsored wars and violence (Peck, 2011). A series of acts, for instance the PATRIOT Act in the US, or the new poli- cies and practices through which states are pushing back refugees (Levitan et al., 2010), position state security above human rights. The changes raise critical questions about who is considered to be part of 'the state', and whose security has to be protected. Core civil and political rights such as the presumption of innocence, the right to be formally charged, and the right to a trial can now be suspended based on the rationale of national security. This same argument also serves as a key mechanism to weaken or repress opposition to the curtailment of liberties. Lubban (2005) points out that framing the curtailment of human rights (and civil rights within nations) as a trade-off during tough times is often politically successful because the rights of groups who are declared as likely to do wrong are seemingly being traded to ensure the liberties of good citizens. Not surprisingly, the liberties that are protected belong to dominant groups in society. Those who are expected to give up their liberties are inevitably the 'other', those who are already marginalized or disenfranchised (Menjivar and Abrego, 2012).

In contrast to this notion of state security, which justifies the curtailment of human rights, the notion of human security highlights the need for expanded substantive rights, including economic and social rights (Sen and Ogata, 2003).[2] The core disagreement around whether or not state security should get precedence over human security speaks centrally to some core social justice principles. As the political and economic structures have swung to emphasize state security, the emphasis on economic, social, and cultural rights has been further eroded through structural adjustment policies and processes. The contrast is evident in the massive increase of state spending on arms globally (Global Arms Trade, 2013). Meanwhile, the ten leading causes of death globally are related to causes such as hunger and diseases (WHO, 2017), which are preventable when one has access to social, economic, and cultural rights. The negative consequences of separating political and civil rights from economic, social, and cultural rights are notable. They further attenuate the claims made by marginalized groups during the inception of UDHR, and consequently the struggle to achieve global human security remains the unattained objective of the 21st century.

Security, Violence, and Human Rights

Much like the early and mid-twentieth centuries, activists and civil groups continue to struggle for human security. They seek a range of political, civil, economic, social, and cultural rights that would enable them to live free from violence, with full access to the rights necessary to build lives of human dignity. However, they do so in the context of 21st-century conflicts and violence.

People who are favourably inclined to the notion of state security, and the curtailment of rights, point out that all wars require a curtailment of rights. This then assumes that at the conclusion of wars, rights will be restored to people in democracies (Ignatieff, 2009). This argument, however, presupposes that wars are the dominant form of conflict, and that wars begin and end. It also assumes that the impacts of such conflicts are faced primarily by combatants, or a few groups that are asked to give up their rights temporarily. Empirical data indicates a different reality. Gleditsch et al. (2002) presented a new database on *Armed Conflict 1946–2001* that showed how, by the turn of the 21st century, intra-state conflict, i.e. conflict that kills at least 25 people annually, has become the dominant form of conflict after the Second World War (Halleberg, 2012). Thus, the boundary between wars and armed conflicts within states has become blurred. Both types of conflict engender the curtailment or suspension of human rights.

America's 'war on terror', along with similar efforts in other countries, has led to the creation of new national and global security regimes and the rise of immigration complexes (Aranda and Vaquera, 2015; Hall, 2010). If the access to human rights was supposed to guarantee some relief from government-sponsored repression and violence, the rapid expansion of security regimes, including the rapid increase of private armies (Dickenson, 2011), the normalization of violence (Pandey, 2006; Purkayastha and Ratcliff, 2014), and the success of state security discourses to justify these expansions, point to the uneasy relationship between violence, security regimes, human rights, and human security in the 21st century.

As in the mid-20th century, groups and individuals have been struggling to challenge the incursion of this rapid expansion of routinized violence in their everyday lives. One example is the fast-unto-death protest by Irom Sharmila in India, between 2000 and 2015, highlighting the relationship between state security regimes, violence, and the suspension of rights (Mehrotra, 2009). In India, the 1956 Armed Forces Special Powers Act (AFPSA) empowered military and paramilitary forces to operate within selected 'disturbed' regions of the country. Manipur, where Irom Sharmila is located, was defined as such a region. Armed forces in these areas were allowed to fire upon their own citizens, after giving a warning, in order to maintain law and order, or to destroy arms caches. They were also allowed to stop people on suspicion, search their vehicles, and arrest people on reasonable suspicion of wrongdoing with no prior warrant required. The officers who acted under AFSPA were also granted immunity for their actions.

Yet these powers are not unique to India. These powers – stop on suspicion, surveillance, and searches without warrants, the legal right to fire upon people on suspicion of threats – have become familiar parts of the national security narrative, and common practices in the Global North in the 21st century. In many, if not most, countries around the world the police forces are now armed and often enjoy significant immunity. The result is the devastating impact of police brutality and violence enacted against marginalized communities (Alexander, 2010; Black Lives Matter, 2016; Chatterji, 2012). The level and range of violence in everyday life has been exacerbated, not only because of the state-sanctioned violence by armed forces, or violence by private security forces hired to protect economic interests, but also by the groups that set themselves up to 'protect their communities' with violence of their own.

The efforts of groups around the world, such as Black Lives Matter (Black Lives Matter, 2016), or the protest of Naga mothers against the violence by Indian military (Purkayastha and Ratcliff, 2014), draws attention to this routinization of violence on the grounds of state security, and the negative effect it has on human security. A large number of groups have also highlighted that the enhanced ability to access superior types of arms, legally or illegally, has inevitably led to the escalation of sexualized violence (cf. Rehn and Sirleaf, 2002; SACW, 2005; Sutton et al., 2008). Many of these groups have asserted the need to resist the normalization of cultures of violence. They have raised questions about the cultural right of people, especially of those who are most likely to experience such violence, to define what constitutes normalcy and to identify the conditions that enable them to exercise their own rights to survival and well-being within contexts of peace (Purkayastha, 2008; 2009b). Thus far, these struggles have been unable to halt the rapid spread of routine violence associated with the securitization of states. However, the continuing use of non-violent struggles to highlight the repressiveness of armed responses keeps the questions about violence and human security at the centre of many struggles.

The escalation of measures to support state security has an additional negative economic and social impact. Scholars such as Watkin (2004) point out that as the mass production of weapons increases dramatically, so also does the range and costs of ordinary people's experiences of such wars. With the ever-increasing production and marketing of arms, it is not difficult to secure arms (Global Arms Trade, 2013). The number of people around the world who are directly and indirectly affected by armed conflicts, even if they are not injured or killed, has been growing rapidly. Such conflicts redirect resources from human welfare to the political economy of warfare. The redirection of resources affects the ability of people to access health, education, jobs, or housing at affordable costs, all of which prevent thousands from dying each day from the preventable social causes of hunger and disease (see Bahuguna, 1990; Barnett, 2008; Bhatt, 2008; Das Gupta, 2010).

Many contemporary struggles attempt to redefine what rights and security mean in the 21st century, and which structures and efforts will either promote or impede large-scale access to human security.

One such effort is Nobel Laureate Wangari Matthei's Green Belt movement intended to draw attention to the depletion of natural resources due to wars and conflicts. Thousands of activists have sought to take back their lands and replenish the earth through planting trees in conflict-torn areas (Matthei, 2003). A similar stand off is under way in the US today as Native Americans attempt to halt the building of an oil pipeline through Standing Rock. They have defined their right 'to protect our water, our sacred places, and all living beings' (Standing Rock, 2016). This is expanding the idea of rights beyond the customary idea of conditions that states or governments might bestow. Instead, they have asserted their right to define these terms with reference to a holistic perspective on political, civil, social, economic, and cultural human rights. Similarly, in India, the Narmada Bacho activists have started protesting the building of large dams on the river Narmada. These dams disrupt the livelihoods of many marginalized groups. The Narmada Bacho have gone on to challenge the state's ability to 'grab their land' (Patkar, 2011).

These various groups and examples connect the dots between the actions of states, powerful international and national economic interests, and the deprivation of human security. Many other groups and individuals have drawn our attention to the connections between the rapid process of privatization and commodification of resources, such as land, seeds, water, and air, and the violent repressions, including deaths, of groups that resist such appropriation of resources (see Pantuliani, 2009; Shiva, 2002, 2005; Zwarteveen et al., 2012). Other activists target the inequalities caused by the rapid privatization of urban space, housing, cutbacks in welfare provisions in countries whose spending on military and state-security continues to grow (Desai, 2002). Whether or not these activists use the specific English words 'human rights', their struggles are for human security and social justice.

Among many struggles for human rights today, the rapidly escalating struggle over water rights reveals the unfinished struggle of access to social, cultural, political, and economic rights. As water is turned into a commodity based on market value, this commodity is increasingly unavailable to ordinary people. Its commodification becomes protected through the deployment of security forces. For many of the activists and scholars, this is an excellent example of a form of routine violence, where security forces begin to restrict the supplies of a resource that was culturally understood to belong equally to all humanity (Shiva, 2002).

Depending on the ability of the powerful group to protect their commodity, private armed guards are not uncommon in places where modern water is pumped and bottled, or where land (with minerals or high values for potential real estate development) can be appropriated in the name of progress. Activists have pointed out that many groups honour cultural norms by quenching someone's thirst – voluntarily, from a common resource of humanity – or consider the land to hold spiritual meanings, so that privatization and commodification of water acts as a form of cultural assault, along with the negative implications on local groups' economic and social rights (Shiva, 2005).

The struggle to access human security is also about defining the terms. Once the neoliberal definitions prevail, governments and powerful private groups can invoke state security to forcibly repress the people who oppose them. Recognizing that the forces of privatization are reshaping resources and rights, groups have begun to expand the definition of human rights to include human and environmental connections, and the rights of collectivities, as a key perspective to understand human rights and human security. The movements for 'earth democracy', for green belts, for sacred places, for non-privatized water, air, and seeds, for rights to lands and livelihoods offer a different language for understanding rights. Similarly, the struggles to stop state-sponsored violence against racial minorities, immigrants, and refugees, or sexual violence against women, are creating new frameworks for understanding rights and security. Challenging the processes that make violence banal, these very diverse struggles across the world offer their beliefs and non-violent strategies and practices as a way of promoting more peaceful human–environmental coexistence, and a more holistic vision of human security and human rights.

Social Justice: A Few Thoughts

Abraham (2012) notes, in her Buenos Aires plenary, that social justice struggles continue to occur around the world. Even though the language or perspective of these millions of struggles extends far beyond the focus on human rights and security, the specific focus on the human rights enterprise approach, at a minimum, draws attention to these terrains of social justice struggles. This approach also offers some lessons that are important for understanding social justice from a scholarly perspective.

The approach draws attention to the multifaceted and prolonged nature of certain struggles. On the one hand, the institutionalization of human rights through the UN represents a significant step in the struggle for justice by people who experience violence and repression. Human rights charters and conventions provide an edifice of laws and policies that can be useful as a way of linking international efforts to struggles within countries. On the other hand, this chapter shows that each victory represents one step within a larger, longer arc of efforts to achieve social justice. The struggles described here indicate both the need to build institutional structures, and to constantly re-define the meanings and parameters of these institutions. The UDHR, its charters and conventions, and its reporting mechanisms provide a set of grounded realities that can be used by various entities around the world, including for the purposes of re-defining or interrupting power.

The human rights gatherings have provided platforms for the networking and agenda setting efforts to keep the institutional structures dynamic. Examining human rights as an enterprise, as a process of struggle – with victories and defeats – allows us to think about human security as part of a larger terrain of struggle for social justice. In other words, the social justice scholarship has to retain a focus on the institutions that emerge through struggles, as well as examining the dynamic relationship of these institutions and the ongoing struggles that act as forces of critique and change within these institutions.

The human rights enterprise approach allows us to look across local, national, and international levels. One important reason to examine these levels is because these structures intersect to create impediments or possibilities for achieving human security. It is equally important to understand how each of these levels – local, national, international – can work in disjunctured ways so that the problems or conflicts at one level might be at odds with the problems and conflicts at another level; for instance the local and international agendas might coalesce but start to diverge from the national agenda. The struggles within countries in the aftermath of the passage of UDHR remind us that claiming rights and achieving social justice may depend on simultaneous yet different approaches and decisions to address diverse local, national, or international contexts. Thus social justice discussions need to examine both the intersecting global–national–local structures that define the terrain of struggle, but also the relationship between the actions taken within disjunctured contexts.

Using the human rights enterprise approach I have highlighted the alliances between states and capitalist interests, which work together to violate human rights. Violence remains a key tool in controlling group access to rights and security. We need to continue to foreground how violence, in its different forms, from routine violence to wars, is a tool of these constellations used to maintain their power. Only then can we fully understand the forces that groups face in their struggle for social justice.

The 21st-century struggles are pitted against states and global security regimes that reach across national borders, often through the use of increasing levels of violence. At the same time, an examination of the terrain of struggle shows that groups seek to challenge these constellations and re-define terms, such as rights, so that the perspective on rights, human security, and social justice is no longer confined to discussions of states and citizens alone. A focus on these struggles draws attention to the multiple entities that use violence and violate rights, and also to the specific efforts under way to resist the normalizing of violence in the context of everyday lives.

Nearly 70 years after UDHR, we continue to remain indebted to the people who have dedicated their lives and energies towards securing social justice via the human rights charters and conventions. The achievement of human security, however, remains within a terrain of ongoing struggles.

Notes

1   Department of Sociology, University of Connecticut, Storrs CT 06269-1068. Bandana.Purkayastha@uconn.edu.

2   The case of cultural rights is more controversial since it has been widely used by fundamentalist groups to assert their power. I have discussed these issues elsewhere (see Iwata and Purkayastha, 2012; Purkayastha, 2003).

References

Abraham, M. (2012) Speech at Buenos Aires. Available at: www.isa-sociology.org/en/conferences/forum/buenos-aires-2012/plenary-sessions-and-open-forum-videos/ (accessed 20 January 2017).

Alexander, M. (2010) *The New Jim Crow: Mass Incarceration in the Age of Colorblindness*. New York, NY: The New Press.

Anderson, C. (2003) *Eyes Off the Prize: The United Nations and the African American Struggle for Human Rights, 1944–1955*. New York, NY: Cambridge University Press.

Aranda, E. and Vaquera, E. (2015) Racism, the immigration enforcement regime, and the implications for racial inequality in the lives of undocumented young adults. *Sociology of Race and Ethnicity*, *1*, 88–104.

Armaline, W., Glasberg, D., and Purkayastha, B. (2012) *Human Rights in our own Backyard: Injustice and Resistance in the US*. Philadelphia, PA: University of Pennsylvania Press.

Armaline, W., Silfen Glasberg, D., and Purkayastha, B. (2015) *The Human Rights Enterprise: The State, Resistance, and Human Rights*. London: Polity Press.

Bahuguna, V. (1990) The Chipko movement. In: I. Sen (ed.), *A Space within the Struggle: Women's Participation in People's Movements* (pp. 111–124). New Delhi: Kali for Women.

Barnett, J. (2008) Peace and development: Towards a new synthesis. *Journal of Peace Research*, *45*, 75–89.

Bhatt, E. (2008) *We are Poor but so Many*. New Delhi: Oxford University Press.

Black Lives Matter (2016) Available at: blacklivesmatter.com (accessed 3 January 2017).

Blow, C. (2016) Denounce the hate, Mr. Trump. *New York Times*, 11 November. Available at: www.nytimes.com/2016/11/11/opinion/denounce-the-hate-mr-trump.html?_r=0 (accessed 20 January 2017).

Chabot, S. (2002) Transnational diffusion and the African American reinvention of the Gandhian repertoire. In: J. Smith and H. Johnston (eds), *Globalization and Resistance: Transnational Dimensions of Social Movements*. Lanham, MD: Rowman & Littlefield.

Chatterji, A. (2012) Witnessing a feminist intervention in India-administered Kashmir. In: A. Loomba and R. Lukose (eds), *South Asian Feminisms*. New Delhi: Zubaan Books.

D'Angelo, R. (2001) *The American Civil Rights Movement*. Guilford, CT: McGraw-Hill/ Dushkin.

Das Gupta, S. (ed.) (2010) *Women's Encounter with Disaster*. Kolkata: Frontpage Publications.

Desai, A. (2002) *We are the Poors: Community Struggles in Post Apartheid South Africa*. New York, NY: Monthly Review Press.

Dickenson, L. (2011) *Outsourcing War and Peace: Preserving Public Values in a World of Privatized Foreign Affairs*. New Haven, CT: Yale University Press.

Donnelly, J. (1982) Human rights and human dignity: An analytical critique of non western conceptions of human rights. *The American Political Science Review*, *76*(2), 303–316.

Ertürk, Y. and Purkayastha, B. (2012) Linking research, policy and action: A look at the work of the special rapporteur on violence against women. *Current Sociology*, *60*, 20–39.

Falcón, S. (2016) *Power Interrupted: Antiracist and Feminist Activism Inside the United Nations*. Seattle, WA: University of Washington Press.

Gleditsch, N., Wallerstein, P., Erikkson, M., Sollenberg, M., and Strand, H. (2002) Armed conflict 1946–2001: A new dataset. *Journal of Peace Research*, *39*(5), 615–637.

Glenn, E.N. (2002) *Unequal Freedom: How Race and Gender Shape American Citizenship*. Cambridge, MA: Harvard University Press.

Global Arms Trade (2013) Available at: www.globalissues.org/article/74/the-arms-trade-is-big-business (accessed 16 August 2013).

Hall, A. (2010). 'These people could be anyone': Fear, contempt (and empathy) in a British immigration removal center. *Journal of Ethnic and Migration Studies*, *36*, 881–898.

Hallberg, J. (2012) PRIO conflict site 1989–2008: A geo-referenced dataset on armed conflict. *Conflict Management and Peace Science*, *29*(2), 219–232.

Horne, G. (2008) *The End of Empires: African Americans and India*. Philadelphia, PA: Temple University Press.

Human Rights Bodies (2016) Available at: www.ohchr.org/EN/HRBodies/Pages/HumanRightsBodies.aspx (accessed 1 August 2013).

Ignatieff, M. (ed.) (2009) *American Exceptionalism and Human Rights*. Princeton, NJ: Princeton University Press.

Ishay, M.R. (2008) *The History of Human Rights: From Ancient Times to the Globalization Era*. Berkeley, CA: University of California Press.

Iwata, M. and Purkayastha, B. (2011) Reflections on cultural human rights. In: W. Armaline, D. Glasberg, and B. Purkayastha (eds), *Human Rights in our Backyard: Injustice and Resistance in the US*. Philadelphia, PA: University of Pennsylvania Press.

Kathrada, A. (2004) *Memories*. Capetown, ZA: Zebra Press.

Kumar, R. (1990) *A History of Doing*. London: Verso.

Lauren, P. (1998) *The Evolution of International Human Rights*. Philadelphia, PA: Temple University Press.

Lawson, S. (1997) *Running for Freedom: Civil Rights and Black Politics in America since 1941*. Boston, MA: McGraw-Hill Press.

Levitan, R., Kaytaz, E., and Durukan, O. (2010) Unwelcome guests: The detention of refugees in Turkey's 'foreigner's guesthouses'. *Refugee*, *26*, 77–90.

Lubban, D. (2005) Eight fallacies about security and liberty. In: R. Wilson (ed.), *Human Rights in the War on Terror*. Cambridge, UK: Cambridge University Press.

Matthei, W. (2003) *The Green Belt Movement: Sharing the Approach and the Experience*. New York, NY: Lantern Books.

Mehrotra, D. (2009) *Burning Bright: Irom Sharmila and the Struggle for Peace in Manipur*. New Delhi: Penguin Books.

Menjivar, C. and Abrego, L. (2012) Legal violence: Immigration law and the lives of central Americans. *American Journal of Sociology*, *117*, 1380–1421.

Morris, A. (1984) *The Origins of the Civil Rights Movement: Black Communities Organizing for Change*. New York, NY: Free Press.

Moyn, S. (2010) *The Last Utopia: Human Rights in History*. Cambridge, MA: Belknap Press.

Mukherjee, M. (2011) *Churchill's Secret War: The British Empire and the Ravaging of India during World War II*. New Delhi: Tranquebar Press.

Naidoo, P. (2006) *156 Hands that Built South Africa*. Durban, ZA: Stephan Phillips Pvt Limited.

Pandey, G. (2006) *Routine Violence: Nations, Fragments, Histories*. Stanford, CA: Stanford University Press.

Pantuliani, S. (ed.) (2009) *Uncharted Territory: Land, Conflict and Humanitarian Action*. Dunsmore: Practical Action Publishing.

Parikh, B. (2001) *Gandhi: A Short Introduction*. New York, NY: Sterling Publishing Company.

Patkar, M. (2011). Available at: www.narmada.org; http://wn.com/narmada_bachao_andolan; http://search.yahoo.com/search;_ylt=AuktwBEsHnoKOZNpBTghtlSbvZx4?p=narmada+

bacho+medha+david+harvey&toggle=1&cop=mss&ei=UTF-8&fr=yfp-t-900 (accessed 5 August 2013).

Pearce, T. (2001) Human rights and sociology: Some observations from Africa. *Social Problems*, *48*, 48–56.

Peck, J. (2011) *Ideal Illusions: How the US Government Co-opted Human Rights*. New York, NY: Henry Holt and Company.

Purkayastha, B. (2003) Looking beyond the individual: Interaction of structural factors and human agency in the empowerment of women. In: A. Mukherjee and K. Bhattacharya (eds), *Conditioning and the Empowerment of Women: A Multidimensional Approach*. New Delhi: Gyan Publishing House.

Purkayastha, B. (2008) Building a fabric of peace: Notes from the field. In: G. Caforio, G. Kuemmel, and B. Purkayastha (eds), *Armed Conflict and Conflict Resolution: Sociological Perspectives* (pp. 393–411). Bingley: Emerald Group.

Purkayastha, B. (2009a) Tagore and human rights. In: C. Sealey and R. Datta (eds), *Celebrating Tagore*. Kolkata: Allied Publishers.

Purkayastha, B. (2009b) Many views on peace. In: G. Caforio (ed.) *Military Sociology, Essays in Memory of Charles Moskos*. Bingley: Emerald Group.

Purkayastha, B. (2012) Human rights, global visions. In: A. Omara-Otunnu, S. Mobilia, and B. Purkayastha (eds), *Human Rights: Voices of World's Young Activists* (pp. 1–9). Kolkata: Frontpage Publications.

Purkayastha, B. and Ratcliff, K. (2014) Routine violence: Intersectionality at the interstices. In: M. Segal and V. Demos (eds), *Advances in Gender Research*, Volume 18B. London: Emerald Publications.

Purkayastha, A., Purkayastha, B. and Waring, C. (2012) From international platforms to local yards: Standing up for the elimination of racial discrimination in the United States. In: W. Armaline, D. Glasberg, and B. Purkayastha (eds), *Human Rights in our Backyard: Injustice and Resistance in the US*. Philadelphia, PA: University of Pennsylvania Press.

Rehn, E. and Sirleaf, E.J. (2002) *Women, War, Peace: The Independent Experts' Assessments on the Impact of Armed Conflict on Women and Women's Role in Peace Building*. Available at: www.unifem.org/materials/item_detaild89f.html (accessed 1 August 2013).

SACW (2005) *Joint Statement by Women's Groups Against Armed Forces Special Powers Act, 1958*. Available at: www.sacw.net/Wmov/JointStatement20012005.html. (accessed 12 January 2008).

Sen, A. and Ogata, S. (2003) *Human Security Now*. Available at: www.unocha.org/humansecurity/chs/index.html (accessed 30 July 2012).

Shiva, V. (2002) *Water Wars: Privatization, Pollution, and Profit*. Boston, MA: South End Press.

Shiva, V. (2005) *Earth Democracy: Justice, Sustainability, and Peace*. Boston, MA: South End Press.

Standing Rock (2016) Available at: http://standwithstandingrock.net/oceti-sakowin/ (accessed 17 January 2017).

Sutton, B., Morgen, S., and Novokov, J. (eds) (2008) *Security Disarmed: Critical Perspectives on Gender, Race, Militarization*. New Brunswick, NJ: Rutgers University Press.

UDHR (1948) Available at: www.wunrn.com/reference/pdf/univ_dec_hum_right.pdf; www.un.org/en/documents/udhr/; http://www.ohchr.org/EN/HRBodies/Pages/Human RightsBodies.aspx.

Walsh, J. (2014) From nation of immigrants to states of intransigence: Temporary migration in Canada and Australia. *International Sociology*, *29*, 584–606.

Watkin, K. (2004) Controlling the use of force: A role for human rights norms in contemporary armed conflict. *The American Journal of International Law*, *98*, 1–34.

WHO (2017) *Mortality and Global Health Estimates*. Available at: www.who.int/gho/ mortality_burden_disease/en/ (accessed 20 January 2017).

Wilson, R. (ed.) (2005. *Human Rights in the War on Terror*. Cambridge, UK: Cambridge University Press.

Zwarteveen, M., Ahmed, S., and Gautam, S. (eds) (2012) *Diverting the Flow: Gender Equity and Water in South Asia*. New Delhi: Zubaan Books.

6

Whistleblowing and Social Justice

The Influence of *Ubuntu* on Whistleblowing Intentions

Tina Uys

Introduction

Issues related to social justice are firmly on the agenda in the 21st century. Similarly, the role of whistleblowers in promoting corporate governance and public accountability is prominent in everyday discourse. In spite of these trends, the articulation between the phenomena of whistleblowing and social justice is seldom explored. It could be argued, however, that the processes linked to whistleblowing, as well as the outcomes flowing from it, are directly related to social justice concerns, in particular those of democratization and human rights.

For the purposes of this chapter, a whistleblower is defined as an organizational insider – someone with privileged access to an organization's information – making a disclosure about perceived non-trivial organizational wrongdoing to someone who is considered to be in a position to address the concern. The whistleblower's concerns could be raised internally, through internal channels. Whistleblowers could also resort to an external authority, such as a regulator, or make their disclosure publicly by talking to the media. Such disclosures generally result in retaliation by members of the organization where the wrongdoing is being exposed.

While whistleblowing is focused on promoting an ethical workplace through an attempt to rectify something that is going wrong in the organization, it is also an issue of rights and justice. Social justice in the organizational context, or organizational justice as it is often referred to, concerns perceptions of fairness within the organization. Greenberg (2011) distinguished four forms of organizational justice. First, distributive justice entails the perception of fairness with regard to the distribution of rights, resources, and costs among group members. Second, procedural justice, or the perceived fairness of the process, is used to regulate the allocation of resources. Third, organizational justice is determined in terms of the perceived fairness with which members of the organization are treated by others. This is referred to as interpersonal or interactional justice. Fourth, and lastly, informational justice concerns the perceptions of organizational members relating to the quality of the information upon which decisions are based (Greenberg, 2011, pp. 67–71).

When it comes to organizational justice, whistleblowing researchers have largely focused on ensuring that all role players perceive the whistle-blowing process as fair. The role players involve the whistleblower as well as a broad range of disclosure recipients, which could include the wrongdoer, the organization employing the whistleblower, or those affected by the whistleblower's disclosures. The emphasis therefore tends to be on the implementation of mechanisms that incentivize observers of perceived wrongdoing to disclose their concerns to the relevant parties. Included in this are the mechanisms that protect those who blow the whis-tle against retaliation, thereby ensuring that organizational justice prevails in the organization. It could be argued, however, that this scope should be broadened from a narrow focus on protecting the whistleblower to a broader emphasis on giving prominence to what whistleblowers would like to achieve with their disclosures. The goal of all of it should be that the workplace is returned to its former (presumably) ethical state as an environment where all role players act in the interests of fairness and the public good.

The focus of this chapter is on considering factors that would encour-age organizational members to take a stand against the abuse of power, thereby ensuring organizational justice for all in the organization. As a point of departure, I discuss Near et al.'s (1993) explanation of the whistleblowing process in terms of power relations and justice theory. They concluded that legalistic organizational protections were preferable to legal protections implemented by the state. The former is more likely to result in perceptions of procedural and distributive justice, both on the part of the whistleblower and the recipients of the disclosures of wrongdoing. Hence, it would be more likely to encourage whistleblowing, as well as inspire a positive response by the organization. Subsequently, I explore the link between belief systems and whistleblowing intentions, which is implicit in the perception of organizational justice held by organizational members. This is followed by an analysis of the influence of culture on whistleblowing intentions, in particular the African philosophy of *ubuntu* and its emphasis on restorative justice. In conclusion, I argue that an analysis of the role of organizational justice in whistleblowing should extend beyond just considering how whistleblowers can be encouraged and protected from retaliation. It should also focus on how the act of whistleblowing contributes to restoring organizational justice in the workplace by strengthening its ethical foundation.

Organizational Justice and the Process of Whistleblowing

Near et al. (1993) employed justice theory to explain why legal state sanctions have been unsuccessful in encouraging whistleblowing, as compared to the relative success of legalistic responses by organizations through the implementation of whistleblowing procedures. They argue that legalistic organizational protections would be more conducive towards encouraging whistleblowing, as well as urging organizational members to respond positively to disclosures, than legal protections implemented by the state. Procedures for whistleblowing put in place by the organizations themselves are more likely to generate perceptions of procedural and distributive justice, both on the part of the whistleblower and the recipients of the disclosures of wrongdoing (Near et al., 1993).

The level of organizational justice and satisfaction experienced by organization members, in general, is directly related to their satisfaction with the system (procedural justice) and/or their satisfaction with the outcomes (distributive justice). Whistleblower satisfaction would be highest if these individuals felt that the procedures followed in dealing with their disclosures were administered fairly, and that the outcomes were positive. This would mean that the wrongdoing was terminated, and there was no retaliation taken against the whistleblower.

Similarly, organization members affected by the whistleblowing would experience the greatest satisfaction if they believed that harm to the organization had been averted, and that fair reporting procedures had been followed. This could include the whistleblower making use of internal channels, rather than airing their concerns publicly, thereby minimizing damage to the organization's reputation. In his study of the likelihood of achieving organizational justice in the Australian police service, Beckley (2014) stressed the importance of creating a positive organizational culture where bullying, ostracism, and intimidation of the whistleblower is not tolerated (2014, p. 180). He concluded that employees in organizations displaying high levels of organizational justice would be more committed to achieving organizational goals and objectives; express higher levels of satisfaction with their work environment; and would show more trust in their profession, resulting in 'good staff retention, good workplace relations, high productivity and performance' (Beckley, 2014, p. 186).

In order to achieve organizational justice, it is important that procedural and distributive justice for the whistleblower, as well as the organization members, should be ensured. Rather than using legal means to reduce the negative impact of retaliation and thereby boost the whistleblower's outcome satisfaction, Near et al. argued that mechanisms should be created improving perceptions of procedural justice and the system satisfaction of the whistleblower as well as those organization members witnessing the whistleblowing activity. They stated:

> we believe that legal stratagems must focus on the system and outcome satisfaction of all the parties involved, including other organization members who are potentially affected by the whistle-blowing, as well as the whistle-blower. (1993, p. 406)

In order to develop the most effective strategies which would enhance all role-players' satisfaction with the procedures and the outcomes, it is important to understand the factors that influence the likelihood of the observer of wrongdoing engaging in whistleblowing. One such explanation flows from the application of Fishbein and Azjen's (2010) Theory of Reasoned Action.

Theory of Reasoned Action: The Link Between Belief Systems and Whistleblowing Intentions

Fishbein and Azjen's (2010) Theory of Reasoned Action (TRA) argues that three types of conceptually independent underlying beliefs about the behavior determine the intention to behave in a particular way, namely behavioral beliefs, injunctive and descriptive normative beliefs, and control beliefs.

Behavioral beliefs, or outcome expectations, relate to actors' views of possible positive or negative outcomes that could flow from engaging in the behavior. Through weighing up the costs and benefits that the behavior could result in, actors develop a favorable or unfavorable attitude towards personally performing said behavior. Observers of wrongdoing in an organization therefore evaluate the possible consequences of making a disclosure or not making a disclosure, on the basis of which they form a favorable or unfavorable attitude towards engaging in whistleblowing (Fishbein and Azjen, 2010, pp. 20–23).

Individuals then develop perceptions with regard to how their significant others would respond should they engage in the same behavior, and whether these significant others are likely to engage in the behavior themselves. Through these injunctive and descriptive normative beliefs actors develop a *perceived norm* (previously called a subjective norm) with regard to the behavior, which refers to the social pressure that actors experience to act in a particular way, as well as the extent to which individuals are motivated to conform to the expectations of significant others. Observers of organizational wrongdoing would therefore be more likely to form an intention to blow the whistle if they felt that people whose opinions they value would approve of them doing so (Fishbein and Azjen, 2010).

Finally, individual assessments of how easy it would be to perform the particular action inform their intention to do so. This entails weighing up whether the resources and opportunities needed to perform certain behaviors are available, as well as the constraints and risks associated with those behaviors. These control beliefs result in the individual developing a sense of *perceived behavioral control* (Fishbein and Azjen, 2010). In the case of whistleblowing, organizational obstacles such as management intentionally ignoring or frustrating the reporting of wrongdoing, the belief that it is impossible to correct the wrongdoing through reporting, and concerns about the possibility of retaliation can all act as control factors that discourage potential whistleblowers.

The combination of people's attitudes, perceived norms, and perceived behavioral control, with regard to a particular change, inform their intention to engage in certain behavior. People with favorable attitudes towards whistleblowing, who perceive the organizational norms to be supportive, and who believe that they are in control of the situation, are therefore more likely to have a strong intention to blow the whistle on organizational wrongdoing. According to Fishbein and Azjen (2010), the stronger the intention to behave in a particular way, the greater the likelihood that the behavior will be executed. The *actual control* that people have over carrying out their intentions, however, particularly whether they have the required skills and abilities to do so, or whether environmental constraints are preventing them from performing the actions, should be taken into account when attempting to predict whether their intentions will translate into actions.

In a study on whistleblowing intentions among Korean police officers, Park and Blenkinsopp (2009) explored how well Ajzen's Theory of Planned Behaviour (the precursor to TRA) predicted internal and external whistleblowing intentions. Park and Blenkinsopp's (2009) research demonstrates that the attitudes toward whistleblowing, subjective norms, and perceived behavioural control are able to significantly predict whistleblowing intentions in the case of internal whistleblowing, while subjective norm alone was the determining factor with regard to external whistleblowing (2009, p. 552). While the results of Park and Blenkinsopp's research have made an important contribution to our understanding of whistleblowing intentions, they argue for the need to conduct further cross-cultural studies. They suggest that the impact of national cultural dimensions, such as individualism or collectivism, on the three determinants of whistleblowing intentions should be investigated.

Influence of Culture on Whistleblowing Intentions

Various studies have explored the influence of culture on the intention to blow the whistle. Park et al. (2008) argued that culture influences people's perceptions on three central issues related to whistleblowing: (i) their perceptions of the kind of activities that qualify to be considered as wrongdoing; (ii) what the appropriate response would be in coming across behavior that is considered to be wrongdoing (i.e. do nothing, confront the transgressor, or blow the whistle); and (iii) what the most appropriate form of whistleblowing (i.e. formal or informal, identified or anonymous, internal or external) would be in those situations where whistleblowing is seen as the appropriate response (2008, p. 930).

According to William de Maria (2005) whistleblowing will only be successful in challenging wrongdoing in the workplace if the basic preconditions of a democratic state are in position. These include the existence of a stable state where the rule of law is generally accepted, and where there is a broad belief that state anti-corruption agencies are effective. Furthermore the public should be confident that disclosures will be effective in combating corruption; freedom of expression should be guaranteed; judicial, regulatory, and state powers should be separated; and the public interest should be foregrounded when it comes to state income and expenditure.

Patel's (2003) comparison of the professional judgments of Australian, Indian, and Chinese-Malaysian accountants concluded that Australian culture is the most conducive towards employing whistleblowing as an internal control mechanism. The study by Park et al. (2005) regarding the effect of Confucian ethics and collectivism on whistleblowing intentions among South Korean public servants demonstrated the complexity of the relationship between whistleblowing and cultural factors. Several other studies have also considered the impact of national and cultural differences on employees' perceptions of, and responses to, wrongdoing (see Brody et al., 1999; Keenan, 2002, 2007; Oktem and Shahbazi, 2012; Sims and Keenan, 1999; Tavakoli et al., 2003).

Most of these studies employed the four distinctions developed by Hofstede (1991) in his theory of international cultures. These are:

1. Power-distance: The extent to which employees are unperturbed about approaching and/or contradicting their superiors. Where power-distance is large, power is centralized and subordinates are expected to comply with instructions without hesitation. In this context management initiates contact, and employees are less likely to challenge the system.

2. Uncertainty avoidance: A high uncertainty avoidance culture evades ambiguity and unpredictability through emphasizing rules and procedures for all situations. In a high avoidance culture employees feel threatened by unknown or uncertain situations. The emphasis on rules and procedures, however, does not necessarily mean that rules are always followed or that they are logical or consistent.

3. Collectivism/individualism: In a collectivistic culture people give precedence to group membership and group achievements above individual well-being. Employees look out for their in-group and place a strong emphasis on the beliefs, views, needs, norms, and duties they have in common, as well as the maintenance of stable and long-term memberships. In contrast, in an individualistic culture, everyone looks out for themselves and their family. Employees tend to maintain an independence from the organization.

4. Femininity/masculinity: A feminine culture values relationships, cooperation, and security, rather than financial success and advancement. Conflicts are resolved through compromise and negotiation. Masculine cultures, on the other hand, resolve conflicts through a struggle between the conflicting parties.

Each of these distinctions has an impact on individual and organizational inclinations towards whistleblowing; on the articulation of perceptions of wrongdoing; on misgivings about possible retaliation; and on the voiced likelihood of blowing the whistle in general. In societies where a high power-distance is dominant, employees are unlikely to challenge established authority patterns through engaging in whistleblowing. In high uncertainty avoidance cultures, employees would be inclined to follow the rules and to discourage unauthorized disclosures of perceived wrongdoing. Collectivist cultures emphasize the promotion and maintenance of harmonious working relationships. In this context it is more likely that whistleblowing would be viewed as an act of betrayal when it exposes organizational wrongdoing rather than individual wrongdoing. Similarly, a feminine culture would avoid direct confrontation in conflict situations and would therefore be less likely to expose perceived wrongdoing through whistleblowing (Vandekerckhove et al., 2014, pp. 46–53).

In their study, Trongmateerut and Sweeney (2013) conducted a cross-cultural investigation of the influence of subjective norms on whistleblowing by comparing the two cultures of Thai collectivism and American individualism. Their findings showed a direct influence of subjective norms and attitudes for whistleblowing on whistleblowing intentions. They also found an indirect effect of subjective norms on whistleblowing intentions through their impact on attitudes. The collectivist Thai participants had significantly stronger subjective norms for whistleblowing than the individualistic American participants and held significantly more favorable attitudes towards whistleblowing than their American counterparts. Also, subjective norms for whistleblowing had a stronger impact on attitudes toward whistleblowing in the Thai group, and both subjective norms for, and attitude towards, whistleblowing impacted more strongly on the intentions of the Thai group to blow the whistle. They also experienced a greater indirect influence of subjective norms on their intentions to blow the whistle than the Americans. While these findings demonstrate that subjective norms strongly influence whistleblowing attitudes and intentions across divergent cultures, the views of referent others seem to play a much more important role in collectivist cultures.

While theoretical and methodological challenges in Hofstede's typology of cultural dimensions have been identified (see Vandekerckhove et al., 2014, pp. 54–55), the typology can be usefully employed to analyze the potential impact of the South African conception of *ubuntu*. Hwang et al. (2008) conducted a study that included the Chinese notion of *guanxi*, which consists of mutual obligations and loyalty linked to influential relationships in social networks. They found that a strong identification with *guanxi* had a negative impact on the intention to blow the whistle. While no similar research has been conducted with regard to *ubuntu*, it could be useful to consider the role that a strong commitment to *ubuntu* would play in whistleblowing intentions.

The African Notion of *Ubuntu*

The collectivist value system espoused by the majority of the South African population (and also across Africa) is reflected in the adherence to the value of *ubuntu*. *Ubuntu* implies that 'we can only be persons in and through other persons' (Prozesky, 2007, p. 54); 'a person is a person through other persons' (Metz, 2007, p. 323). It includes an emphasis on 'morality, humaneness, compassion, care, understanding and empathy' (Boon, 2007, p. 25).

Metz (2007) identifies the core of *ubuntu* as being about the production of harmony and reduction of discord, where harmony means embracing a fusion of identity and solidarity (2007, p. 340). Solidarity entails the moral obligation to be concerned about the wellbeing of others, while identity relates to associating oneself with a group and participating in its activities. *Ubuntu* therefore has both a communal and a relational element that entails the requirement that one should look for positive community opportunities for living in harmony with others. In particular *ubuntu* prioritizes familial relationships and the importance of valuing and promoting these wherever it is possible (Metz and Gaie, 2010, pp. 275–276).

In an article constructing *ubuntu* as a normative moral theory of right action, Metz (2007) identified a number of moral judgments that are more likely to be held by adherents of *ubuntu* than westerners who live in developed constitutional democracies. It could be argued that some of these moral judgments display features of Hofstede's typology of cultural dimensions. In particular, this indicates that *ubuntu* exhibits a tendency towards collectivism, a feminine culture, and high uncertainty avoidance.

Metz (2007) distinguished two moral judgments that could arguably be said to demonstrate a feminine culture. The first is that policy decisions should be taken on the basis of consensus, where compromise and agreement by all concerned is achieved. The second is the aim of ensuring that the criminal justice system seeks reconciliation, rather than retribution. This includes seeking restorative justice, while limiting punitive measures to those instances where it would foster harmonious relationships. An *ubuntu* ethic values enhancing relationships, and promoting cooperation and consensus.

Ubuntu displays a tendency toward uncertainty avoidance through stressing the importance of upholding communal norms and traditions, acknowledging others, and participating in rituals (Metz 2007, p. 327). The most important aspect of *ubuntu*, when considering issues related to whistleblowing, is its collective emphasis. This is particularly evident in its emphasis on the creation of wealth on a cooperative basis and in the interest of the community, rather than a competitive one. Similarly, it holds the view that the distribution of wealth should take account of its impact on communal relationships, and that it should include the moral obligation to help others. Wealth therefore should be distributed on the basis of need, rather than individual rights (Metz, 2007, pp. 326–327; Metz and Gaie, 2010, pp. 277–278).

The emphasis that *ubuntu* places on promoting the principles of communal relations, harmony, and consensus seems to preclude the generally individualistic act of whistleblowing, where perceived organizational wrongdoing is exposed in the interest of the more abstract ideal of promoting the public interest.

When Would Ubuntu Impede Whistleblowing?

In terms of Hofstede's conceptual scheme, *ubuntu* implies a collectivistic and feminine culture with moderate uncertainty avoidance. This implies a low inclination towards whistleblowing. On the other hand, Boon (2007) argued, 'it was accepted [in traditional African culture] that there was a collective responsibility to uphold the law. If an individual saw a wrong being done and did nothing to stop it, or did not report it, then that individual incurred responsibility for the act' (2007, p. 44). How do we explain the presumed reluctance to report wrongdoing? Three issues are of particular importance in understanding the relationship between *ubuntu* and whistleblowing: the perception of wrongdoing, informing versus whistleblowing, and inclusion and exclusion.

Perception of Wrongdoing, Particularly Corruption

The act of whistleblowing requires the awareness that some questionable behavior has occurred, or that some policy is problematic. Members of the organization must be exposed to information about wrongful activities (McLain and Keenan, 1999, pp. 259–260), and must then display the necessary ethical sensitivity that enables them to identify a particular act as unacceptable or harmful (Ponemon, 1994, p. 121). Recognizing that an activity is wrongful usually flows from the realization that the observed behavior conflicts with one's values or expectations about what should happen in an organization (Henik, 2005, p. 113; Near and Miceli, 1985, p. 4). Organizational members are therefore likely to perceive behavior as wrongdoing only if it conflicts with their views of procedural or distributive justice.

Research has also shown that members are significantly more likely to blow the whistle when they feel that they are personally victimized (Cassematis and Wortley, 2013, p. 628). This is the point at which interpersonal justice comes into play. Physical proximity to the wrongdoer could also make it more likely that someone will become aware of something going awry in the workplace (Mesmer-Magnus and Viswesvaran, 2005, p. 291).

Individuals' perceptions around what constitutes wrongdoing are often considered straightforward and unambiguous, while in reality they are subject to vast variation (Blenkinsopp and Edwards, 2008, pp. 183–184). A number of explanations for differences of interpretation can be identified. Observers of questionable activity often have only partial or ambiguous information at their disposal upon which to base their judgment. McLain and Keenan (1999) stressed the importance of quality information in strengthening observers' confidence that their conclusions about the wrongfulness of actions are valid. Ensuring that decisions are based on quality information will strengthen informational justice in the organization (1999, p. 261).

Likewise, wrongdoing is sometimes not recognized as such because of the processes of normalizing and rationalizing that socialize people into believing that morally dubious practices are actually the correct and proper way to carry out the business of the organization. Various researchers have pointed out that co-workers in the immediate work group play an important role in influencing the perceptions of their peers with regard to the wrongfulness of particular behaviors (Blenkinsopp and Edwards, 2008, p. 200; Greenberger et al., 1987, p. 531; Miceli et al., 2012, p. 938). The views of the group will be especially influential if the majority agrees that the particular activity is acceptable and the group is perceived to be a credible source of information (Greenberger et al., 1987, pp. 528–531; Henik, 2005, p. 112).

Cultural variations also play a role in what is viewed as being wrongdoing, as well as what the appropriate response should be. In his cross-cultural comparison of whistleblowing as an internal control mechanism, Patel (2003) contrasted the multiple standards of morality evident in Chinese culture, with ethical standards being decided collectively in Indian culture (depending on the people and the context), and the Australian emphasis on individuality, independence, equality, and egalitarianism. This study demonstrated that cultural issues are of particular importance when considering the relationship between *ubuntu* and whistleblowing.

Corruption is arguably one of the central forms of organizational wrongdoing that necessitates reporting to authorities. Corruption is a contested concept, however, and could be viewed as a social construction (Pavarala, 1993, p. 408). It can be argued that corruption is generally condemned worldwide, as Chabal and Daloz (1999) wrote, 'officially, all African societies have accepted Western norms in respect of this phenomenon, which is why the local press regularly exposes the most blatant cases of venality and illegal deals' (1999, p. 104). On the other hand, Chabal and Daloz also argued that corruption is 'an integral part of the social fabric of life' where it is endemic in nature and the distinction between the private and public spheres has become muted (1999, p. 99). Corruption is a phenomenon evident at all levels of the social strata, from those at the lower end whose only means of survival are selling the small amount of power they possess, to those at higher levels for whom

> extortion is one of the many avenues of enrichment; it facilitates social advancement and the upholding of one's position. As we have seen, it enables the political elites to fulfil their duties, to meet the expectations of their clients and, hence, to enhance their status. (Chabal and Daloz, 1999, p. 99)

A commitment to *ubuntu* conflicts especially strongly with the likelihood of blowing the whistle when potentially corrupt practices are viewed as being 'the obligations of mutual support, the imperatives of reciprocity, the importance of gift exchange, the payment of tribute, the need to redistribute' (Chabal and Daloz, 1999, p. 100). Difficulties arise when trying to determine whether gift giving is an expression of the culturally accepted practice of mutual obligation flowing from the network of relationships established in terms of *ubuntu*, or whether it is actually a bribe.

Chabal and Daloz argued that condemnation of corruption only tends to follow if 'its fruits are [not] deemed to have been suitably and vigorously redistributed according to the logic of patronage' (1999, p. 100). Whistleblowing that goes against this understanding would be seen as contradicting the tenets of social justice put forward by *ubuntu*, and would thus be denounced. Corruption is a systemic problem and should be studied by focusing on understanding the cultural context wherein it occurs, including its social and structural roots. It must be understood how each occurrence of corruption forms a key element of the 'instrumentalization of disorder' (Chabal and Daloz, 1999, p. 103). Rather than highlighting the 'corrupt African', the focus should be on understanding systems in trouble, by considering the conditions of poverty, disease, and exploitation that characterize Africa (de Maria, 2005, pp. 5–6).

Attempts to root out corruption through whistleblowing should keep in mind how features of the social system, in a particular society, could promote different combinations of opportunity, motivation, and justification that are the preconditions for corruption to occur (Aguilera and Vadera, 2007, p. 432). It is important to determine whether whistleblowing is perceived as promoting the interests of social justice, or whether it is seen as going against the grain of established practices in a particular society.

Informing Versus Whistleblowing

Ubuntu is also likely to inhibit whistleblowing as long as the general public tend to draw parallels between whistleblowing and informing. Even highly regarded management experts, such as Peter Drucker (as quoted in Orr, 1981, p. 4), argue that whistleblowing is simply another word for informing. He (in Orr, 1981) states forcefully

> the only societies in Western history that encouraged informers were bloody and infamous tyrannies – Tiberius and Nero in Rome, the Inquisition in the Spain of Philip II, the French Terror, and Stalin. And furthermore under 'whistleblowing,' under the regime of the 'informer,' no mutual trust, no interdependencies, and no ethics are possible. (Drucker in Orr, 1981, p. 4)

In a country like South Africa with its history of domination and oppression, it is especially important to draw a clear distinction between whistleblowing and informing, particularly in light of the past role played by those *impimpi* who betrayed the struggle against the apartheid regime in South Africa by informing on their associates to the police and security structures (Uys, 2010, p. 122). Confounding whistleblowing with informing sometimes leads to people discrediting whistleblowing as being counter-revolutionary.

Informers are those individuals who secretively provide privileged information about a person or organization to a state agency, usually the police, the army, the judiciary, or security services (Dudai, 2012, p. 34). The anonymous nature of the disclosure, as well as the financial or other benefits that informers stand to gain from their actions, ensure that community perceptions of informers are generally negative. During the time of apartheid the betrayal of the struggle against apartheid by so-called impimpi was often punished by necklacing in which a tyre filled with fuel was placed around the informer's neck and set alight (Uys, 2010, pp. 122–123).

A clear distinction, therefore, needs to be made between informers and whistleblowers. Near and Miceli (1996) suggested that the fundamental difference lies in what they call the whistleblower's 'reasonable supposition of success' of terminating the wrongdoing through their disclosure (1996, p. 510). In contrast, informants reveal information with little regard for the purposes for which the recipient requires or will use the information.

Another important distinction between whistleblowing and informing relates to differences in power relations. De Maria wrote, '[Informing] is the powerless reporting to the powerful on the misdeeds of the powerless. Whistleblowing, on the other hand, is the powerless disclosing the misconduct of the powerful' (1999, p. 32). Informers, therefore, promote the interests of the powerful, often receiving a reward of some kind, while whistleblowers raise concerns about illegal, unethical, or dangerous practices of the powerful. In contrast to informers who are the, sometimes unwilling, lackeys of the powerful, whistleblowers voluntarily attempt to restrain the abuse of power. While informers disclose information in order to support those in power, whistleblowers make disclosures that challenge those in power. As the speakers of truth to power, whistleblowers disrupt the status quo, and generally find themselves at the losing end as the playing fields are never level.

Inclusion and Exclusion

Another issue that relates to the restrictions that a strong commitment to *ubuntu* could place on the inclination towards whistleblowing has to do with the boundaries of the group that people identify with and relate to. Who is included when we are talking about *ubuntu* and who *can* be included? Metz and Gaie stressed the importance of the obligation to familial relationships encompassed within *ubuntu* (2010, p. 276). Cherishing and promoting one's existing familial relationships wherever possible is seen as creating an environment where 'all human beings are seen as potential members of an ideal family' (Metz and Gaie, 2010, p. 276). Actual friendly relationships, however, are prioritized above those that could potentially come into being in the future, and those that do not exist or are not likely to exist in the future. The community and solidarity of *ubuntu* is therefore more circumscribed than the whistleblower's focus on the abstract notion of the public interest.

This tendency to favor one's own group, however, is not restricted to adherents of *ubuntu* alone. Research conducted in the United Kingdom and Australia has shown a similar pattern towards considering reporting wrongdoing by those in positions of authority to be more acceptable than reporting wrongdoing by colleagues and peers. The least acceptable is considered to be reporting wrongdoing by family and friends (Vandekerckhove et al., 2014, p. 59).

The prospective whistleblower in an environment with a high commitment to *ubuntu* struggles with the demands of competing loyalties. Whistleblowers are often under the impression that they are acting in the best interests of the organization. They believe that as loyal employees the organization expects them to disclose suspicions of wrongdoing, so that problems can be investigated before they escalate and result in major harm to the organization's reputation. In contrast, the employer often views the revelations of the whistleblower to be disloyal to the organization, especially when they are revealing entrusted information that the employer does not want revealed (Uys and Senekal, 2008, p. 40).

Organizational loyalty is a complex issue. It is often understood as flowing from the employee's relationships within the organization, as well as their identification with the organization as members. In terms of the social contract existing between employers and employees, the latter is expected to act in ways that demonstrate their good faith and enhance the best interests of the organization. This entails that reasonable instructions should be carried out, one's actions should be consistent with the values and norms of the organization, one should defend the organization's reputation, and confidentiality should be maintained (Uys, 2008, p. 907).

The way in which the majority of organizations worldwide respond to whistleblowers demonstrates that they place organizational loyalty above any considerations of public interest or corporate governance. Whistleblowing is regarded as a violation of trust, and a form of betrayal, which threatens the profitability and damages the reputation of organizations.

When Would Ubuntu Foster Whistleblowing?

The difficult choice before observers of wrongdoing in the workplace is whether to disclose their suspicions or whether to remain silent. This is exacerbated in an organizational context where a high premium is placed on the values of *ubuntu*. To a certain extent, one could argue that the emphasis placed by a 'new managerialism' (Powell, 1998, p. 165), introduced in the 1980s, around the values of 'corporate culture', 'family', and 'team', reflects *ubuntu*'s commitment to identification and solidarity with one's in-group. This includes an overarching loyalty to the organization. In this context, observers of wrongdoing need to decide whether their loyalty to a particular person, a group of people, or to the organization is paramount, and therefore remain silent, or whether the universally acceptable rules applicable to that particular context should apply and that they should therefore expose the wrongdoing. Observers of wrongdoing with a high commitment to *ubuntu* will only be able to choose the latter route, if an enabling organizational culture is established where *ubuntu* is made more inclusive and the boundaries of group identification are broadened.

This necessitates a conceptualization of organizational loyalty as rational loyalty, where loyalty entails being loyal to the explicit values and norms of the organization. The implementation of formal whistleblowing procedures and an open communication structure would enable the perceiver of organizational wrongdoing to comply with the 'duty not to radically upset norms central to the community's self-conception' (Metz and Gaie, 2010, p. 280). In this context, blowing the whistle would then necessarily imply acting in the best interests of the organization.

A high commitment to *ubuntu* will also foster whistleblowing if community members are made to understand that corruption usually has a harsher impact on the poor than on the wealthy. Corruption often requires the poor to spend large portions of their resources on survival bribes that will at best maintain the status quo, while the wealthy enhance their powerful positions when paying influence bribes. Funds appropriated by the corrupt are usually those intended to improve the circumstances of the poor (Green, 2013, pp. 23–24). Rather than just displaying an emotional and practical concern for the wellbeing of those with whom one has a direct relationship, the scope of *ubuntu* should be broadened to include a shared identity with, and goodwill towards, the poor, the powerless, and the marginal. Exposing corruption through whistleblowing will then foster the harmonious relationships that *ubuntu* prizes above all.

In his analysis of the relationship between *ubuntu* and public governance, Metz (2009) argued that *ubuntu* prohibits the awarding of state resources to individuals on the basis of family or political affiliations, as these may jeopardize harmonious relationships. Where such nepotism or preferential hiring occur, a commitment to *ubuntu* should therefore encourage observers of this behavior to blow the whistle. A correct understanding of the tenets of *ubuntu* should enable the observer of wrongdoing in the workplace to blow the whistle and therefore contribute towards restoring social justice.

Ubuntu will be more conducive to whistleblowing if organizations manage the whistleblowing process in terms of an emphasis on restorative justice. This entails that justice is achieved through community restoration. Such a process would include the involvement of all stakeholders in collectively deciding and dealing with the aftermath of the disclosure and its future implications, in ways that restore organizational justice through the return to an ethical workplace where the wellbeing and dignity of all role players are ensured (Daly, 2016, p. 16; Mangena, 2015).

Conclusion

Ultimately, whistleblowing can be viewed as the attempt to pursue social justice through rectifying possible wrongs, and thereby ensuring the fairness of processes, outcomes, and the treatment of organizational members. An ethical workplace is fundamentally one that implements principles of fairness. Organizational justice can only be sustained or restored in organizations with mechanisms in place that allow for perceived wrongdoing to be disclosed and dealt with in a manner that promotes all four elements of organizational justice: procedural, distributive, interactional, and informational. How this is to be achieved should be the focus of future research.

References

Aguilera, A.V. and Vadera, A.K. (2007) The dark side of authority: Antecedents, mechanisms, and outcomes of organizational corruption. *Journal of Business Ethics, 77,* 431–449.

Beckley, A. (2014) Organisational justice: Is the police service ready for it? *Journal of Policing, Intelligence and Counter Terrorism, 9*(2), 176–190.

Blenkinsopp, J. and Edwards, M.S. (2008) On not blowing the whistle: Quiescent silence as an emotion episode. *Research on Emotion in Organizations, 4,* 181–206.

Boon, M. (2007) *The African Way: The Power of Interactive Leadership.* Cape Town: Zebra Press.

Brody, R.G., Coulter, J.M., and Lin, S. (1999) The effect of national culture on whistle-blowing perceptions. *Teaching Business Ethics, 3*(4), 385–400.

Cassematis, P.G. and Wortley, R. (2013) Prediction of whistleblowing or non-reporting observation: The role of personal and situational factors. *Journal of Business Ethics, 117,* 615–634.

Chabal, P. and Daloz, J. (1999) *Africa Works: Disorder as Political Instrument.* London: Villiers Publications.

Daly, K. (2016) What is restorative justice? Fresh answers to a vexed question. *Victims & Offenders, 11*(1), 9–29.

De Maria, W. (1999) *Deadly Disclosures: Whistleblowing and the Ethical Meltdown of Australia.* Kent Town: Wakefield Press.

De Maria, W. (2005) Whistleblower protection: Is Africa ready? *Public Administration and Development, 25,* 217–226.

Dudai, R. (2012) Informers and the transition in Northern Ireland. *British Journal of Criminology, 52*(1), 32–54.

Fishbein, M. and Azjen, I. (2010) *Predicting and Changing Behavior: The Reasoned Action Approach.* New York, NY: Psychology Press, Taylor & Francis.

Green, V.E. (2013) *Corruption in the Twenty-first Century: Combating Unethical Practices in Government, Commerce, and Society.* Bloomington, IN: iUniverse.

Greenberg, J. (2011) *Behavior in Organizations,* 10th edn. Boston, MA: Pearson.

Greenberger, D.B., Miceli, M.P., and Cohen, D. (1987) Oppositionists and group norms: The reciprocal influence of whistle-blowers and co-workers. *Journal of Business Ethics, 6,* 527–542.

Henik, E. (2005) *Ethical Decision-making in the Domain of Whistle-blowing: How Issue Characteristics Affect Judgments and Intentions.* Available at: https://escholarship.org/uc/item/3q38f5bh (accessed 9 May 2014).

Hofstede, G. (1991) *Cultures and Organizations: Software of the Mind.* London: McGraw-Hill.

Hwang, D., Staley, B., Chen, T., and Lan, J.S. (2008) Confucian culture and whistle-blowing by professional accountants: An exploratory study. *Managerial Auditing Journal, 23*(5), 504–526.

Keenan, J.P. (2002) Comparing Indian and American managers on whistleblowing. *Employee Responsibilities and Rights Journal, 14*(2/3), 79–89.

Keenan, J.P. (2007) Comparing Chinese and American managers on whistleblowing. *Employee Responsibilities and Rights Journal, 19*(2), 85–94.

Mangena, F. (2015) Restorative justice's deep roots in Africa. *South African Journal of Philosophy, 34*(1), 1–12.

McLain, D.A. and Keenan, J.P. (1999) Risk, information, and the decision about response to wrongdoing in an organization. *Journal of Business Ethics, 19*(3), 255–271.

Mesmer-Magnus, J.R. and Viswesvaran, C. (2005) Whistleblowing in organizations: An examination of correlates of whistleblowing intentions, actions, and retaliation. *Journal of Business Ethics, 62*(3), 277–297.

Metz, T. (2007) Towards an African moral theory. *The Journal of Political Philosophy, 15*(3), 321–341.

Metz, T. (2009) African moral theory and public governance: Nepotism, preferential hiring and other partiality. In: F.M. Munyaradzi (ed.), *African Ethics: An Anthology for Comparative and Applied Ethics*, pp. 335–56. Pietermaritzburg: University of KwaZulu-Natal Press.

Metz, T. and Gaie, J.B.R. (2010) The African ethic of ubuntu/botho: Implications for research on morality. *Journal of Moral Education*, *39*(3), 273–290.

Miceli, M.P., Near, J.P., Rehg, M.T., and Van Scotter, J.R. (2012) Predicting employee reactions to perceived organizational wrongdoing: Demoralization, justice, proactive personality and whistleblowing. *Human Relations*, *65*(8), 923–954.

Near, J.P. and Miceli, M.P. (1985) Organizational dissidence: The case of whistle-blowing. *Journal of Business Ethics*, *4*, 1–16.

Near, J.P., Dworkin, T.M., and Miceli, M.P. (1993) Explaining the whistle-blowing process: Suggestions from power theory and justice theory. *Organization Science*, *4*(3), 393–411.

Near, J.P. and Miceli, M.P. (1996) Whistle-blowing: myth and reality. *Journal of Management*, *22*(3): 507–526.

Oktem, M.K. and Shahbazi, G. (2012) Attitudes toward different forms of whistleblowing in Turkey and Iran. *Middle-East Journal of Scientific Research*, *12*(7), 945–951.

Orr, L.W. (1981) Is whistleblowing the same as informing? *Business and Society Review*, Fall, 4–17.

Park, H. and Blenkinsopp, J. (2009) Whistleblowing as planned behavior – a survey of South Korean police officers. *Journal of Business Ethics*, *85*(4), 545–556.

Park, H., Rehg, M.T., and Lee, D. (2005) The influence of Confucian ethics and collectivism on whistleblowing intentions: A study of South Korean public employees. *Journal of Business Ethics*, *58*, 387–403.

Park, H., Blenkinsopp, J., Oktem, K.M., and Omurgonulsen, U. (2008) Cultural orientation and attitudes toward different forms of whistleblowing: A comparison of South Korea, Turkey, and the UK. *Journal of Business Ethics*, *82*(4), 929–939.

Patel, C. (2003) Some cross-cultural evidence on whistle-blowing as an internal control mechanism. *Journal of International Accounting Research*, *2*, 69–96.

Pavarala, V. (1993) Corruption as a site for contested meaning: elite constructions in India. *Qualitative Sociology*, *16*(4), 405–422.

Ponemon, L. (1994) Whistle-blowing an internal control mechanism: Individual and organizational considerations. *Auditing: A Journal of Practice and Theory*, *13*(2), 118–130.

Powell, R. (1998) Managerial procedure and professional practice in social work. In: G. Hunt (ed.), *Whistleblowing in the Social Services: Public Accountability and Professional Practice*. London: Arnold.

Prozesky, M. (2007) *Conscience: Ethical Intelligence for Global Well-being*. Scottsville: University of KwaZulu-Natal Press.

Sims, R.L. and Keenan, J.P. (1999) A cross-cultural comparison of managers' whistleblowing tendencies. *International Journal of Value-Based Management*, *12*(2), 137–151.

Tavakoli, A.A., Keenan, J.P., and Crnjak-Karanovic, B. (2003) Culture and whistleblowing: An empirical study of Croatian and United States managers utilizing Hofstede's cultural dimensions. *Journal of Business Ethics*, *43*, 49–64.

Trongmateerut, P. and Sweeney, J.T. (2013) The influence of subjective norms on whistle-blowing: A cross-cultural investigation. *Journal of Business Ethics, 112*, 437–451.

Uys, T. (2008) Rational loyalty and whistleblowing: The South African context. *Current Sociology, 56*(6), 907–924.

Uys, T. (2010) Speaking truth to power: The whistleblower as organizational citizen in South Africa. In: D. Lewis (ed.) *A Global Approach to Public Interest Disclosure Legislation? The Lessons to be Learned from Existing Statutory Provisions and Research*. London: Edward Elgar.

Uys, T. and Senekal, A. (2008) Morality of principle versus morality of loyalty: The case of whistleblowing. *African Journal of Business Ethics, 3*(1), 38–44.

Vandekerckhove, W., Uys, T., Rehg, M., and Brown, A.J. (2014) Understandings of whistleblowing: Dilemmas of societal culture. In: A.J. Brown, D. Lewis, R.E. Moberly, and W. Vandekerckhove (eds), *International Handbook on Whistleblowing Research*. Cheltenham: Edward Elgar.

7

Equal Schools, Global Power and Hungry Markets

Sociology in the Long Struggle for Social Justice in Education

Raewyn Connell

Mass Schooling and the Sociology of Education in the Global Metropole

In the sociology of education, the main object of knowledge is state-controlled public schooling – its institutions, pupils, workforce, and informal life. Mass elementary school systems were created, in the imperial centres and in some colonies, during the 19th century. School systems greatly expanded in the 20th century, adding mass secondary education in rich countries, and extending primary education and adult literacy in most of the developing world.

Considering their funding, control, and support mechanisms, mass school systems make up one of the great institutional complexes of modernity. They represent a huge shift of the social labour concerned with children and youth, from the informal contexts of family, farm, and neighbourhood into the world of paid labour, formal organization, and public surveillance. Great social debates have swirled around mass schooling, including fierce controversies about exclusion, selection, and social justice.

In this chapter I begin with the sociology of education in the global North, i.e. Europe and the United States. I will use the term 'global metropole' to recognize the role of these societies as the centres of empire in the last 500 years. I then move on to thinking about education and society in the (much larger) global periphery, the colonized and semi-colonized world and the postcolonial societies that grew from it.

Schooling on a mass scale thus embodies a very large commitment of labour, time, and social resources. As economists view modern economies, education is a major industry, and school teaching is one of the largest professions.

A combination of cultural and technical arguments persuaded imperial and colonial governments to find so much money for education. In the early 19th century, it was thought that inculcating literacy, religion, and orderliness would help to tame unruly popular classes, create moral uplift, and, in the colonial context specifically, help spread the Gospel and culture of the colonizers. In the later 19th century, governments led by the rising industrial power of Germany began to fund technical education as a tool for economic development and military power.

One product of this early investment in education was a legacy of magnificent school buildings. Often these would be the finest examples of architecture, and the largest institutions, found in working-class and rural communities. Another product, however, was a legacy of deep social division. The political purpose and conflicts surrounding the formation of these institutions meant that mass school systems were born segregated. They continue to be segregated in multiple ways, along the lines of class, race, gender, religion, and region. Ruling-class schooling has always been separated from working-class schooling. Likewise, in colonial contexts separate schools were provided for colonizers and the colonized. Historically, where girls were allowed schooling, separate classes were usual, and often enough, separate schools. Various churches have created their own schools, both for missionary purposes and for the general education of their followers. Rural schools are often very different from urban. It is not by chance that a social history of schooling in South Australia was called *The Long Division* (Miller, 1986).

This profoundly unequal, yet potent, institutional system became the focus of social struggles and projects of reform almost everywhere it was established. Indeed, the history of education is often written as a story of reforms and reformers. Behind the famous names, the Kay-Shuttleworths, the Deweys, and the Makarenkos, are complex social changes and powerful social interests. These formed the background, and increasingly the foreground, subject matter of the sociology of education when this field of research emerged during the 20th century.

The Comtean-framed sociology of c. 1850–1920 attempted vast theorizations of social progress, in which education was of limited interest. Curiously, Émile Durkheim's initial university appointment was as a lecturer in pedagogy. He developed an abstract doctrine of education as being the inculcation of norms in the interest of social solidarity. In his main sociological work, however, Durkheim left the issue behind. Typical of that generation was *The Principles of Sociology*, by the influential

US sociologist Franklin Giddings (1896). This book contained only four trivial mentions of education in its grand account of the whole field of sociology.

Education really became a sociological concern after the collapse of evolutionary sociology. In the decades after the Great War, the discipline was re-focussed on problems of social difference and conflict within the society of the metropole (Connell, 2007).

This moment can be seen in Willard Waller's (1932) *The Sociology of Teaching*, an intelligent attempt to describe the occupational world of teachers in the United States, using 'literary realism' rather than fieldwork. Teachers were presented as cultural transmitters, mostly conformist, occupying a modest but dignified social position, and embedded in a network of social relationships with pupils, parents, and colleagues. The liveliest part of Waller's work was his account of everyday life in schools, including primary groups among the children, and tensions between pupils and teachers. The political agenda at this time was mild school improvement, a kind of washed-out progressivism, recommending less formalism and more naturalism. Questions of social justice had not yet come into focus.

They did come into sharp focus with the next generation, when the sociology of education finally crystallized in the global metropole. Pivotal texts from this moment were Allison Davis's (1948) *Social-Class Influences upon Learning*, a brilliant social critique of school curricula and mental testing; and Warner et al.'s (1944) *Who Shall Be Educated? The Challenge of Unequal Opportunities.* This polemic work, dedicated to the Chicago School sociologist Robert Park, stressed schooling's potential for social mobility. These texts brought the then-new US empirical sociology of stratification to bear on educational practices and outcomes. They documented massive class differences. However, their interpretation was compromised, in Warner et al.'s case, by a functionalist acceptance of the need for social stratification.

The same moment was marked in England by Floud et al.'s (1956) *Social Class and Educational Opportunity*, the first of a series of studies in which A.H. Halsey developed a 'political arithmetic' of education and became a major figure in sociology. A generation later than the United States, the state had created a mass secondary school system in England, but had stratified it, using paper-and-pencil tests supposed to measure pure academic potential. Halsey and his colleagues showed that this was a cruel illusion. What was actually happening was class discrimination, with working-class children being under-resourced and filtered out of academic streams and advanced education regardless of their talent and potential.

For the next two decades, sociologists studying education in the global metropole wrestled with this dilemma, the appearance of equal provision versus. the actuality of social inequality. Basil Bernstein, in Britain, published a series of papers pointing to differences between working-class and middle-class language patterns, and their different relationships with the formal language of the school (Bernstein, 1971). Pierre Bourdieu, in France, likewise published a series of reports about cultural differences between working-class and middle-class families, translating into a systematically biased selection process and leading to the reproduction of social privilege (Bourdieu, 1966; Bourdieu and Passeron, 1964). At the same time, James Coleman led a massive statistical investigation of racial inequalities in education in the United States that produced the famous 1966 report *Equality of Educational Opportunity*, and a fierce debate about the reality of 'school effects' (Coleman, 1990).

The Coleman report, commissioned by the US federal government, fed directly into public policy around desegregation. Halsey's work also directly influenced policy, supporting a shift towards comprehensive high schools in Britain. Together with the concept of a 'culture of poverty', which came from social anthropology, reformist sociologists of education collectively shaped the 'war on poverty' of the 1960s and 1970s in the global metropole. Their stratificationist sociology lay behind the strategy of 'compensatory education' for disadvantaged communities. Halsey, for instance, became a key figure in the 'Educational Priority Area' strategy in Britain (Halsey, 1972).

Compensatory education in practice, however, had limited effects. Its political support withered with the advent of neoliberalism. Coleman moved towards the political right, Bernstein became preoccupied with increasingly abstract analyses, and the darker vision of Bourdieu, suggesting the inescapability of 'social reproduction', became more and more influential. Meanwhile a younger generation of sociologists emerged who saw the reformism of their elders as naïve. They were sceptical of hopes for social mobility without deep structural change in society. A harder-edged structuralist Marxism underpinned the educational sociology of the Birmingham school in Britain. One of its more famous proponents was Paul Willis (1977), who wrote *Learning to Labour: How Working Class Kids Get Working Class Jobs*. Marxism also guided a new wave of US research led by Samuel Bowles and Herbert Gintis' (1976) work

Schooling in Capitalist America, and Michael Apple's (1979) *Ideology and Curriculum*.

The Marxist-inspired 'new sociology of education' of the 1970s in turn came under fire for its one-sided focus on class issues and its economic determinism. Its radicalism, however, opened a space in which several new intellectual projects flourished. One was an exploration of gender inequalities in education, launched by the new feminism. This created extensive documentation of the school experience of girls and policy issues about gender equity. It was brought together in Britain by Madeleine Arnot et al.'s (1999) definitive work *Closing the Gender Gap*.

A second group of researchers took a fresh look at the everyday realities of school life, informed by sharper thinking about gender, race, and class. This resulted in classic school ethnographies such as Barrie Thorne's (1993) *Gender Play* and Philip Wexler's (1992) *Becoming Somebody*, both from the United States. Post-structuralist thought added a concern with embodiment in schools and the complexities of identity.

A third project took a closer look at teachers, their industrial realities and career structures, as well as their occupational culture. A key study in this project was Gerald Grace's (1978) *Teachers, Ideology and Control*, a look at urban schools in London. In the best of this research, teachers, although still facing social controls, no longer appeared as puppets of conservative culture or of grand social structures. Indeed, Henry Giroux (1988) published a significant book called *Teachers as Intellectuals*, giving far more social agency to their role.

A fourth project, strongly influenced by Apple's (1979) analysis and Ivor Goodson's (1988) research in curriculum history, explored the highly political process of making curricula, compiling textbooks, and setting up testing regimes.

From the 1970s to the 1990s, then, the sociology of education in the global metropole became multidimensional in its understanding of social structure, and more concrete and subtle in its picturing of educational processes. Yet this increasingly sophisticated social science had diminishing influence on what happened in school systems. No sociologist of the subsequent generations had the educational policy impact of Havighurst, Halsey, or Coleman, though most of them were far more committed to social justice goals.

Partly this lack of efficacy was due to the shift in radical attitudes towards the state in the global metropole. Enthusiasm for the welfare state was replaced by suspicion, which persisted even though feminist scholars were drawn into policy work, and socialist scholars often worked with teacher unions. More importantly, the discipline of sociology as a whole lost influence because the political climate changed. By the 1980s the welfare state of the metropole was under challenge from an ascendant neoliberalism. Under Kohl, Thatcher, and Reagan, social equality ceased to be a policy goal; indeed, economic inequality began to rise again, and has continued since. Reagan himself once quipped that the US had a war on poverty, and poverty won. By the 1990s, even labour and centrist parties in the metropole had gone neoliberal. The main policy intellectuals of the new dispensation were neoclassical economists, who cared little for social justice and a great deal for private property and free markets.

What is Socially Just Education?

The sociology of education has not had much to say about the nature of education itself, or what its purposes should be. There is a definite tendency to bracket these questions, while getting on with studies of the groups engaged in education, and studies of unequal access or injustices perpetrated through educational institutions.

One reason for this wariness may be that statements of the aims of education have usually been framed in conservative and individualist terms: 'to help boys and girls to achieve the highest degree of individual development of which they are capable', to quote the British establishment figure, Sir Percy Nunn (1945, p. 5). Another reason is that when sociological theorists have grappled with the meaning of education, they have usually defined it in functionalist terms as a form of social reproduction – a view shared by Talcott Parsons and Pierre Bourdieu, not to mention Louis Althusser. For teachers, this is even more discouraging than outright individualism. At least Sir Percy gave teachers something to try for!

It would be hard to find, in the recent sociology of education, a statement comparable in boldness to George Counts' (1932) *Dare the School Build a New Social Order?* Counts, a US progressive, was already one of the pioneers of empirical social research on schooling. He became a radical critic of the timidity of Dewey's progressive education. In the depths of the great depression, Counts proposed that teachers themselves must contest capitalist control of schooling, transform the schools as an agency to regenerate democracy, and prepare children to participate in the vast social changes of modernity. Some of his ideas were echoed in the 'critical pedagogy' movement 50 years later, but the sociology of education never undertook a sweeping agenda like that.

Nevertheless, there are ideas in the sociology of education relevant to thinking about the nature of education and the meaning of social justice in education. Even the ideas of 'social reproduction' or the 'transmission of culture' can be made relevant, if we combine them with the empirical findings of the sociology of curriculum. Curricula are socially produced and are always selective. Power is exerted in the course of this production, and power can be contested. The cultural content of teaching and learning, that is to say, is embedded in a dynamic social process.

The sifting and sorting that goes on in school systems, i.e. the selection of *people*, is also accomplished by specific social mechanisms, especially through testing and streaming. The formation of specific skills, central to ideas of education as a mechanism of economic development, is dependent on the social construction of qualifications and technologies, for instance the institutionalization of apprenticeships, or the legal definition of university degrees. The idea of education as a form of human emancipation, for instance in Paulo Freire's (1972/1968) *Pedagogy of the Oppressed* (written in exile from a brutal dictatorship), implies a repressive social structure and a collective process that transcends its effects.

What the more sophisticated sociological accounts of educational processes have in common is a concept of education as the social process that forms not behaviours, attitudes, or values directly (as in theories of 'socialization'), but *capacities for practice* (Connell, 1995). Education is a generative part of the historical process. In education, the social practices through which we respond to our situation generate a new situation and a new social reality, changing structures through time. That is to say, education is an *ontoformative* process, to use the expression of the Czech philosopher Karel Kosík (1976).

There are three features of the process of forming capacities for practice that are important for thinking about social justice in education. First, it is crucial to see this as a complex and fully social process. We must not fall into the familiar dualist formulas of social theory that pair (individual) action with (collective) structure, and thus make concepts of 'action' or 'practice' the micro end of a micro/macro duality. (This is the logical structure of role theory, socialization theory, and concepts of habitus.) Practice is also collective. That is a lesson that goes back to the early days of the labour movement. It is highly relevant to the modern economy. Production and exchange involves such extensive and intricate webs of interdependent work, involving literally thousands of people in apparently simple transactions, that individual effects cannot rationally be measured. The formation of capacities for practice includes (and this is vital in the early stages of education) the capacities for coordination with others that will generate collective practice. The shift in childhood from 'parallel play', characteristic of ages 2 to 3, to interactive play with other children, is one of the fascinating moments in this formation.

The second crucial feature of the formation of capacities for practice is its historical specificity. The ontoformative process is located and transformed in time and space. We cannot produce abstract universal truths about this process, as functionalist sociology and market ideology hope to do. We always need to be concerned with the historical setting of educational processes. By no means can we simply project the metropolitan sociology of education onto postcolonial societies. But we can always ask historical questions about power dynamics that are projected across space and which link together historical chains of social practice. So we are not confined to the local; we can formulate questions about colonialism, imperial systems, neo-colonial relations, and global power structures, as influences on education.

The third crucial feature is that different dynamics in the formation of capacities for practice do have different consequences. Our actions matter; we have some ability to steer the historical process. We can, therefore, meaningfully debate the aims of educational processes. We cannot expect easy agreement on these aims. Official statements on the goals of education range from the banal to the incoherent (e.g. Australian Education Council, 1989), that is, when they are not actively toxic.

But we can distinguish practices that expand the collective capacity for practice from those that diminish it – whether by imposing responses to situations (various forms of authoritarianism), or killing, maiming, or imprisoning the participants in society (various forms of militarism). There is a vector here that actually has a wide application. The imposition of practices often goes under the name of 'training', and that has become widespread in corporate and NGO settings as a substitute for education. The surveillance and terrorization of populations, by official or unofficial forces, is an endemic feature of contemporary life. Hence we have CCT, drones, assassinations, femicide, not to mention the continuation of a global nuclear threat.

A fully social conception of education allows us to deepen the understanding of justice in education, beyond the distributive-justice idea that has dominated policy debates. Education is dangerous. Authoritarian governments and religions have persistently tried to control the content of education as well as to ration its distribution. Education is dangerous because schools and colleges do not just 'reproduce' culture. As Counts (1932) realized, they do shape the new society that is coming into existence all around us. Social justice in education therefore not only concerns equality in the distribution of an educational service, it concerns the nature of the service itself, and its consequences for society through time.

Just social relations involve mutual responsibility, and a just society contains dense webs of mutual responsibility – especially, shared responsibility for children. Currently, much of our mutual responsibility for children (and for adult learners) is mediated through a school system. Just education can be regarded as a set of arrangements designed to make this responsibility effective. The neoliberal turn in education is ethically damaging precisely because it undermines this web of responsibility.

In this historical context, socially just education is education that emphasizes mutual responsibility. It does so institutionally, in the form of a public school and university system rather than a privatized one, and pedagogically, in classrooms that emphasize mutual aid in learning and development.

Mutual responsibility does not imply standardization. On the contrary, justice in education means responding to the deep diversity that actually exists in large school-going populations. The equity campaigns of the last few decades have familiarized us with a list of educationally relevant differences: poverty, gender, ethnicity, disability, rurality, sexuality, migrant status, etc. The response required is not just one of recognizing human rights. This is only the beginning with issues of justice. What is needed are educational responses to deep diversity.

This means we have to meet at least two requirements. The first is *curricular justice*. This means a curriculum organized around the experience, culture, and needs of the least advantaged members of the society – rather than the most advantaged, as things stand now (Connell, 1993). Socially just curriculum should draw extensively on indigenous knowledge, working-class experience, women's experience, immigrant cultures, multiple languages, and so on; aiming for richness rather than standardized testability.

This is impossible unless the primary decision-making process around curriculum is decentralized, and face-to-face teaching is separated from the audit mechanisms of competitive testing. Decentralized decision making, however, needs solid institutional support. Teacher education, for instance, needs to be shaped around the skills and resources needed for producing such curriculum. Educational research needs to explore, in depth, the generative mechanisms underlying curriculum.

The second requirement is to emphasize, in policy as well as philosophy, the *social encounters* that make up an educational system. The sociology of education now has a wealth of knowledge about these encounters. It is teachers, however, who have to turn the possibilities of mutual aid into shared learning and creative experiences. Encounters between people, and encounters between groups, are the means of building culture. Just education becomes a means by which culture regenerates itself from below, rather than through commercialization or other strategies of power.

Encounters between people and groups only become educationally productive if there is mutual respect. Philosophers in the last few decades have emphasized that justice not only refers to material equality, but also to recognition, respect, and the overcoming of oppression (Fraser, 1995; Young, 1990). A just education system does not define some students as being good clients and others as rabble; it does not under-invest in some social groups while over-investing in others.

A just education system can allow itself to trust: to trust learners, without the whip of examination, and to trust teachers, without the club of auditing. It seeks security rather than insecurity, knowing that the basic security of this trust allows both deep learning, and intellectual and cultural adventuring, to occur. This has been possible in the past for privileged minorities such as ruling classes; however, an education system based on privilege is a corrupt form of education. We know how to do better.

Education and Social Justice in the Changing World Order

The sociology of education discussed in the first section of this chapter made familiar one set of inequalities in school systems. While class is undoubtedly relevant, there are also inequalities of gender and race, and other patterns of exclusion, that exist within the society of the metropole. What has not always been appreciated is that the mechanisms of inequality themselves vary across the world and change historically. From early days, the class and gender inequalities of the metropole were accompanied by massive racial and gender exclusions in the colonial school systems. These, in turn, have been replaced by new, differently configured, class and ethnic privileges in postcolonial regimes. The locus of gender privilege shifts; the boundaries between public and private education are re-drawn; educational privilege may be sought globally as well as locally. No systems model of education will work consistently in this shifting historical reality.

The period of the formation of modern mass schooling was also the high point of European imperialism, and of course this social technology was used in colonies as well as the metropole. In settler colonies such as Australia and the western United States, something like universal primary education was approached in the late 19th century, *among the settler population*. Indigenous populations were, at best, given a thin missionary education to make them Christian and fit for abject positions within the economy.

In colonies of conquest, including India, much of the Arab world, most of Africa, and, in an earlier period, Spanish and Portuguese America, most of the indigenous population were at first left to their own educational practices, while the colonial economy steadily destroyed the social order in which that education was grounded. The colonizers, however, soon brought local elites into their formal education, whether state or missionary, in a strategy articulated by a high British official's famous *Minute on Indian Education*:

> It is impossible for us, with our limited means, to attempt to educate the body of the people. We must at present do our best to form a class who may be interpreters between us and the millions whom we govern; a class of persons, Indian in blood and colour, but English in taste, in opinions, in morals, and in intellect. (Macaulay, 1835)

It didn't entirely work to the colonizers' advantage. Among the beneficiaries of this strategy were Mohandas Gandhi, Sun Yat-sen, Jomo Kenyatta, Kwame Nkrumah, in fact a large part of the leadership of republican and independence movements in the 20th century.

The colonizers did implant the model of formal schooling, however, which became the template for mass school systems later on. From the 1950s, schooling in postcolonial countries, supplemented by adult literacy programmes, expanded on a very large scale. Universal, free, and compulsory elementary education was written into the 1948 Universal Declaration of Human Rights, expanded by later conventions, and its worldwide implementation was brought under the aegis of UNESCO (Hodgson, 1998). Developmentalist state elites gradually became persuaded of a kind of human-capital argument, even before that idea became a central doctrine in the metropole and for the World Bank. Western-style education met opposition, for instance from some groups of *ulama* in the Muslim world who had their own model of education. The colonizer's model of schooling, however, was also claimed by some oppressed groups as a means of empowerment, such as the *dalits* in India, the untouchable or excluded castes.

There is no doubt that this expansion produced tremendous gains in popular literacy, dramatically so among rural populations and women. At the same time, research in postcolonial contexts persistently showed that social class selectivity accompanied the spread of schooling, especially at the secondary level (Foster, 1980; Chisholm, 2004). Indeed, to many observers the advanced levels of formal schooling became a key mechanism in the *formation* (rather than the reproduction) of an indigenous middle class among colonized and formerly colonized peoples. With the global integration of skilled labour markets and corporate management, internationalized education (in English language schools) is now being seen as a key to the formation of a transnational or global 'middle class'.

This process of class formation is itself being shaped by a new political-economic context, the advent of neoliberal market agendas across much of the world (Harvey, 2005; Braedley and Luxton, 2010). Currently a major shift is happening from old forms of inequality based on institutional segregation, to new forms of inequality based on market mechanisms. Under neoliberal regimes, schools and colleges are being re-defined as firms and forced to compete; while students are being re-defined as competitive individuals. Even the teaching workforce is made more hierarchical and entrepreneurial, and payment-by-results emerges from the gloom of history to become the newest bright idea (Connell, 2009). Education becomes a zone of manufactured insecurity, with individual achievement through competition the only recognized form of success.

The neoliberal market agenda, reducing all areas of life to market-like forms and stressing competition, needs measures of success and failure. In education this means a competitive testing regime. In the last generation, immense effort has been invested to build up such regimes, producing 'league tables' of schools and universities. They now operate on an international scale, helped by a competitive testing system, the euphemistically named Program for International Student Assessment (PISA).

PISA was launched in 1997 by the neoliberal think-tank of wealthy countries, the OECD, and is used to produce league tables of national educational 'performance'. Large-scale quantitative testing creates pressures toward a standardization of curriculum, to produce common performances that can be tested in this way. This hoists curricular decision-making out of the local settings and attaches it to centres of social power. The underlying attitude is made clear on the OECD's website, announcing in corporate-speak how well the one-party state of Singapore, a hub for transnational capital, does on these tests:

> A strong education system has enabled Singapore to develop a modern vibrant economy. Well trained and highly motivated teachers are central to its success. (OECD. Available at: www.oecd.org/pisa/, accessed 20 January 2013)

The PISA research can in fact provide some information about inequalities in school systems. But this isn't what attracts the headlines, or the policy interest. What gets attention is each country's position in an international ranking of performance.

That isn't entirely a matter of journalistic flag-waving. Neoliberalism has been global from the start, though this isn't always recognized. Neoliberalism represents a re-structuring of the world economy. It gained its grip as an alternative strategy of growth for postcolonial economies (Connell and Dados, 2014). This strategy rests on the search for comparative advantage in global markets. It is associated with a huge surge in world trade, de-industrialization in many economies, and the integration of national economies via deregulation and the operation of global finance and transnational corporations.

In the neoliberal world, mass education isn't the universal growth formula that it seemed in the 1950s and 1960s. If a country has something else to sell on the world market, such as oil, arms, or diamonds, its regime may get away with under-investment or even dis-investment in education. The Australian government, for instance, has disinvested in universities (in real terms) and watched school participation rates plateau since the 1990s, while the country's coal and iron-ore mines (leased at peppercorn rent to transnational corporations and local billionaires) have grown at a staggering pace. The ruling groups may be quite content for public education systems to decay, provided they get the education they want for their own children – a service that is increasingly provided by private schools and universities. For the rich in developing countries, this often means sending children to private education in the global North.

The market is hungry and seeks new services to commodify. Education has been one of the market's major spheres of expansion in the last three decades. Commodification of access to educational services is very much in agreement with 'user-pays' neoliberal ideology, according to which the market is always more efficient than the state. The fact that the market, pricing educational services according to what the privileged can pay, also serves as a powerful device to exclude children of the masses from having contact with children of the rich is just a bonus.

The new world of global markets, uneven development, and commodification has been registering in the sociology of education. UNESCO's 'education for all' strategy has produced some excellent analysis of gender issues (UNESCO, 2003). Elaine Unterhalter's (2007) *Gender, Schooling and Global Social Justice* is a model of relational gender sociology addressing education on a world scale. Close examination of educational markets and their effects on schooling and social relations is well under way, with illuminating studies such as Simon Marginson's (1997) *Markets in Education* and Stephen Ball's (2003) *Class Strategies and the Education Market*.

Remaking Sociology's Relationship to Education

In an illuminating study of the 'water wars' in Bolivia, where local residents contested the privatization of water supplies and the takeover by transnational corporations, Nina Laurie (2005) forcefully argues that globalization research in the South cannot presuppose the consolidated gender regime, coherent across the society, that gender theory in the global North does presuppose. This observation applies to other issues besides gender and is relevant right across the postcolonial world.

The colonial encounter was ontoformative, on a very large scale. It disrupted existing social structures and created social realities that had not existed before. This has been described with particular clarity by Valentine Mudimbe (1988) in *The Invention of Africa*. Conquest installed a colonizing structure, whose tasks were to dominate space, reform the natives' minds, and integrate the local economies into global capitalism. This launched the creation of colonial states, the intervention of missionaries, and the sudden transformation of ecosystems by plantation economies and colonial pastoralism. Colonialism generated struggles for independence, postcolonial civil wars, industrial development projects, urban growth on an unprecedented scale, and the exploitation of dependent economies by predatory alliances of local elites with transnational capital that has been well described for Africa by Moeletsi Mbeki (2009).

A social science based on the social experience of the imperial centres alone is not adequate to such a history. I have shown in *Southern Theory* (Connell, 2007) how even the most influential sociological theories (taking Giddens, Coleman, and Bourdieu as examples) are shaped, and limited, by their unexamined geopolitical background. The same is true of the sociology of education. Concepts such as 'social mobility', 'ideology', 'socialization', 'social reproduction', and 'habitus', and the idea of teaching as a 'semi-profession' in a stratified but stable social order, all reflect the experience, the social order, and the specific problems of the societies of the global metropole.

These concepts and frameworks from the metropole have been applied, without very much reflection, in a great deal of research in the global periphery, whether in rich or poor parts of the periphery. I will give an example close to home: I live in Australia, a settler-colonial society, which, like its sister dominion Canada, has produced significant social research on education. The local research traditions in both of these countries are deeply concerned with social justice. This can be seen in the superb Canadian research by David Livingstone (1999), *The Education–Jobs Gap: Underemployment or Economic Democracy*, or in the Australian project in which I shared, *Making the Difference: Schools, Families and Social Division* (Connell et al., 1982). Some very innovative work has come out of these countries, such as the wonderful book by Bronwyn Davies (1989), *Frogs and Snails and Feminist Tales*.

It is no denigration of the creativity here to observe that the intellectual framing of the sociology of education in these two countries is overwhelmingly from Europe and the USA. Australia and Canada have faithfully followed metropolitan intellectual trends from stratificationism to structuralism to poststructuralism. Reliance on metropolitan framing has left the sociology of education in these countries weak in addressing indigenous education, and (until recently) the consequences of global neo-liberalism in a dependent economy.

It is important, then, that we are beginning to see a critique of Northern hegemony in studies of education, as well as in sociology more broadly. There is now a growing concern to build on the work of researchers, activists, and theorists from the periphery.

I will briefly mention four contributions to this emerging project. Shailaja Fennell and Madeleine Arnot (2008) have posed the problem of 'decentering hegemonic gender theory' from the North, finding intellectual resources in Africa and South Asia for re-thinking gender issues in education. Anne Hickling-Hudson (2009) has made a broad claim for the importance of Southern social theory for understanding issues in postcolonial education and leadership in education. A postcolonial perspective has now emerged in comparative education (Takayama et al., 2017). Debbie Epstein and Robert Morrell (2012), returning to the question of gender, examine South African educational experience and thought, and map the multiple intellectual frameworks that have emerged in the global dynamics of knowledge.

Change is still in its early days. Yet if we agree that postcolonial thought (Chakrabarty, 2000), indigenous knowledge (Odora Hoppers, 2002), decolonial perspectives (Mignolo, 2005), Southern theory (Connell, 2007), and sciences from below (Harding, 2008) are all important, not only for curricular justice in schools but also for social science's knowledge about education, then this is a fruitful beginning. It opens up a real prospect of moving beyond the Eurocentric framing that has so far dominated the sociology of education.

To move beyond Eurocentrism does not mean abandoning the achievements of Northern intellectuals in understanding education or in analysing social justice. That would be an appalling waste. It does, however, mean that we interrogate their work as being a product of metropolitan society. Above all, it means being willing to plunge into the complications of knowledge in the postcolonial world – where the majority of the world's people and educational experiences are found.

The complications of knowledge include the downstream practical consequences of colonialism, the interplay of diverse intellectual traditions, and the deep problems of dependence and global hegemony in intellectual production (Mignolo, 2005; Alatas, 2006). The sociology of education that prioritizes the experience of the global South cannot be based on either simple pluralism or traditional knowledge. It has to grapple with unprecedented realities: the educational consequences of mega-cities from São Paulo to Guangdong, huge informal economies, mass migration, the collapse of subsistence agriculture, not to mention new media, industrialization, and climate change. A tremendous effort of imagination and intellectual integration, as well as severe realism, is required in our thinking about education now.

Sociology has long had a divided self-image. On the one hand, it imagined itself as being a social physics, cool, objective, the study of 'the phenomena of association and of social organization', to quote Giddings

(1896, pp. iii, v), in his summary of what 'the scientific description of society' is all about. On the other hand, sociology has also seen itself as being engaged, critical, illuminating, humane, even revolutionary, addressing the big issues in social life. That was what C. Wright Mills (1959) meant by 'classical sociology' in *The Sociological Imagination*. Somewhere between these poles is where most sociologists actually live. A combination of these ideas can be used to define a social purpose for sociology, assembling the knowledge needed for a democratic society to work.

I say 'assembling the knowledge', not to invoke a postmodern bricolage of fragments, but to stress that the construction of knowledge, like the making of society, is a historical process. We are constantly building on what is already known, criticizing and revising it, compiling information, making guesses, testing, and sometimes abandoning new ideas. Heroic syntheses, from Ibn Khaldun's (1377) *Muqaddimah* to Sylvia Walby's (2009) *Globalization and Inequalities*, are always welcome, making new connections and stimulating imagination. They are not themselves the goal, however. Social science is not an orderly business. Its sweet disorder is purposeful. Knowledge can grow, and knowledge constantly plays back into social processes such as education.

An agenda for the sociology of education might be concisely defined as being what democratic movements concerned with education need to know. That, however, is not a simple definition. Movements are plural, the social dynamics of education have worldwide dimensions, and the repressive and exploiting powers that democratic movements confront are globally connected.

I am going to end this chapter with a political illustration. In settler-colonial Australia we have periodic debates about poverty and education. In the past we have borrowed some ideas about compensatory education from the United States, and some ideas about social inclusion from neoliberal Europe. We have abolished the only national programme (the very creative Disadvantaged Schools Programme) that emphasized local knowledge. Neoliberal policymakers are now reading the national test scores, scratching their heads, and have proposed to pay some 'super-principals' extra high salaries to parachute in and solve the problems of poor people.

Several years ago, I was invited to contribute by an education magazine to write an essay on how to fix disadvantage. I tried to think sociologically and practically, and, with some light editing, this is what I argued for:

1. Rethinking the curriculum to make it work for the full range of social groups within the education system, prioritizing the least advantaged. This is the principle I call 'curricular justice'. It means building curriculum from the knowledge and skills, and around the needs, of groups who are currently marginalized – including Aboriginal students, a process already under way; including immigrant students, for whom the process is not so well advanced; and rural students who are often disregarded. Rethinking curriculum also means rethinking assessment. We need to throw out the primitive, monocultural, abstracted tests upon which media and policymakers place so much reliance. Alternative forms of assessment and evaluation already exist, in school practice.

2. Designing initiatives to make full use of the creativity and collective skills of teachers. 'Mandated' programmes, where a rigid teaching method and top-down auditing are required to get funding for disadvantaged students, are guaranteed to choke off teaching initiatives. Teaching is a daily process of improvisation. A teacher's capacity to judge the needs of students, to tailor curriculum to their needs, to cooperate with one another in developing materials and methods, are of the essence in making education systems work well.

3. Focussing resources where they are most needed. This is a simple principle, but we do not do it. Factoring in selective drop-out, and the higher cost of advanced levels of education, far more money is spent on the education of middle-class and ruling-class students, for whom the system is already designed, than on the education of working-class students. Government subsidies for elite private schools are merely the most scandalous part of wider funding inequalities. I doubt that curricular justice can be achieved without greater economic justice in the education sector.

4. Renovating technical and vocational education. Australia has had an astonishing number of enquiries and reports, while technical and further education colleges have been torn apart by neoliberal restructuring. Yet, after primary schooling, vocational education is the field where there is the most chance of immediate gains in social inclusiveness. If technical and vocational educations are seen as a core responsibility of public education, rather than another target for privatization, it could be the driver of wider educational change.

5. Developing schools as community resources. Elite private schools currently perform this role for the privileged. They provide a focus for networking, and that is an important reason why rich families fund them. Public schools can serve local communities in multiple ways – as cultural centres, as adult education centres, as social centres, as points of delivery for other public services. The more a school is embedded in local society, the more resources it will have, and the more pupils will feel familiarity and ownership with it.

There is no short-term solution to inequalities in education. But I would argue that work along these lines has the best chance of shifting a school system in democratic directions.

Acknowledgements

Part of the second section of this chapter is based on Raewyn Connell, 'Just education', *Journal of Education Policy*, 2012, 27(5), 681–683; the concluding passage is adapted from Raewyn Connell, 'Fixing disadvantage in education', *EQ Australia*, Autumn 2009, 7–8. I am grateful for the help of Rebecca Pearse and John Fisher. Andrew Fraser's doctoral thesis *Just Education: Teachers' Voices on Social Justice, Advantage and Disadvantage: A Study Undertaken in Sydney Catholic Schools in Neoliberal Times* (University of Sydney, 2012) encouraged me to think much harder about these issues.

References

Alatas, S.F. (2006) *Alternative Discourses in Asian Social Science: Responses to Eurocentrism*. New Delhi: Sage.

Apple, M. (1979) *Ideology and Curriculum*. London: RKP.

Arnot, M., David, M., and Weiner, G. (1999) *Closing the Gender Gap: Postwar Education and Social Change*. Cambridge: Polity.

Australian Education Council (1989) *Common and Agreed National Goals for Schooling in Australia* [The 'Hobart Declaration']. Canberra: Australian Education Council [now MCEETYA].

Ball, S.J. (2003) *Class Strategies and the Education Market: The Middle Classes and Social Advantage*. London: Routledge Falmer.

Bernstein, B. (1971) *Class, Codes and Control*. London: Routledge & Kegan Paul.

Bourdieu, P. (1966) L'école conservatrice. *Revue Française de Sociologie*, 7, 325–347.

Bourdieu, P. and Passeron, J.C. (1964) *Les héritiers: Les étudiants et la culture*. Paris: Minuit.

Bowles, S. and Gintis, H. (1976) *Schooling in Capitalist America: Educational Reform and the Contradictions of Economic Life*. London: RKP.

Braedley, S. and Luxton, M. (ed.) (2010) *Neoliberalism and Everyday Life*. Montreal: McGill-Queen's University Press.

Chakrabarty, D. (2000) *Provincializing Europe: Postcolonial Thought and Historical Difference*. Princeton, NJ: Princeton University Press.

Chisholm, L. (ed.) (2004) *Changing Class: Education and Social Change in Post-apartheid South Africa*. Cape Town: HSRC Press.

Coleman, J.S. (1966) *Equality of Educational Opportunity*. Washington, DC: US Department of Health, Education, and Welfare.

Coleman, J.S. (1990) *Equality and Achievement in Education*. Boulder, CO: Westview Press.

Connell, R. (1993) *Schools and Social Justice*. Toronto, ON: Our Schools Ourselves.

Connell, R. (1995) Transformative labour: Theorizing the politics of teachers' work. In: Mark. B. Ginsburg (ed.), *The Politics of Educators' Work and Lives* (pp. 91–114). New York, NY: Garland Publishing.

Connell, R. (2007) *Southern Theory: The Global Dynamics of Knowledge in Social Science*. Cambridge: Polity Press.

Connell, R. (2009) Good teachers on dangerous ground: Towards a new view of teacher quality and professionalism. *Critical Studies in Education, 50*(3), 213–229.

Connell, R. and Dados, N. (2014) Where in the world does neoliberalism come from? The market agenda in southern perspective. *Theory and Society, 43*(2), 117–138.

Connell, R., Ashenden, D., Kessler, S., and Dowsett, G. (1982) *Making the Difference: Schools, Families and Social Division*. Sydney: Allen & Unwin Australia.

Counts, G.S. (1932) *Dare the School Build a New Social Order?* New York, NY: Day.

Davies, B. (1989) *Frogs and Snails and Feminist Tales: Preschool Children and Gender*. Sydney: Allen & Unwin Australia.

Davis, A. (1948) *Social-class Influences upon Learning*. Cambridge, MA: Harvard University Press.

Epstein, D. and Morrell, R. (2012) Approaching southern theory: Explorations of gender in South African education. *Gender and Education, 24*(5), 469–482.

Fennell, S. and Arnot, M. (2008) Decentring hegemonic gender theory: The implications for educational research. *Compare, 38*(5), 525–538.

Floud, J., Halsey, A.H., and Martin, F. (1956) *Social Class and Educational Opportunity*. London: Heinemann.

Foster, P. (1980) Education and social inequality in sub-Saharan Africa. *Journal of Modern African Studies, 18*(2), 201–236.

Fraser, N. (1995) From redistribution to recognition? Dilemmas of justice in a 'post-socialist' age. *New Left Review, 212*, 68–93.

Freire, P. (1972 [1968]) *Pedagogy of the Oppressed* (Myra Bergman Ramos, trans.). Harmondsworth: Penguin.

Giddings, F.H. (1896) *The Principles of Sociology: An Analysis of the Phenomena of Association and of Social Organization*. New York, NY: Macmillan.

Giroux, H.A. (1988) *Teachers as Intellectuals: Toward a Critical Pedagogy of Learning*. Granby, MA: Bergin & Garvey.

Goodson, I.F. (1988) *The Making of Curriculum: Collected Essays*. London: Falmer.

Grace, G. (1978) *Teachers, Ideology and Control: A Study in Urban Education*. London: Routledge & Kegan Paul.

Halsey, A.H. (ed.) (1972) *Educational Priority. Vol. I: EPA Problems and Policies*. London: HMSO.

Harding, S. (2008) *Sciences from Below: Feminisms, Postcolonialities, and Modernities*. Durham, NC: Duke University Press.

Harvey, D. (2005) *A Brief History of Neoliberalism*. Oxford: Oxford University Press.

Hickling-Hudson, A.R. (2009) Southern theory and its dynamics for postcolonial education. In: Roland Sintos Coloma (ed.), *Postcolonial Challenges in Education* (pp. 365–376). New York, NY: Peter Lang.

Hodgson, D. (1998) *The Human Right to Education*. Aldershot: Dartmouth Publishing.

Ibn Khaldun (1377 [1958]) *The Muqaddimah: An Introduction to History* (F. Rosenthal, trans.). London: Routledge & Kegan Paul.

Kosík, K. (1976) *Dialectics of the Concrete*. Dordrecht: Reidel.

Laurie, N. (2005) Establishing development orthodoxy: Negotiating masculinities in the water sector. *Development and Change*, *36*(3), 527–549.

Livingstone, D.W. (1999) *The Education–Jobs Gap: Underemployment or Economic Democracy*. Toronto, ON: Garamond Press.

Macaulay, T.B. (1835) Minutes of 2 February 1835 on Indian education. In: George M. Young (ed.) (1957) *Macaulay, Prose and Poetry* (pp. 721–729). Cambridge, MA: Harvard University Press.

Marginson, S. (1997) *Markets in Education*. Sydney: Allen & Unwin Australia.

Mbeki, M. (2009) *Architects of Poverty: Why African Capitalism Needs Changing*. Johannesburg: Picador Africa.

Mignolo, W.D. (2005) *The Idea of Latin America*. Oxford: Blackwell.

Miller, P. (1986) *The Long Division: State Schooling in South Australian Society*. Adelaide: Wakefield Press.

Mills, C.W. (1959) *The Sociological Imagination*. New York, NY: Oxford University Press.

Mudimbe, V.Y. (1988) *The Invention of Africa: Gnosis, Philosophy, and the Order of Knowledge*. Bloomington, IN: Indiana University Press.

Nunn, P. (1945) *Education: Its Data and First Principles*, 3rd edn. London: Edward Arnold.

Odora Hoppers, C.A. (ed.) (2002) *Indigenous Knowledge and the Integration of Knowledge Systems*. Claremont: New Africa Books.

Takayama, K., Sriprakash, A., and Connell, R. (eds) (2017) *Contesting Coloniality: Rethinking Knowledge Production and Circulation in Comparative and International Education*, Supplement to *Comparative Education Review*, *61*, (S1).

Thorne, B. (1993) *Gender Play: Girls and Boys in School*. New Brunswick, NJ: Rutgers University Press.

UNESCO (United Nations Educational, Scientific and Cultural Organization) (2003) *Gender and Education for All: The Leap to Equality*. Paris: UNESCO Publishing.

Unterhalter, E. (2007) *Gender, Schooling and Global Social Justice*. London: Routledge.

Walby, S. (2009) *Globalization and Inequalities: Complexity and Contested Modernities*. London: Sage.

Waller, W. (1932) *The Sociology of Teaching*. New York, NY: Wiley.

Warner, W.L., Havighurst, R.J., and Loeb, M.B. (1944) *Who Shall Be Educated? The Challenge of Unequal Opportunities*. New York, NY: Harper.

Wexler, P. (1992) *Becoming Somebody: Toward a Social Psychology of School*. London: Falmer.

Willis, P. (1977) *Learning to Labour: How Working Class Kids Get Working Class Jobs*. Farnborough: Saxon House.

Young, I.M. (1990) *Justice and the Politics of Difference*. Princeton, NJ: Princeton University Press.

8

Suicide or Murder?

Apple, Foxconn, and China's Workers

Ngai Pun, Jenny Chan and Mark Selden

Introduction

At approximately 8 am on 17 March 2010, Tian Yu, a 17-year-old worker, went to the window of her fourth-floor dorm room at the Foxconn factory and jumped.[1] She survived, and lives paralyzed from the waist down. Many more have followed Yu's attempt, and have tried to end their lives, even as fans of Apple consume new generations of electronic products as if there were no tomorrow. In 2010, 18 young rural migrant workers attempted to commit suicide at Foxconn facilities in Shenzhen and other Chinese cities, resulting in 14 deaths; four survived with crippling injuries. The workers who attempted or committed suicide ranged in age between 17 and 25 – in the prime of youth (Pun and Chan, 2012; Chan, 2013). What drove them to take such desperate acts? Is suicide an extreme form of labor protest chosen by some to expose an intolerable and oppressive production regime, in which rural migrant workers are deprived of dignified work and life?

The internationalization of electronics production poses challenges to workers and their supporters from Greater China (including mainland China, Hong Kong, and Taiwan) and around the world. We contend that the responsibility for the spate of individual worker suicides is not Foxconn's alone, although as the manufacturer of more than 50% of the world's electronic products (Dinges, 2010), it is an enormous player and bears direct responsibility. The labor crises are by no means limited to the Foxconn workers. They extend far beyond the factory floor, to the profit squeeze that Foxconn and other supplier factories face from such multinational corporate giants as Apple, Microsoft, IBM, Google, Samsung, HP, and Dell (Chan et al., 2015, 2016). As activist academics, based in Hong Kong and the United States, in the face of the Foxconn suicide tragedy and the waves of labor protests over the past seven years, we ask two major questions: How to strengthen workers' power through organizing a global anti-sweat-shop campaign? How to connect grassroots labor struggles that spring from the point of production, to student and consumer campaigns that can impact international consciousness and the sphere of consumption?

Scholars and activists envisage a future in which 'each new generation of technical improvements in electronic products should include parallel and proportional improvements in environment, health and safety, and social justice attributes' (Smith et al., 2006, p. 11). With a shift in the location of world manufacturers from Europe and North America to China, and other low-income industrializing countries since the 1970s, China has risen to become the world's factory. During the 2008 Global Financial Crisis, foreign firms accounted for 'nearly 60 percent of all exports and 90 percent of exports designated "high tech" by the Chinese government' (Kroeber, 2008, p. 33). Of the foreign-invested electronics manufacturers, Foxconn was, and remains, the leader of high tech exports.

The Rise of Foxconn as the World's Largest Electronics Manufacturer

In the course of China's reform and opening, large foreign-invested enterprises have secured favorable terms from local governments. With access to industrial land and human resources, Foxconn has fine-tuned and assembled personal computers, mobile phones, video-game consoles, and other consumer electronics products for global brands, soon outstripping Western and other Asian manufacturers in providing low-cost, efficient services. By the end of the 1990s, Apple, Lucent Technologies, Nortel, Alcatel, Ericsson, and many other technology manufacturers had 'sold off most, if not all, of their in-house manufacturing capacity – both at home and abroad – to a cadre of large and highly capable US-based contract manufacturers', and international manufacturers led by Foxconn (Sturgeon et al., 2011, p. 236).

Like many other foreign-funded enterprises in South China, in 1988, Foxconn began with a small workforce of 150 Chinese rural migrants, approximately 100 of them young women. Unmarried female middle-school graduates were particularly prized by managers, who saw them as having such desirable feminine attributes as dexterity and docility; making them ideally suited to assembly work. According to one estimate, in the 1980s approximately 70% of the factory labor force in the Shenzhen

Special Economic Zone in Guangdong province was female, typical of the gendered division of labor at export-oriented industries (Andors, 1988).

Foxconn's expansion, built on strong foundations of manufacturing and assembly for export, can be aptly summarized in a corporate slogan: 'China rooted, global footprint' (Foxconn Technology Group, 2013, p. 4). The Taiwanese-owned company currently has production facilities in 29 countries on five continents, including: Taiwan, China, Japan, South Korea, Australia, New Zealand, Indonesia, Malaysia, Singapore, Vietnam, India, United Arab Emirates, Finland, Sweden, Denmark, the Netherlands, Austria, Germany, Russia, the Czech Republic, Slovakia, Hungary, Turkey, Ireland, Scotland, Brazil, Mexico, Canada, and the United States. The heart of its industrial empire, however, is in China. Taiwanese scholar Tse-Kang Leng estimated that by the early 2000s '90 percent of Hon Hai's net profit' had been generated from 'its business in China' (2005, p. 70). Hon Hai Precision Industry Company, founded in 1974, is the Taipei-based parent company of Foxconn.

Between 2003 and 2004, Foxconn acquired handset assembly plants owned by Motorola, in Mexico, and by Nokia, in Finland, and merged with Ambit Microsystems Corporation in Taiwan, enabling it to branch out from computer to mobile communications equipment manufacturing (Hon Hai Precision Industry Company, 2017). *CommonWealth Magazine* reported that Terry Gou, founder and chief executive officer of Hon Hai and Foxconn, 'presided over successive lightning quick acquisitions across Scandinavia, South America and Asia, becoming Taiwan's first business chief to complete mergers on three different continents within a single year' (Huang, 2014). *The Harvard Business Review* (2016) elevated Gou to the ranks of the best CEOs around the globe: ranked 40th out of 100.

Today, the large contract manufacturers for Apple include Foxconn, Pegatron, Quanta Computer, Flextronics, BYD, Compal Electronics, Inventec Appliances, and Wistron, among others. Jeff Williams, Apple's senior vice president of operations, confirmed that in 2014 'more than 1,400 talented engineers and managers were stationed in China', to manage engineering and manufacturing operations at large production sites; they worked and lived 'in the factories constantly' (BBC, 2014). According to information provided by an Apple University researcher, in 2016, in China alone, Apple has 'more than 2,000 large and small suppliers, including first-tier and sub-tier suppliers of parts and components, materials and equipment'.[2] This data suggests that China has become the center of globalized electronics production.

Behind the 'Made in China' label is a vast network of global brands and their suppliers. When the calculation of the value of the products is credited entirely to China, however, the picture is distorted. The largest share of profits is retained by American, European, Japanese, and South Korean corporations that designed and manufactured the most technologically advanced parts. In 2010, Apple's corporate strength was well illustrated by its ability to capture an extraordinary 58.5% of the sales price of the iPhone, an unparalleled achievement in world manufacturing (see Figure 8.1). Particularly notable is that labor costs in China accounted for the smallest share, only 1.8%, or nearly US$10, of the US$549 retail price of the iPhone 4 at that time. Other major component providers captured slightly over 14% of the value of the iPhone. The cost of raw materials was just over one-fifth of the total value (21.9%). Above all, it is industrial design, global marketing, and business acumen that reap the richest rewards for Apple, with a large share of the profit is generated by Japanese, South Korean, European, and American suppliers of sophisticated components for the iPhone. In this international division of labor there is relatively little value created by the workers in electronics processing and assembly.

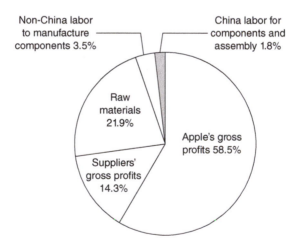

Figure 8.1   Distribution of value for the iPhone 4, 2010

Note: The percentage is calculated on the iPhone 4's retail price at US$549 in 2010. No amount for 'distribution and retail' is shown because Apple is paid directly by a cellular company, such as AT&T or Verizon, which handles the final stage of the sale.

Source: Adapted from Kraemer et al. (2011, p. 5).

Sean Starrs highlights the fact that now more than ever, 'it is more important to investigate who ultimately profits from the production and sale of goods and services rather than where their production or sale is geographically located' (2015, p. 19). Global brands, like Apple and Foxconn, should be held as accountable as any foreign government for conditions in the factories that produce their products and their profits.

Labor and the Apple–Foxconn Production Chain

The centralization and concentration of giant industrial capital, with Chinese workers providing the core labor force, has directly contributed to Apple's, and other tech multinationals', global success (Chan et al., 2013). Foxconn has the ability to transform Apple designs into efficiently manufactured and assembled products, working with Japanese, South Korean, and other manufacturers of sophisticated components, with the final product honed and assembled by Chinese workers and shipped to the world. It has also perfected another important skill. Because of the large-scale of production and the hundreds of thousands of jobs at its largest plants, Foxconn has been able to negotiate effectively with local governments to obtain lucrative terms that maximize both its own and Apple's profits (Barboza, 2016).

Apple contracted Foxconn to build most of its products in southeastern China, beginning in 2002, with facilities later expanding throughout the country. More than a dozen business groups compete within Foxconn, working on speed, quality, efficiency, engineering services, and added value to maximize profits. Two 'Apple business groups' – iDPBG (integrated Digital Product Business Group) and iDSBG (innovation Digital System Business Group) – have risen to become the 'superstars' at Foxconn. With more than one million workers in 30-plus production sites in China alone, while producing iPhones and a wide array of best-selling electronic products, Foxconn simultaneously produces a working class, and its policies provoke labor struggles.

In the wake of the Foxconn suicide wave in 2010, Apple tightened the noose on Foxconn by splitting iPhone orders with Pegatron to minimize reputational risks, and also to maximize profits. Faced with Apple's pressures for products to meet demand, Foxconn was compelled to further increase overtime work, resulting in 60–70-hour work weeks during the busy time (far beyond the normal 40-hour work week stipulated under the national Chinese labor law). An ever-shorter production cycle, accelerated finishing time, and heavy overtime requirements placed intense pressures on assembly-line workers even when many of them were desperate for overtime wages.

Surviving Foxconn and Apple

The iPhone is the signature Apple product. Apple sold one million units of the digital music player iPod in two years, but it took just 74 days to reach that milestone with the introduction of the original iPhone in 2007, and a sprint of just three days to surpass sales of 1.7 million of the updated iPhone 4 in June 2010 (Apple, 2010). During the same period, Foxconn workers toiled day and night to ramp up iPhone production. Foxconn – until the 2010 suicide cluster – was the sole manufacturer of iPhones (Chan and Pun, 2010).

In the hospital, in July 2010, suicide survivor Tian Yu talked about her family background, the circumstances that led to her employment at Foxconn, and her experiences working on the assembly line and living in the factory dormitory. During interviews with Yu and her family, it became

 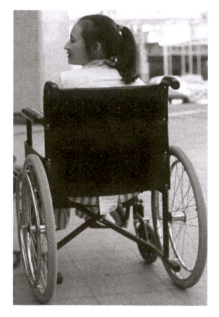

Figure 8.2 and 8.3　Tian Yu in the Shenzhen Longhua People's Hospital in Guangdong province. Half-paralyzed, she is confined to bed or a wheelchair.

clear that her story had much in common with that of many Foxconn employees, who comprise the new generation of Chinese workers.[3]

Yu belongs to the generation of 'left-behind children', as the out-migration wave enveloped China's countryside. 'I was born into a farming family in February1993 in a village', Yu relates. What was recently a village is now part of Laohekou (Old River Mouth) city in Hubei province, which has a population of 530,000.

Yu's grandmother brought her up while her parents were far from home supporting the family as migrant factory workers. Like many of the children who were left behind, she spent her early years playing with other neighborhood children. There was little parental guidance. Eventually, her parents returned home to resume farming with just enough money to renovate the house. Yu, the eldest child, has a sister and a brother. She hoped, in the future, to be able to help look after her 12-year-old brother who was born deaf. 'At best my family could earn about 15,000 yuan on the land in a year, hardly enough to sustain six people. Growing corn and wheat on tiny parcels of land and keeping a few pigs and chickens might not leave us hungry,' Yu said, 'but making a better life is challenging if one seeks to eke out a living on the small family plot.'

China's accession to the World Trade Organization (WTO) in 2001 brought about new challenges to villagers, who faced a flood of cheap subsidized crops being imported from overseas. Despite gains associated with the elimination of agricultural taxes in 2005, and the subsequent establishment of a social insurance scheme under the new socialist countryside campaign, with the departure of most young people for the cities, the prospects for household-based agriculture and rural development generally have remained dim. Sporadic efforts toward cooperative rural construction and alternative development initiatives aside, opportunities for sustainable farming and lucrative non-farm work opportunities in the remote villages are scarce.

After graduating from junior secondary school and completing a short course at the local vocational school, Yu decided to leave home to find a job. For her cohort of rural youth, the future, the only hope, lay in the cities. By 2010, TV and especially Internet technology and mobile communications had opened a window onto the real and imagined city lifestyle. 'Almost all the young people of my age had gone off to work, and I was excited to see the world outside, too', Yu explained.

Soon after the Spring Festival, the Chinese New Year, in early February 2010, Yu's father gave her 500 yuan to tide her over while searching for

work in the coastal Guangdong province, the heart of the burgeoning electronics industry. He also provided a second-hand cell phone so that she
could call home. He asked her to stay safe.

From Farm to Factory

'My cousin brought me to the long-distance bus station', Yu recalls her
departure for the city. 'For the first time in my life I was far away from
home. Getting off the bus, my first impression of the industrial town was
that Shenzhen was nothing like what I had seen on TV.'

On 8 February, at the recruitment center, Yu recalls: 'I queued up for
the whole morning, filled out the job application form, pressed my finger-
tips onto the electronic reader, scanned my identity card, and took a blood
test to complete the health check procedures. Foxconn assigned me staff
number F9347140.' Yu also received a color-printed Foxconn Employee
Handbook, which is replete with upbeat language for new workers: 'Hurry
toward your finest dreams, pursue a magnificent life. At Foxconn, you can
expand your knowledge and accumulate experience. Your dreams extend
from here until tomorrow.'[4]

At employee orientation, a human resources manager told a group of
new recruits including Yu, 'Your potential is only limited by your aspirations! There's no choosing your birth, but here you will reach your destiny.
Here you need only dream, and you will soar!' He told stories of entre-
preneurs like Apple chief Steve Jobs (1955–2011), Intel Chairman and
CEO Andrew Grove (1936–2016), and Microsoft co-founder Bill Gates
(1955–), to inspire new workers.

Yu remembers, 'Then, I and hundreds of other new workers were taken
from Foxconn's recruitment center to the factory, about an hour's ride on
the company bus. The setting sun bathed the Foxconn facilities in golden
light.'

Foxconn is a key node in the global production network, where production, assembly, and shipment of finished products to world consumers
continues around the clock 24 hours a day, 365 days a year. Yu joined the
ranks of 400,000 Foxconn Longhua workers. The 'campus', as the managers like to call it, organizes production and daily reproduction activities in
a densely populated environment. The gigantic Longhua complex includes
multi-storey factories, dormitories, warehouses, two hospitals, two librar-
ies, a book store, a kindergarten, an educational institute (known as the
Foxconn University), a post office, a fire brigade with two fire engines,

an exclusive television network, banks, soccer fields, basketball courts, tennis courts, track and field, swimming pools, cyber theaters, shops, supermarkets, cafeterias, restaurants, guest houses, and even a wedding dress shop. Container trucks and forklifts rumble nonstop, serving a grid of factories that churn out iPhones, iPads, and other electronics products for Apple, and many global electronics giants.

'I arrived late for my first day of work. The factory was so big, and I got lost. I spent a long time looking for the workshop', Yu recalls. The factory directory shows that there are ten zones, listed from A to H, J, and L, and they are further subdivided into A1, A2, A3, J20, L6, L7, and so on. It takes almost an hour to walk from the south main gate to the north main gate, and another hour to walk from the east to the west gate. Yu did not know what each building was, nor did she know the meaning of the English acronyms that could be seen written everywhere.

Sisters or Strangers?

'Hand in hand, heart to heart, Foxconn and I grow together', reads a bright red Foxconn banner above the production line. It suggests that workers and the company share a common destiny. In contrast to the corporate image of 'a warm family with a loving heart', however, Foxconn workers frequently experience isolation and loneliness, some of it deliberately created by managerial staff to prevent the formation of strong social bonds among workers.

Managers and foremen prohibit conversation during working hours in the workshop. 'I woke up at 6:30 am, attended a morning meeting at 7:20 am, started work at 7:40 am, went to lunch at 11 am, and then usually skipped the evening meal to work overtime until 7:40 pm', Yu adds. 'Friendly chit-chat among co-workers is not very common even during the break. Everyone rushes to queue up for lunch and eat quickly.' A long work day of enforced silence, punctuated only by the noise of the machines, is the norm.

On top of the 'standard' 12-hour shifts during busy periods, like all other workers, Yu attended compulsory unpaid work meetings every day. 'I reported to the line leaders 15 to 20 minutes earlier for roll call. Leaders exhorted us to maintain high productivity, reach daily output targets, and keep discipline.' The assembly lines ran on a 24-hour non-stop basis. The well-lit factory floor was visible throughout the night from afar. Yu felt that there was no way to say no to overtime.

Working on one of the Apple product lines, Yu was responsible for spot inspections of glass screens to see whether they were scratched. During the month or more that Yu worked on the production line, she made no friends. Foxconn's practice of rotating day and night shifts on a monthly basis not only effects workers' rest, but it also hinders their ability to make friends and establish networks of social support. Yu said, 'I was switched to the night shift in March. Checking the screens of the products made my eyes feel intense pain.'

The factory dormitory incorporates a massive migrant labor force without the support of family networks. Whether single or married, the worker is assigned a bunk space (upper or lower bunk) for one person. The 'private space' consists simply of one's own bed behind a self-made curtain with little common living space. With roommates assigned to different departments and often working different shifts, it was difficult to socialize. When speaking of her roommates, Yu said, 'We were not close'.

Foxconn houses most of its employees in multi-storey dormitories, at or close to the factory. The workplace and living space are compressed to facilitate high-speed round-the-clock production. Although eight girls were housed in the same room, Yu said, 'We were strangers to each other. Some of us had just moved in as others moved out. None of the roommates was from Hubei.' Yu's father explained the significance of this: 'When she first came to Shenzhen, sometimes when others spoke, she couldn't understand much.'

Random dormitory allocations break up friendships and localistic networks. 'At Foxconn, when I felt lonely, I would sometimes chat on QQ[5] online', Yu remarks. But those chatting on the QQ online community often remain far apart in time, space, and experience.

The Accumulation of Despair

New workers, like Yu, are often reprimanded for working 'too slowly' on the line, regardless of their efforts to keep up with the 'standard work pace'. Emphasizing the company's claim to produce the world's best products for global customers, the maximum allowable rate of defective products is set low. Yu said, several times, that she had made no mistakes on the screens, but the line leader blamed her anyway. With only a single day off every second week, or two rest days during the whole month, there was no spare time for Yu to use the Olympic-sized swimming pool in 'the factory city'.

Yu recalls, 'After I had worked a month, when it was time to distribute wages, everyone else got their wage debit cards, but I did not'. Yu was deeply troubled. She asked the line leader what had happened. Although she worked at Longhua, she was told that there was no record of her personal information at Longhua.

At Foxconn, the cash flow required for workers' wages is huge, and payment is done by a banking system through wage debit cards rather than giving out cash to individual workers. A debit card is a bank card, with which a worker can deposit, withdraw, and transfer money from 24-hour ATM machines that are accessible from within the Longhua complex. But where was her debit card?

Yu had been interviewed at the recruitment center in Foxconn Guanlan before being sent to the Longhua facility. Unbeknownst to Yu, the Human Resources Department at Guanlan had kept her personnel file and failed to transfer the documents to Longhua, where she actually worked. The result was that her debit card system at Foxconn Longhua had never been set up. 'I had no choice but to take a bus to Foxconn Guanlan on my own.' Yu recounted her experience that day. The Guanlan factory, which began production in 2007, employed 130,000 workers in early 2010. Entering an unfamiliar factory compound, 'I went to Block C10, B1, B2, and from floor to floor of building after building to inquire about my wage card'. After a fruitless day of searching for the right office, with managers and administrators deflecting responsibility, Yu was unable to find information about her wage card. 'I went from office to office by myself but no one would point me in the right direction. They all brushed me off, telling me to ask someone else.'

Yu had not been paid for a month of work, approximately 1,400 yuan consisting of basic pay of 900 yuan plus overtime premiums. By then it was the middle of March, and after more than one month in Shenzhen, she had spent all of the money her parents had given her. 'Where could I borrow money? At this moment of crisis my cell phone broke, and I was unable to get in touch with my cousin in Shenzhen.'

Yu had reached the breaking point. The exhausting assembly line, harsh factory discipline and friendless dormitory, together with the difficulty she faced contacting her family, were compounded by the exhaustion of her funds and the company's failure to pay her. Her testimony reveals how overwhelmed she felt. 'I was so desperate that my mind went blank.'

In the early morning on 17 March, Yu jumped from her dormitory building in despair. After 12 days in a coma, she awoke to find that she had become paralyzed from the waist down. Yu is now confined to bed or a wheelchair for the rest of her life.

One Life to Live

In October 2010, facing mounting public anger over the multiple worker suicides and the company's callous handling of the cases, Foxconn disbursed a one-off 'humanitarian payment of 180,000 yuan to help the Tian family to go home'. This gesture was made in a bid to end its corporate responsibility, and to remove the problem from the eyes of the Chinese and the international press.

Foxconn sent Yu's parents home in exchange for their silence about management's negligence. In the words of Yu's father, 'It was as if they were buying and selling a thing'.

When Yu left the hospital, however, she also left us, as researchers, with some troubling questions about the lives of one million Foxconn workers, and the responsibilities of corporations and the Chinese government to protect workers.

Suicide as Protest

Suicide involves an intensely personal, and social, struggle on the part of the individual. In November 1970, in South Korea, 22-year-old textile worker Chun Tae-il poured gasoline on himself and set himself afire as a means of rallying fellow workers and calling on the dictatorial government of Park Chung-hee to protect worker rights. His suicide inspired the labor and democratic movements that followed, and helped transform the South Korean dictatorship, galvanizing 'collective action by mobilizing the "hearts and minds" of the target audience' (Kim, 2008, p. 549). Did Chinese workers at Foxconn, not unlike their Korean counterparts, take their lives to mobilize for social justice?

Behind the façade of prosperity, exemplified by the Shenzhen skyline, Foxconn worker Xu Lizhi (1990–2014) ended his life on 30 September 2014. He was 24 years old. A native of rural Guangdong, his multiple attempts to find employment that would allow him to escape from the assembly line, such as a position as a librarian in the factory, had failed. He left this, his last poem, next to his deathbed.

On My Deathbed

I want to take another look at the ocean,

Behold the vastness of tears from half a lifetime

I want to climb another mountain,

Try to call back the soul that I've lost

I want to touch the sky,

Feel that blueness so light

But unable to do any of these, I'm leaving this world.

Everyone who's heard of me

Shouldn't be surprised at my leaving

Even less should you sigh or grieve

I was fine when I came, and fine when I left.

– Xu Lizhi, 30 September 2014[6]

While Lizhi worked and lived, he was never able to find a comfortable niche in the Foxconn world of labor, or to escape it to find a better life. Another of his poems reflects this.

Rented Room

A space of ten square meters

Cramped and damp, no sunlight all year

Here I eat, sleep, shit, and think

Cough, get headaches, grow old, get sick but still fail to die

Under the dull yellow light again I stare blankly, chuckling like an idiot

I pace back and forth, singing softly, reading, writing poems

Every time I open the window or the wicker gate

I seem like a dead man

Slowly pushing open the lid of a coffin

– Xu Lizhi, 2 December 2013

Some of his most poignant poetry conveys a sense of life on the assembly line. In this next poem he is capturing the exhaustion of workers on the line, falling asleep while standing.

Falling Asleep While Standing

The paper before my eyes fades to yellow

With a steel pen I chisel on it uneven black

Full of working words

Workshop, assembly line, machine, work card, overtime, wages ...

They've trained me to become docile

Don't know how to shout or rebel

Don't know who to complain to or denounce

Only how to silently endure exhaustion

When I first set foot in this place

I hoped only for that grey pay slip on the tenth of each month

To grant me some belated solace

For this I had to grind away my rough edges, grind away my words

Refuse to skip work

Refuse to take sick leave

Refuse leave for private reasons

Refuse to be late

Refuse to leave early.

By the assembly line I stood straight as iron, with versatile hands

On many days, many nights

I fell asleep while standing

– Xu Lizhi, 20 August 2011

Later Lizhi wrote of a screw that fell to the ground, in perhaps his most desolate reflection on life and death at Foxconn.

A Screw Fell to the Ground

A screw fell to the ground

In this dark night of overtime

Plunging vertically, lightly clinking

It won't attract anyone's attention

Just like last time

On a night like this

When someone plunged to the ground

                                        – Xu Lizhi, 9 January 2014

As Lizhi here recorded, respect for human life could never be earned on the line.

When *Time* magazine nominated 'workers in China' as runner-up in the 2009 Person of the Year, the editor commented that they have brightened the future of humanity by 'leading the world to economic recovery' (Ramzy, 2009). But what of those who sacrificed to help usher in economic recovery?

In their defiant deaths the Foxconn workers call on the Chinese nation – and international society – to wake up before more lives are sacrificed. Throwing their tender, still not full-grown bodies from dormitory buildings is an act of frustration and defiance. Neither in China nor internationally, however, should anyone have to make sacrifices of this kind. In our view, each suicide was tantamount to murder.

Apple's Outsourcing and its Global Supplier Responsibility Program

How have image-conscious companies such as Apple responded to Foxconn worker suicides, and subsequent worker strikes and protests? In February 2011, Apple released its Supplier Responsibility Progress Report to show the remedial measures taken by Foxconn in the aftermath of suicides. Apple's auditing team was quick to applaud Foxconn's emergency responses:

> The team commended Foxconn for taking quick action on several fronts simultaneously, including hiring a large number of psychological counselors, establishing a 24-hour care center, and even attaching large nets to the factory buildings to prevent impulsive suicides. (Apple, 2011, p. 19)

What is striking about these 'remedial measures' is that all were put in place only after the negative publicity that followed the suicide cluster.

Moreover, none of them address such core issues as speedup, and illegal levels of compulsory overtime work in Foxconn factories. Nowhere does it mention Apple's own direct responsibility in demanding immediate delivery of new models.

In transnational production, Apple's competitiveness is predicated on its ability to design and market innovative products to meet ever-changing consumer demand. Tracking demand worldwide, it adjusts production forecasts daily. As Apple CEO, Tim Cook, who succeeded the late Steve Jobs in August 2011, puts it, 'Nobody wants to buy sour milk' (Satariano and Burrows, 2011). Streamlining and controlling the global supply chain on the principle of 'competition against time' is Apple supply-chain management's goal. As a result, compressed delivery time of new products has repeatedly taken precedence over worker health and safety and rights protection, at times with tragic consequences. Under such circumstances, whatever the stepped-up audits, the tremendous pressure by Apple on suppliers to cut corners continues.

In this self-policing – or more accurately public relations – mode of corporate social responsibility, Apple failed to address the issues that arose from its own ordering practices, which contributed directly to blatant rights violations by supplier factories (Drahokoupil et al., 2016). Moreover, Apple is not alone. Apple and other leading corporate members moved to resolve the public relations crisis in a quick fix, while ignoring the problematic production conditions that gave rise to the contentious labor relations in their supply chains.

Holding Apple and Foxconn Accountable for Workers' Rights

On 18 May 2010, nine mainland Chinese and Hong Kong academics issued an open letter calling on Foxconn and the Chinese government to do justice to the young generation of migrant workers. The statement reads:

> From the moment they [the new generation of rural migrant workers] step beyond the doors of their houses, they never think of going back to farming like their parents. ... The moment they see there is little possibility of building a home in the city through hard work, the very meaning of their work collapses. The path ahead is blocked, and the road to retreat is closed. Trapped in this situation, the workers face a serious identity crisis and this

magnifies psychological and emotional problems. Digging into this deeper level of societal and structural conditions, we come closer to understanding the 'no way back' mentality of these Foxconn employees. (Chan and Pun, 2010)

In late May 2010, our Hong Kong-based research partner, Students and Scholars Against Corporate Misbehavior (SACOM), created a blog dedicated to the Foxconn worker victims and their families, with the theme song 'Grief' spreading quickly throughout the web. Across the Straits, in June, more than 300 Taiwanese issued another open statement and held a press conference to condemn Hon Hai/Foxconn management and its brutality toward mainland workers. On the basis of these two open statements, linking scholars and students from mainland China, Hong Kong, and Taiwan, a large-scale collective investigation of Foxconn began in the summer of 2010.

SACOM, the non-governmental organization formed by Hong Kong university students and scholars in 2005, has striven to advance labor rights in mainland China and the world. On 8 June 2010, the date of Foxconn's annual shareholder meeting in Hong Kong, SACOM launched the 'Global Day of Remembrance for Victims of Foxconn'. Foxconn workers in Guadalajara, Mexico, on 8 June 2010, demonstrated in solidarity to protest against oppression in China, setting up a makeshift cemetery to let the workers rest in peace and draw media attention at home and abroad (CEREAL, 2010).[7] It was a moment when the hearts and minds of worker supporters were mobilized.

On 14 June 2010, United Students Against Sweatshops (USAS), working through a nationwide network of over 150 American college and high school chapters, sent an open letter urging the then Apple CEO, Steve Jobs, to 'address the problems in Shenzhen by ensuring payment of living wages, legal working hours, and democratic union elections in Foxconn supplier factories' (USAS, 2010). The letter was copied to our research partners and campaign allies, including SACOM, San Francisco Chinese Progressive Alliance, and Washington, DC-based Worker Rights Consortium (an independent labor rights monitoring organization that conducts investigations of working conditions in factories around the globe). Nevertheless, they received no response from Apple.

Can a moral appeal to humanity, and a universal call to guarantee labor rights, be closely linked to the struggle for social justice of Chinese workers?

Conclusion

Apple celebrated the tenth anniversary of iPhone's debut on 9 January 2017 – *iPhone at Ten: The Revolution Continues* (Apple, 2017). Wait. Viewed from the perspective of workers, we must ask: what's worth celebrating? Are workers who produce the most profitable product in the electronics world enjoying improved working and living conditions? Have they secured fundamental labor rights including collective bargaining, the right to strike, and to organize autonomous unions at Apple's suppliers all over the world? SACOM marks 2017, the year of the global anti-sweatshop campaign, *iSlave at Ten: The Campaign Continues* (Chan, 2017).

Foxconn workers, as a notable example, have gained some support of students and scholars, workers, and consumers in Greater China, the United States, Mexico, and the world. The challenge of labor has also compelled the stability-obsessed state to make certain concessions, such as the increase of local statutory minimum wages and the betterment of the conditions of the most vulnerable workers (Chan and Selden, 2017; Pringle, 2017). It is crucial for workers, and their supporters, to carry on their collective struggles to build a more just society.

Corporate and state strategies to date have effectively restricted worker activism to the local level (Friedman, 2014; Lee, 2016). The core question remains whether Foxconn workers and their counterparts in workplaces throughout China will succeed in strengthening their protests as part of a national and global labor movement. That would of course require not only the growth of Chinese labor struggles, but labor struggles and support movements centered on the developed countries as well as the Global South.

Notes

1   Tian Yu is her real name. Her attempted suicide was reported in local Chinese media.

2   Jenny Chan and Mark Selden's Skype interview with the Apple University researcher on 9 August 2016.

3   Unless otherwise stated, our research team interviewed Tian Yu during summer 2010 in Shenzhen city, Guangdong. Translations ours.

4   The Foxconn Employee Handbook is on file with the authors. Translations ours.

5   QQ is a Chinese instant messaging program owned by the Chinese corporate giant Tencent. QQ.com hosts an online community of hundreds of millions of users, most of them Chinese.

6   The poems written by Xu Lizhi were translated into English by Matthew A. Hale and his colleagues, and published on the Nao blog (Friends of the Nao Project, 2014). Xu Lizhi's poems in the original Chinese are selected and edited by Qin Xiaoyu, entitled *Xin de Yi Tian* [A New Day], and was published posthumously in 2015 by the Writers Publishing House.

7   'Protesta contra suicidios en Foxconn' [Protest Against Suicides in Foxconn], Guadalajara, Mexico, 10 June 2010. Available at: www.youtube.com/watch?v=4ikF9vD3R_A (accessed 19 April 2018) (10 minutes; narrated in Spanish).

References

Andors, P. (1988) Women and work in Shenzhen. *Bulletin of Concerned Asian Scholars*, *20*(3), 22–41.

Apple (2010) *iPhone 4 sales top 1.7 million*, 28 June. Available at: www.apple.com/pr/library/2010/06/28iPhone-4-Sales-Top-1-7-Million.html (accessed 18 April 2018).

Apple (2011) *Apple supplier responsibility: 2011 progress report*. Available at: http://images.apple.com/supplier-responsibility/pdf/Apple_SR_2011_Progress_Report.pdf (accessed 18 April 2018).

Apple (2017) *iPhone at ten: The revolution continues*, 8 January. Available at: www.apple.com/newsroom/2017/01/iphone-at-ten-the-revolution-continues/ (accessed 18 April 2018).

Barboza, D. (2016) How China built 'iPhone City' with billions in perks for Apple's partner. *The New York Times*, 29 December. Available at: www.nytimes.com/2016/12/29/technology/apple-iphone-china-foxconn.html (accessed 18 April 2018).

BBC (2014) Apple 'deeply offended' by BBC investigation, 19 December. Available at: www.bbc.co.uk/news/technology-30548468 (accessed 18 April 2018).

CEREAL (Centre for Reflection and Action on Labor Rights) (2010) Mexican Foxconn workers support their Chinese colleagues. Available at: https://goodelectronics.org/mexican-foxconn-workers-support-their-chinese-colleagues/ (accessed 3 May 2018).

Chan, J. (2013) A suicide survivor: The life of a Chinese worker. *New Technology, Work and Employment*, *28*(2), 84–99.

Chan, J. (2017) #iSlaveat10. *Made in China: A Quarterly on Chinese Labour, Civil Society, and Rights, 2* (3), 20–23, July–September. Available at: http://www.chinoiresie.info/PDF/Made-in-China_3_2017.pdf (accessed 26 June 2018).

Chan, J. and Pun, N. (2010) Suicide as protest for the new generation of Chinese migrant workers: Foxconn, global capital, and the state. *The Asia-Pacific Journal*, 13 September. Available at: http://japanfocus.org/-Jenny-Chan/3408 (accessed 18 April 2018).

Chan, J., Pun, N., and Selden, M. (2013) The politics of global production: Apple, Foxconn, and China's new working class. *New Technology, Work and Employment*, *28*(2), 100–115.

Chan, J., Pun, N., and Selden, M. (2015) Apple's iPad city: Subcontracting exploitation to China. In: K. van der Pijl (ed.), *Handbook of the International Political Economy of Production* (pp. 76–97). Cheltenham: Edward Elgar.

Chan, J., Pun, N., and Selden, M. (2016) Chinese labor protest and trade unions. In: R. Maxwell (ed.), *The Routledge Companion to Labor and Media* (pp. 290–302). New York, NY: Routledge.

Chan, J. and Selden, M. (2017) The labour politics of China's rural migrant workers. *Globalizations*, *14*(2), 259–271.

Dinges, T. (2010) Foxconn rides partnership with Apple to take 50 percent of EMS [Electronics Manufacturing Services] market in 2011. *IHS Technology*, 27 July. Available at: www.isuppli.com/Manufacturing-and-Pricing/News/Pages/Foxconn-Rides-Partnership-with-Apple-to-Take-50-Percent-of-EMS-Market-in-2011.aspx (accessed 18 April 2018).

Drahokoupil, J., Andrijasevic, R., and Sacchetto, D. (eds) (2016) *Flexible Workforces and Low Profit Margins: Electronics Assembly between Europe and China*. Brussels: ETUI (European Trade Union Institute).

Foxconn Technology Group (2013) *2012 Corporate Social and Environmental Responsibility Annual Report*. Available at: www.foxconn.com (accessed 18 April 2018).

Friedman, E. (2014) *Insurgency Trap: Labor Politics in Postsocialist China*. Ithaca, NY: Cornell University Press.

Friends of the Nao Project (2014) *The Poetry and Brief Life of a Foxconn Worker: Xu Lizhi (1990–2014)*. Available at: https://libcom.org/blog/xulizhi-foxconn-suicide-poetry (accessed 18 April 2018).

Hon Hai Precision Industry Company (2017) *Company Milestones*. Available at: www.foxconn.com/GroupProfile_En/CompanyMilestones.html (accessed 18 April 2018).

Huang, E. (2014) Hon Hai Precision: You are your own greatest enemy. *Common Wealth Magazine*, 16 October. Available at: https://english.cw.com.tw/article/article.action?id=340 (accessed 3 May 2018).

Kim, H. (2008) Micromobilization and suicide protest in South Korea, 1970–2004. *Social Research*, *75*(2), 543–578.

Kraemer, K.L., Linden, G., and Dedrick, J. (2011) *Capturing Value in Global Networks: Apple's iPad and iPhone*. Available at: http://econ.sciences-po.fr/sites/default/files/file/Value_iPad_iPhone.pdf (accessed 18 April 2018).

Kroeber, A. (2008) Rising China and the liberal west. *China Economic Quarterly* (March), 29–44.

Lee, C.K. (2016) Precarization or empowerment? Reflections on recent labor unrest in China. *The Journal of Asian Studies*, *75*(2), 317–333.

Leng, T.K. (2005) State and business in the era of globalization: The case of cross-strait linkages in the computer industry. *The China Journal*, *53* (January), 63–79.

Pringle, T. (2017) A class against capital: Class and collective bargaining in Guangdong. *Globalizations*, *14*(2), 245–258.

Pun, N. and Chan, J. (2012) Global capital, the state, and Chinese workers: The Foxconn experience. *Modern China*, *38*(4), 383–410.

Ramzy, A. (2009) Person of the year 2009, runners-up: The Chinese worker. *Time*, 16 December. Available at: www.time.com/time/specials/packages/article/0,28804,1946375_1947252_1947256,00.html (accessed 18 April 2018).

Satariano, A. and Burrows, P. (2011) Apple's supply-chain secret? Hoard lasers. *Bloomberg Businessweek*, 3 November. Available at: www.businessweek.com/magazine/apples-supplychain-secret-hoard-lasers-11032011.html (accessed 18 April 2018).

Smith, T., Sonnenfeld, D.A., and Pellow, D.N. (eds) (2006) *Challenging the Chip: Labor Rights and Environmental Justice in the Global Electronics Industry*. Philadelphia, PA: Temple University Press.

Starrs, S. (2015) China's rise is designed in America, assembled in China. *China's World*, *2*(2), 11–23.

Sturgeon, T., Humphrey, J., and Gereffi, G. (2011) Making the global supply base. In: G.G. Hamilton, M. Petrovic and B. Senauer (eds), *The Market Makers: How Retailers are Reshaping the Global Economy* (pp. 231–254). Oxford: Oxford University Press.

USAS (United Students Against Sweatshops) (2010) *Open Letter to Apple CEO Steve Jobs*, 14 June. Available at: http://usas.org/files/2010/06/20100617_mahoney_to_apple_061410.pdf (accessed 18 April 2018).

9

Protest Suicides, Social Justice, and Public Sociology[1]

Margaret Abraham and Mathew John

In our deeply troubled world, fraught with problems of inequality, violence, and social exclusion, we pose the question: should the sociologist maintain an apathetic distance from the conflicts and contestations of our social world, or should we rather mobilize sociology, through analysis and action for social justice? Considering that sociology is primarily concerned with civil society, we suggest that one of its key functions should be to proactively address issues of social justice. Sociological silence, amidst the political and social upheavals of our time, is tantamount to being indifferent to and even complicit in injustice.

The importance of the sociological perspective is not to be underestimated. Charles Wright Mills (1959) writes,

> It is by means of the sociological imagination that men hope to grasp what is going on in the world and to understand what is happening in themselves as minute points of the intersections of biography and history within society. (1959, p. 7)

Given the discipline's deep understanding of society, its knowledge of theoretical and conceptual frameworks, and its commitment to technical rigor, sociologists are eminently suited to the task of engaging with the public on matters that affect their lives. It is therefore appropriate that the sociological perspective(s) be available to civil society, especially when it can make a difference and contribute to meaningful action by influencing policy and creating meaningful change in the search for a better and more just world. Mills continues to argue that sociologists by their intervention represent the best chance 'to make reason democratically relevant to human affairs in a free society' (1959, p. 194).

Sociology does not become less serious or insightful for its being more accessible. As our job is to study socially relevant matters we surely need to share our analyses with society's main stakeholders, i.e. the public. The building of professional knowledge as an end in itself is invaluable on its own. Often what is ignored by the critics of public sociology is that the scientific truths of professional and other sociologies provide the intellectual ballast that enables the public sociologist to effectively spread and share scientific knowledge with the broader society, of which we all are and must be a part.

The raison d'être for public sociology is succinctly stated by Michael Burawoy (2005): 'Public sociology represents the interests of humanity.' The interests of humanity are best served when social justice is a key guiding principle informing human social exchange. At its core, social justice suggests a social solidarity premised on the principle that every human being matters, that every person has the right to equality and fundamental liberties, to security and dignity. To address injustices is to advocate for social justice, be it at the local, national, transnational, or global level. It is to share in the collective responsibility to transform the institutions that oppress. It is to fight for the most vulnerable members of society, and to ensure the rights of the marginalized. By doing this we help build a more just society. This is the measure of our humaneness.

Social justice is the soul of public and global sociology. It invokes a moral and social responsibility for sociologists to generate and share knowledge and engage in collective action for equality, fairness, and justice for social change. Karl Marx perhaps had the sociologist's mission in mind when he said, 'the task is not just to understand the world but to change it'.

Suicides and the Search for Social Justice

Time and again the world has witnessed suicides that resonate beyond the personal and draw attention to larger issues of social injustice and inequality (Durkheim, 1897). Recently, we have seen suicides in different parts of the world stemming from foreclosures, economic crisis, austerity measures, political repression, forced migration, and the agrarian crisis. While suicide needs to be addressed at the individual level, it also behooves us to consider suicide in the global context of growing social inequalities, heightened economic hardships, and the displacement and dispossession of people.

In this chapter we focus on suicides that have bolstered collective action for social justice in India. We limit ourselves, however, to addressing the social, cultural, and political significance of certain protest suicides that have nothing to do with killing others, and that have raised public consciousness regarding the iniquities. A separate yet connected issue is the critical role played by public sociologists in deconstructing the dynamics of such suicides and their societal implications, as well as helping to bring about transformative change in collaboration with civil society.

A Student Scholar's Suicide, and Struggles for Social Justice

A recent suicide in India and the protests that followed have laid bare the fault lines of a society with myriad contestations revolving around class, caste, community, region, and religion. The trigger for the protests was the death by suicide of Rohith Vemula, a PhD scholar of Hyderabad University, on 17 January 2015, at a time when he was under suspension along with four others for being, allegedly, 'casteist, extremist, and anti-nationalist'. The cruel irony was that for much of his aborted adult life he had actually fought against caste terrorism, communalism, and majoritarian nationalism. Describing his own outcast dalit status as a 'fatal accident', which meant tolerating relentless inequality and cruelty, Rohith's suicide note is a searing indictment of an oppressive, caste-ridden society where, in his words, 'the value of man is reduced to a vote, a number, a thing'. In its helpless poignancy, the suicide note shames a society where caste continues to determine one's place in the social hierarchy. It is also a resounding repudiation of the deeply entrenched system of entitlement and exclusion based on caste and religion.

Rohith's suicide set off countrywide protests, particularly in universities and colleges. These have unsettled the right-wing government, held by the nationalist Bharatiya Janata Party (BJP), under whose watch there have been unprecedented assaults on free speech, and on concessions for the disadvantaged, and minority rights. Likewise, the coercive instruments of the police and judiciary have been used to quell dissent. In an environment of extreme intolerance, intellectuals have been targeted and even killed by right-wing thugs, draconian sedition laws have been invoked against those protesting the agenda of Hindutva, and peaceful demonstrators fighting for the right to freedoms granted under the Indian Constitution have been attacked by mobs.

Youthful insurgents, however, are fighting 'for the soul of India', as feminist writer Nivedita Menon put it. They represent hope that the glaring iniquities in the system will no longer go unchallenged by educated young people.[2] They have been joined in this struggle for social justice by a cross-section of academics, social activists, and writers, both nationally and internationally. One cannot overlook the linkages between this movement and earlier protests by writers, artists, and others who en masse returned the awards and citations conferred by the Indian Government to register their dismay at the frontal assault on basic freedoms in the country.

It is significant that in this movement for social justice, sociologists together with academics, artists, and activists, have been actively participating in protest marches, issuing statements, publishing thought-provoking articles, and giving public lectures on what nationalism and patriotism mean in a humane society. Two sociologists, Professors Vivek Kumar and Rajesh Misra, were physically attacked by thugs of the ruling Bharatiya Janata Party for speaking out against curbs on freedom of expression and growing intolerance. In questioning the hegemony and majoritarian worldview of the ruling elite, the community of sociologists has underlined the importance of real time sociological perspectives in grappling with the problems of the world. Their proactive and impactful involvement in the struggle is an emphatic assertion that sociology matters. It shows that sociologists can play a transformational role in creating a just society. The public sociologist is here to stay.

Farmer Suicides, Social Justice, and the Role of Public Sociology

A suicide does not have to be 'public' in order to resonate beyond the personal and draw attention to issues of social injustice and inequality. Take, for example, the complex phenomenon of suicides by Indian farmers, where the sheer magnitude of these cumulative deaths brings into focus their persisting oppression and the need for social justice and change.

In the context of suicides in relation to social justice, an important subject for public sociology is the unending wave of farmer suicides haunting rural India, where 68 percent of its 1.27 billion people live. These farmer suicides highlight the historical, structural, and relational dimensions of domination and oppression that underlie and contribute to current conditions of inequality and injustice. It also shows how local conditions are shaped by the global forces of neoliberalism.

One of the primary missions of sociology, in the context of farmer suicides, is to study human relations and human related problems within the existing social structures. As such, the sociological perspective is critically important in unraveling this persisting human tragedy, for it is the sociologist who has the vantage point to frame the issues and make sense of the cultural and social processes, the tensions and contradictions that have caused this continuing trauma in the farming community. Public sociology, with its concern for civil society, can play a critical role, through rigorous analysis, highlighting the conditions that contribute to farmer suicides. They can likewise share solutions for social justice to bring about transformative change in building a more just society.

Farmer Suicides: India's Grievous Fault Line

Primarily, the farmers who commit suicide are at the lower end of the many hierarchies that define Indian society. Their deaths are some of the most tragic manifestations of the oppression and injustice that persists in rural India. This ongoing crisis in India's countryside has been taken up for study not only because it features the largest wave of suicides by any one occupational group anywhere in the world, but also because it encapsulates the dilemmas of our time: the formidable impediments in our search for social justice. It is a narrative of power and powerlessness, of displacement and migration, of dominance and exclusion, of the unequal exchange between village and city. Ultimately it expresses the dissonance between the local and the global. Still in the grip of an obdurate caste system and dysfunctional institutions, India's villages have to deal with the neoliberal juggernaut that is indifferent to the concerns of the disadvantaged. The Indian farmers are fighting an unequal battle that has a powerful resonance among the millions in the Global South who have been similarly diminished by the entrenched systems of power.

This complex social, humanitarian crisis has seen more than 300,000 Indian farmers commit suicide in the last 20 years. Even this astounding figure is a gross underestimation, due to extensive manipulation in the compilation of suicide data.[3] The governing class in India, however, seems to be unaware or uncaring about the dimensions of this tragedy, as, until recently, this humanitarian crisis has rarely been mentioned in public debates or in the media (with one of the few exceptions being journalist

P. Sainath, 2014). It was ultimately the public suicide of a farmer, Gajendra Singh, at a political rally in New Delhi in April 2015 that propelled the plight of farmers to center stage, and forcefully reminded the nation's power elite about the unremitting agrarian crisis. Faced with this inconvenient reality, the Agriculture Minister trivialized the issue when he stated in the Indian Parliament in July 2015 that farmer suicides were due to 'debt, family problems, illness, dowry ... love affairs and impotency'. The political class and mainstream media have oversimplified this deeply problematic epidemic of suicides and have attributed this phenomenon almost exclusively to personal financial setbacks and individual angst, ignoring the oppressive social and structural conditions in rural India. Ineffective government interventions have done little to alleviate the distress of these farmers.

It is significant that amidst the callous indifference and relative silence around these suicides by Indian farmers, Indian sociologists and social scientists have ploughed a lonely furrow for several years, working tirelessly to draw attention to the dismal agrarian conditions that led to these deaths (Deshpande and Arora, 2010; Mohanty, 2013; Mohanty and Shroff, 2004; Padhi, 2012; Parthasarathy and Shameem, 1998; TISS, 2005). They have produced insightful analyses of the crisis by generating field research that has enriched our understanding of problems in the farming sector. Regrettably, their painstaking research, analyses, and findings tend to be tucked away in academic journals or books that are frequently out of sight for the public and public policy makers. This is unfortunate because as key interlocutors on behalf of the farming community, sociologists are crucial to bringing about transformative changes in rural India. They are also important as informed intermediaries for communicating the root causes for the farmers' angst to publics across the globe.

Farmer suicides have far-reaching implications for their families, particularly the women who are trapped in the vortex of unpaid debts and daunting family responsibilities in a blatantly patriarchal society (Center for Human Rights and Global Justice, 2011; Padhi, 2012). The grim dimensions of this persisting tragedy underline the need to understand the cultural context, the social ramifications, and the institutional frameworks undergirding rural India that lend background to this cycle of suicides. The challenge for public sociologists is to use our sociological imagination and professional expertise to unravel the causes of this human tragedy and thereby contribute meaningfully through policies' creation and action to build a better world rooted in social justice and a shared humanity.

Agriculture, a Neglected Area

Sociologists have identified a close link between the neglect of the agricultural sector, particularly around the interests of small farmers, and the propensity for farmers to commit suicide. From being almost totally dependent on American largesse through PL-480 imports for its food requirements in the 1950s and 1960s, India today is totally self-sufficient in agriculture and is also the largest exporter of rice in the world, the largest producer of milk, and the second largest producer of fruits and vegetables. Although groundbreaking technologies and innovative agricultural methods have contributed to this success, the credit really goes to the farming community that has toiled to make it happen. What have they received in return? Instead there is an iniquitous system where high productivity and bumper harvests have never ensured a reasonable income for the majority of farmers; where almost half the farm land is still rain-fed, leaving a large swathe of farmers at nature's mercy, and a lack of insurance against the vagaries of nature or the volatility of the market. Likewise, there are inadequate storage and transportation facilities, meaning the small farmers, in particular, suffer losses even when they produce plentifully. The government's focus agriculturally is on containing food inflation in the cities with hardly a thought to whether the food producer is adequately being remunerated. The governing elite obsesses about a high-tech military force, the creation of smart cities, and landing on the moon, bullet trains and glitzy metros, even as rural India remains without basic physical and social infrastructure.

Town Versus Village and a Changing Village Ethos

In a country preoccupied with elitist, urban, and metro-centric concerns, there has developed a glaring and socially calamitous disparity between urban and rural India. The impoverishment of the majority of people living in the countryside has been analyzed by sociologists as being an important contributory factor for the large-scale suicides among farmers. Haphazard 'modernizing' interventions by the state have exacerbated inequalities and social tensions in the villages. The sharpest indictment of the Indian state's priorities and policies is the Government's Socio-Economic and Caste Census (2011). In 74 percent of households (assuming five members in each) throughout rural India, the monthly income of the highest earning household member is less than 5000 Rupees (the equivalent of

80 USD). The corresponding figure for urban India is yet to be released by the government, but according to media reports 35 percent of households in urban India share a similar plight. Physical and social infrastructure in the villages is abysmal.

John Rawls, in *A Theory of Justice*, defines justice as being fairness in the distribution of life chances. In the most literal sense, life chances in the villages of rural India are considerably precarious. According to the India Human Development Report (2011), the average life expectancy in rural India is 60.96 years compared to 67.60 years for urban India. Likewise, the infant mortality rate is 55 per 1000 live births in the rural segment of the population, compared to 34 per 1000 in urban areas; the under-five mortality rate is 71 in rural India compared to 41 in urban areas.

The disparities in opportunities between village and town stand out in the sphere of education also, which is central to the development of human capability and to the process of economic and social progress. The literacy rate in rural India is 67 percent compared to 84.3 percent in urban areas. The rural female literacy rate is a dismal 56.7 percent, with the added dimension of caste discrimination reflected in Scheduled Caste (the group lowest in the caste hierarchy) female literacy rate of only 49.9 percent.

Low levels of literacy, however, do not reveal the whole story of state affairs in rural education. The Annual Status of Education Report (2014) prepared by the non-profit Pratham Education Foundation, based on a survey of 577 rural districts, shows abysmal educational outcomes at all levels. The survey revealed that 40 percent of grade three students could read only the alphabet, or nothing, and only 25.3 percent of them could do simple subtraction math. It is ironic that a country that provides its elite with an education comparable with the best in the world cannot ensure that the majority of its citizens living in rural areas are even functionally literate. The stark reality is that the farming community constitutes India's permanent underclass. It provides cheap unorganized labor that capitalist structures thrive on. Significantly, in the last two decades, there has been a mass exodus of several million peasants from the villages to the towns. This increased migration is poignant testimony to the harsh realities of rural life, which have compelled millions to forsake their roots and swell the ranks of the urban underclass.

Sociologists have identified a link between farmer suicides and the disintegration of the village as an institution that fosters social cohesion and a sense of belonging, despite the absence of hierarchical equivalence among castes. Far from being 'the real pure India' of Mahatma Gandhi's reckoning, the village nevertheless had, in the past, support systems and close kinship ties. With commercialization impinging on institutions and human relationships, however, even the age-old joint family structure that shielded the most vulnerable has now disintegrated. The tyranny of the market has not only destroyed social solidarity and valuable traditions, but it has also unleashed processes of exclusion, discrimination, and displacement that have further marginalized the poor farmers.

In 2014, the percentage share of farmer suicides by land-holding status showed that 27.9 percent and 44.5 percent were marginal and small farmers, compared to 25 percent medium and 2.3 percent large farmers. In this capitalist milieu, the village elite, mainly from the upper and intermediate castes, have cornered the state-sponsored benefits of subsidized power, water, fertilizers, and credit, whereas the small farmers survive on nature's mercy and usurious moneylenders. This oppressive environment drives many of the poorer castes and classes out of the village, forcing them to become rootless migrants in the cities.

An Oppressive Caste System

A discussion of farmer suicides is incomplete without briefly interrogating caste discrimination, which is at the core of the social order in India, and is one of its most disruptive, iniquitous fault lines. The hierarchical division of society through the caste structure has thwarted mobilization of the oppressed along class lines. Despite state welfare programs, myriad social reform movements, and laws against caste-based iniquities, caste still defines social relations in the village and remains the primary determinant of domination, exploitation, and bondage. Although some believe that caste has lost its salience, caste consciousness at the village level continues to be entrenched. The popular engagement in electoral politics is essentially along caste lines, with leaders who are focused on garnering benefits for themselves and their individual constituencies, rather than engaging with larger issues of injustice and oppression in the farming communities.

The upper castes, historically advantaged for centuries, have retained their ascendancy despite growing individual empowerment and resistance to traditional forms of domination. A recent study based on 11 years of fieldwork among sugarcane cutters and brick kiln workers in several districts across the state of Tamilnadu, in southern India, most of whom are former agricultural labor, shows that the majority of the exploited, ill-paid labor is among the Scheduled Caste (lowest in the caste hierarchy), whereas their employers are from the higher castes. These employers often maintain their control over their laborers through debt-bondage (Guerin et al., 2015). This study validates empirically the proposition that oppression is rooted in the caste hierarchy, and that caste and debt are potent ingredients for exploitation and domination in rural India.

The Stranglehold of Debt in the Neoliberal State

While the personal motivations for each suicide are complex, the common thread running throughout the various sociological and research studies done on farmer suicides is indebtedness as a primary cause (Deshpande and Arora, 2010; Kennedy and King, 2014; Mohanty and Shroff, 2004). It is impossible to discount the apparent nexus between farmer suicides and deprivation caused by crop failure, unviable small holdings, fluctuating prices, heavy input costs, and dependency on bank loans, microcredit institutions, and moneylenders, all leading to crushing debt. According to the National Crime Records Bureau's data on farmer suicides (2015), of the over 3,000 farmers who committed suicides across the country due to debt and bankruptcy, 2,474 took out loans from banks or microfinance institutions. A study done by researchers from Cambridge University and UCLA analyzed suicide figures from 18 Indian states and they concluded that the farmers most prone to suicide are those with land ownership of less than one hectare, excessive reliance on cash crops, and a debt of 300 Rupees or more (Kennedy and King, 2014). Given the nature of social and economic relations in rural India, it is hardly surprising that the small and marginal farmers from the lower castes are caught in this predicament and constitute the majority of those committing suicide.

Solidarity among the dominant castes, the moneylenders, the traders, and the commission agents ensures that the power elite can continue to exercise control over the lives of poor farmers, manipulating and even coercing them into submission. The exploitation of these farmers comes in different guises. Traders in seeds, fertilizers, and pesticides provide credit to farmers to purchase inputs, and in return the farmers are obliged to purchase their requirements from those same creditors who then pass on sub-standard products to them. Most of the small and marginal farmers are denied loans from the banks, driving them toward moneylenders for loans at financially ruinous interest rates of up to 60 percent annually. The methods employed by moneylenders to recover loans are brutal and often become the immediate provocation for farmer suicides. This corruption and exploitation are most tragically highlighted in the heart-rending tales of indigent farmers selling their kidneys in order to pay off debts, and even this money, which is earned at the cost of risking their lives, is then compulsorily split with the middlemen who organized the illegal sale.[4]

The socially unequal, economically marginalized, unsettled, and pauperized agrarian world has been further devastated by the neoliberal forces that focus on profit and are unmindful of the concerns of the disadvantaged. The multinational corporations, instead of rejecting these exploitative commercial structures in the villages, have been feeding on the iniquities in the system. The seed companies select seed distributors from the village itself. These chosen distributors are the large farmers who are part of the ruling dispensation and have a say in decision making for the village, thereby perpetuating the unequal, exploitative system. In this era of global integration, reduced tariffs, liberalized import duties, volatile markets, and the absence of a proper regulatory mechanism to protect the weak, the vulnerabilities of the farmers and their families have steadily increased.

The reduced role of the state has exacerbated the miseries of rural India. Various neoliberal reforms have resulted in a decline in the public investment on infrastructure, and particularly irrigation. The government's staple response to the agrarian distress is a periodic debt waiver, which essentially helps only the better off farmers who are able to access credit from institutional sources. Corruption and exploitation have made a mockery of most government schemes. It is clear that unless the systemic deficiencies in the agricultural sector are addressed, the poor and marginalized farmers will continue to be oppressed and many will commit suicide.

The study of farmer suicides in India has underlined the importance of the sociological perspective that is sensitive to the social, cultural, and political undercurrents in society for understanding and grappling with the pressing and seemingly intractable maladies of our time. It has also drawn attention to the fact that to be effective catalysts for social change, sociologists must emerge out from their academic cells and go 'public' so that their findings and insights can become available to civil society where they can actually make the difference, and contribute to meaningful action in our search for a more just world.

Conclusion: Some Reflections

History teaches us that there can be no peace without social justice, but despite centuries of striving, the just society remains elusive. The suicides that we have discussed highlight the tragic reality that inequalities and injustices are pervasive in rural India, but also in our larger violent and polarized world. Today, confronted by the ongoing forces of globalization, which have led to growing inequalities and injustices, we need to work toward the elimination of the structural inequalities that are embedded and experienced in the lived realities of people in local, national, transnational, and global contexts.

The times we live in need more equitable, collaborative relationships between sociologists and the larger public, if we wish to contribute to the promotion of social justice. Activists theorize and have forms of knowledge often devalued in academia, particularly mainstream academia, although this is slowly changing. Collaborations with movements and communities make our scholarship more relevant, but also more rigorous. We have and can strengthen our theories and methods by partnering with communities, to document social injustices, human rights violations, political and economic inequality, corruption, and government and corporate collusion, and also to offer paths toward global fairness. Sociology can help to develop effective strategies for social change. In this search for a better world, the sociological perspective, which is sensitive to all voices, has a critical role to play in deepening our understanding of the challenges faced and the changes needed in our conflict-ridden world.

A protest suicide draws attention to injustice, but it is civil society's response to such a tragedy that determines the outcome for radical change and social justice. The best-known instance of a protest suicide that shook the world and led to the removal of a dictator was the public self-immolation of Thich Quang Duc in Vietnam in 1963. In sharp contrast, the suicides by scores of Tibetan monks have not aroused their fellow citizens, or the rest of the world, to act against Chinese oppression. What is apparent is the randomness and sheer unpredictability of society's response to a protest suicide. The world has witnessed suicide's radical potential to ignite resistance movements for social justice. Conversely, civil society's indifference to issues of social justice is what oppressors have wished for and reveled in.

A potent and dangerous dimension to 'people's power' is when the silent majority is co-opted by the establishment and gives vent to its basest majoritarian impulses. Then democracy metamorphs into majority authoritarianism and human nature becomes genocidal. India has witnessed such programs, executions by Hindu lynch mobs in northern India in 1984 against the Sikh minority, in 2002 in Gujarat, and in 2013 in Muzaffarnagar against the Muslim minority. Elsewhere in the world, the horrific genocide in Rwanda in the 1990s is a poignant example of a large swathe of society being mobilized to commit mass murder.

It is our view that despite the deeply troubling aspects of certain types of 'third estate' (anti-) social engagement, the hope for a more just world ultimately rests with civil society. Throughout history it has primarily been mass movements that have disrupted the status quo, transformed societies, and brought about change for the better. Ordinary people have used the power of non-violent direct action to drive out oppressive colonial powers, to force tyrants to flee, to convert the vilest dictatorships into democracies, and to compel corporations to amend their exploitative ways. India's Freedom movement, the Civil Rights movement, the anti-Apartheid movement, these were fueled by citizens demanding freedom, equality, and social justice. Inspirational leaders have harnessed the power of the people, not guns and bombs, to overwhelm and bring down the most tyrannical governments and effect radical social and structural changes for the common good. To quote Arundhati Roy, 'Radical change cannot and will not be negotiated by governments; it can only be enforced by people. By the public. A public who can link hands across national borders' (2006, p. 297). With the exponential increase in inequality and social injustice in recent years, the 99 percent will need to come together to create a better, more just world. The public sociologist too must strengthen sociology's commitment to social justice and actively collaborate in this endeavor.

Notes

1   An earlier version of this chapter was published in *Öffentliche Soziologie*, edited by Brigitte Aulenbacher, Michael Burawoy, Klaus Dörre, and Johanna Sittel, February 2017, Campus Verlag, Frankfurt/New York.

2   See: https://isaforum2016.wordpress.com/2016/03/21/indias-student-protests-struggle-for-a-better-world/; The JNU Nationalism Lectures, 2016; Praveen Donthi, 2016; Teltumbde, 2016.

3   The National Crime Records Bureau, custodian of suicide records in the country, prefaced its 2014 report with the disclaimer that it is not responsible for the authenticity of the information furnished. This is prudent as the data is based on police records that

are known for their lack of rigor in compiling suicide statistics. Further, by limiting the definition of 'farmer' only to those who own land, this data excludes many women whose land is rarely in their names. The waters have been further muddied by the incorrect classification of suicides by women as being dowry deaths or accidents. The categorization of suicides by profession is also problematic, as it has amorphous groups like 'daily wage earner', 'unemployed', 'self-employed', and 'others', many of whom arguably have farming links. Significantly, in the 2014 report, out of a total of 131,666 suicides, housewives accounted for 20,148 or 15.3 percent, however, nowhere have the number of housewives belonging to farming households who committed suicide been specified, although women on farms are integral to farm activities. The credibility of the official figures has also been severely dented by provincial and state governments manipulating the numbers to show improvement.

4   See: http://news.sky.com/story/india-farmers-plan-to-sell-organs-to-pay-debt-10438044.

References

Annual Status of Education Report (2014) Pratham Education Foundation, http://img.aser centre.org/docs/Publications/ASER%20Reports/ASER%202014/National%20PPTs/aser2014indiaenglish.pdf

Burawoy, M. (2005) 2004 American Sociological Association Presidential Address: For public sociology. *The British Journal of Sociology*, *56*(2), 259–294.

CHRGJ – Center for Human Rights and Global Justice (2011) *Every Thirty Minutes: Farmer Suicides, Human Rights and Agrarian Crisis in India*. New York, NY: New York University School of Law.

Deshpande, R. and Arora, S. (eds) (2010) *Agrarian Crisis and Farmer Suicides*. New Delhi: Sage Publications India.

Donthi, P. (2016) From shadows to the stars. *Caravan Magazine*, 1 May. Available at: www.caravanmagazine.in/reportage/from-shadows-to-the-stars-rohith-vemula (accessed 19 April 2018).

Durkheim, É. (1897/1957) *Suicide: A Study in Sociology*. New York, NY: Free Press.

Guerin, I., Venkatasubramanian, G., and Kumar, S. (2015) Debt bondage and the tricks of capital. *Economic and Political Weekly*, *L*(26–27), 11–18.

Human Development Report (2011) *Towards Social Inclusion*. Institute of Applied Manpower Research, Planning Commission, Government of India.

JNU Nationalism Lectures (2016) *What the Nation Really Needs to Know*. New Delhi: HarperCollins India.

Kennedy, J. and King, L. (2014) The political economy of farmers' suicides in India: Indebted cash-crop farmers with marginal landholdings explain state-level variation in suicide rates. *Globalization and Health*, *10*, 16.

Mills, C.W. (1959) *The Sociological Imagination*. New York, NY: Oxford University Press.

Mohanty, B.B. (2013) Farmer suicides in India. *Economic and Political Weekly*, *48*(21), 45–54.

Mohanty, B.B. and Shroff, S. (2004) Farmer's suicides in Maharashtra. *Economic and Political Weekly*, *39*(52), 5599–5606.

NCRB – National Crime Records Bureau (2015) *Accidental Deaths and Suicides in India (ADSI) Report*. Available at: http://ncrb.gov.in/ (accessed 19 April 2018).

Padhi, R. (2012) *Those Who Did Not Die: Impact of the Agrarian Crisis on Women in Punjab*. New Delhi: Sage Publications India.

Parthasarathy, G. and Shameem (1998) Suicides of cotton farmers in Andhra Pradesh. *Economic and Political Weekly*, *33*(13), 720.

Rawls, J. (1979) *A Theory of Justice*. Cambridge, MA: Belknap Press.

Roy, A. (2006) *An Ordinary Person's Guide to Empire*. New Delhi: Penguin Books.

Sainath, P. (2014) How states fudge the data on declining farmer suicides. *Rediff News*, 18 January. Available at: www.rediff.com.

Teltumbde, A. (2016) Rohith Vemula's death: Exposing the political criminality of Hindutva. *Journal of People's Studies*, *1*(3): 53–57.

TISS – Tata Institute of Social Sciences (2005) *Causes of Farmers' Suicide in Maharashtra: An Enquiry*. Submitted to Mumbai High Court in 2005.

10

Engaging Society

How Public Sociology Contributes to Overcoming Inequalities and Injustice

Marta Soler-Gallart

Introduction

We are living in times of deep social and economic crisis worldwide, in which the former models of society that used to guarantee people's rights and dignities have been questioned, at their very roots. Sociology was born with the democratic revolutions, to develop scientific knowledge that can help people govern themselves towards a more just and equal society. Today, sociology and the social sciences in general are more necessary than ever. Sociology provides knowledge about the possible ways to reduce our current inequalities and injustices, and the consequent loss of meaning that is being experienced by many. Public sociology is now taking on this challenge, by serving the public good through transcending the academy, as Burawoy says, through bringing sociology into a conversation with publics (2005, p. 7).

This public perspective enhances an open dialogue where both researchers and social actors can participate together in the construction of social theories that go beyond descriptive analyses of society. Rather, they contribute to understanding possible pathways towards social justice. We need social science research to provide scientific knowledge that can ground solutions for a more just society. This was, in fact, the origin of sociology, to improve society and the human condition, and this is what public sociology can do, and is doing, through engaging with a diverse public, that is, with society. If we answer questions such as 'knowledge for whom' and 'for what', we must reflect on our role as social scientists, and our positioning as scholars. There are many different possible answers ranging from a motivation to gain knowledge for the academia, or for ourselves, to the noble pursuit of knowledge for the improvement of society.

In this chapter I will discuss the relevance of doing public sociology today. I will look at how it contributes to reducing inequalities and injustice, by engaging with the narratives of individuals and groups who have historically experienced disenfranchisement and marginalization. I will do so through the example of two women: Carmen and Lola. They both represent what Puigvert (2005) calls, 'the other women' (De Botton et al., 2005, p. xviii). These are women with no academic degree, who represent the majority of women in the world, and who are organized at the grassroots level. They embody many feminist struggles in their private spheres. These women have been traditionally invisible in the scholarly feminist debates.

I will also write about academic women engaging with these 'other women' (Beck-Gernsheim et al., 2003), and explore the impact of their dialogues on social science research, sociology, and gender studies. This chapter will argue that these 'other women' have contributed important insights and steps toward overcoming gender violence and inequality. They have also participated in the development of feminist theory and have influenced the promotion of more egalitarian relationships with the researchers and scholars who work for social justice with them. This public sociology includes professional, critical, and policy sociology. When the dialogue between social science researchers and social actors takes place in a rigorous and reliable way for the improvement of society and social policy, all benefit.

The communicative methodology in researching inequality is a good example of this. Through the communicative perspective of research, social scientists can better engage with social actors who suffer from exclusion. They create egalitarian dialogues in which researchers contribute knowledge from the scientific community and social actors contribute their lived experience on the same phenomena, reaching together a better understanding of reality. The communicative methodology ends therefore with the traditional approach of doing social research upon this same public, and sheds light on new pathways for overcoming inequalities and advancing social justice. Finally, I will introduce the case of a public institute doing public sociology, which has actually worked with these 'other women'.

The Dialogue Between the 'Other Women' and Sociologists in Academia

Carmen is a Roma grandmother. She is a person of respect in her community. She is an activist, and president of a Roma Women's Association through which she advocates for the education and labor rights of all Roma, particularly young Romaní women and girls. She is illiterate, from a marginalized ghetto in the city of Barcelona, but this does not stop her personal and collective struggle. In 2001 Carmen participated in the Conference 'Women and Social Transformation' at the University of Barcelona. Renowned feminist scholars such as Judith Butler, Elisabeth Beck-Gernsheim, and Lidia Puigvert all participated and were invited to give lectures. Women like Carmen were also invited to speak, in plenary sessions: they were non-academic migrant and Roma women, working-class women in domestic cleaning, women from adult learning centers, etc. The dialogues between the academics and the other women transcended just the few days of the conference, going on to contributing to an advance in feminist theory. Some of these women argued that a new feminism should radicalize solidarity among women. They explained how often they clean the houses of professional women who struggle against labor discrimination from men, but then treat them with disdain. Non-academic women had been invisible to mainstream feminist struggles, and now, in dialogue, they were developing a feminism of all women.

The inclusion of a diversity of female voices in debates about central feminist issues has been shown to contribute to gains both in the understanding of the sociological questions under exploration, and in the development of collective social struggles. Exchanges between all women help feminist research link to feminist action, a task that challenges researchers who have traditionally worked far from women experiencing such inequality (Gopal, 2012). This essay presents a communicative paradigm as being a tool to address such challenges, and to create sociological knowledge that seeks to be socially useful (for the public), precisely because it has been elaborated acknowledging a diversity of viewpoints (with the public).

Judith Butler was impressed by the conversation with Carmen, about her personal struggles. She knew that the Roma people were excluded, but through their conversation was able to better understand Carmen's experience of constantly fighting against this situation (Beck-Gernsheim et al., 2003). After the conference, Butler emailed our research center (CREA) saying: 'It was a beautiful and moving experience that will change me and my work. You have returned me to my most basic sense of why feminism is urgent, moving and creative' (Soler-Gallart, 2017). Butler's dialogues with Carmen impacted her academic work. After that meaningful encounter, Butler started to include issues of human rights and anti-discrimination in her lectures and scholarly work. She realized that addressing difference, and naming the non-spoken, was directly linked to the daily lives and struggles of many women, and the need to use social theory to openly speak about this link in the defense of their most basic rights. Actually, those non-academic, marginalized women wanted research and theories that dealt with gender, class, or race discrimination, but not only to provide better analyses of such inequalities, but also to develop sociological knowledge that can inform social and political actions that can reduce injustice and improve their lives.

Nine years later, in another conference, titled 'Gender and Diversity of Voices', also in Barcelona, Butler was discussing how social movements must necessarily include a defense of some universals of global justice, which all can agree upon (Butler, 2006). As an example, she said that the gay movement must be deeply anti-racist, meaning that she could not understand a social movement struggling for particular cultural rights but rather for the rights of all those discriminated against. The dialogic perspective she started to develop, engaging with the women at these conferences who were not academics, the 'other women', will make a difference to many women worldwide.

These conversations – the engagement of 'other women' in conversation with intellectuals – also influenced Carmen and the other women like her. Carmen and the Roma Association of Women, which she belongs to, participated in a public sociology research project grounded in communicative methodology. The results from this research were presented at the European Parliament in a dialogue between public sociologists, policy makers, and Roma organizations, Carmen among them. The conclusions were later approved by the Parliament unanimously, thus leading to strategic plans and concrete policies addressing the improvement of Roma education, labor opportunities, and living conditions. Beyond just this impact on policy, Carmen herself, through direct participation in the research, obtained the scientific knowledge that allowed her, at a grassroots level, to enhance the potentials in her own community for success in education, labor, and life.

From a communicative methodological approach, Carmen was engaged throughout the research process in the creation of knowledge, from the definition of the research questions, to the data collection, analysis, and dissemination activities. In this way, she was not only contributing to the work of the researchers, but was also getting from them, and indirectly from the scientific community, new knowledge about actions that had been successful elsewhere in creating better living conditions. In this way the communicative paradigm contributes to social justice, not only by means of including the voices of vulnerable groups in dialogue with researchers, but also through conducting an analysis of data (communicative analysis) that is not oriented to a description of barriers, but rather to identifying the actions that transform these barriers.

For each barrier, a proposal for transformative action is defined, which builds upon the insights of social agents, contrasted with knowledge from the scientific literature and the scientific evidences of these transformations. Later, this is presented and discussed among social researchers, end-users, and policy-makers, in a process characterized by egalitarian relationships among all. The results are then taken up by governments in their development of recommendations and policies addressed to increase social justice and the improvement of human living conditions. The effective results of this process are applied in a number of competitive projects targeting social justice issues. This has led to an expansion of the use of the communicative research methodology in the work of public sociologists.

In the analysis of Roma insertion in the labor market, there is the assumption that Roma women only enroll in vocational training courses to obtain welfare, and that they do not seek real job opportunities. Stereotypes, like being lazy and opportunistic, or that associate freedom with lack of work commitment, are common among the public and mainstream media (Hancock, 2002). Similar labeling has been applied to black populations in the United States. African American women have had to face many injustices related to their gender, class, and race (Collins, 1998).

In the dialogue between Carmen's Roma Association and the public sociologists, it became clear that most of the vocational training offered to these women was not linked to real jobs. Even after completion, the Roma women would later bump into barriers of racism and exclusion in the open labor market. In response to this insight, the Association designed vocational training courses for school services (such as canteen workers), which many Roma mothers could later use to become contracted by primary schools in their neighborhoods. These mothers then became part of the staff at schools where before their children could not have found any Roma reference point. The program has been strongly successful, not only for the high rate of labor insertion of the Roma women learners, but also for the transformation provoked in their families and communities. This well illustrates the process of knowledge creation following a communicative orientation of public sociology, and the impact it can achieve at various levels, including both political and personal. The presence of these mothers has transformed the school context, making visible in the building Roma adults who were before blocked from participation; discrimination that has been historically experienced by the Roma in schools around the world. Moreover, the training has created the emergence of new academic interactions between these Roma women and their children, both in the school and in other spaces of the community. These are spaces that have now become more truly public.

In the poorest neighborhood in Spain a Roma woman is now the president of a newly created cooperative. La Milagrosa barrio was originally characterized by extreme poverty, unemployment, crime, drugs, and strong housing and health problems. Through a dialogic process (the dialogic inclusion contract), citizens from this ghetto conversed with researchers who provided them with successful actions to create employment, based upon research done in other contexts. Instead of welfare assistance, this dialogic process supported the recreation of best practices in La Milagrosa's context. Consequently, there has been a self-creation of the cooperative. They now offer domestic cleaning services, school services, construction and repair services, and harvesting (i.e. garlic, onion), and operate on the democratic management model of workers' owned cooperatives. In only one year La Milagrosa has grown and has 12 working members of the cooperative, which provides employment for 150 people from their community. Most of these people now have, for the first time, a decent job.

Amartya Sen (1999) argues that economic development is related to enhancing people's capacities. Public sociologists have been crucial in providing knowledge about various successful actions, which have then enhanced the Roma entrepreneurial capacities. Rather than victimizing the Roma, or taking a paternalistic approach, collaboration has helped these Roma people appropriate the successful actions themselves and build upon their own capacities. It has therefore contributed to greater social and economic justice for the people living in a place that, little by little, will not be defined as a ghetto anymore.

Lola is another one of these 'other women' who attended a lecture on the 'Intercultural Discourse of Human Rights', which Jürgen Habermas gave at the University of Barcelona in 1997. During the lecture, Lola asked a question about women's labor rights. She is a non-academic woman and her language and way of expression showed it. Half of the almost entirely academic audience reacted, laughing at her intervention. Aware that she was not the standard participant expected at this kind of event, Lola responded, 'I don't talk like an intellectual but I know what I mean' (Flecha, 2000, p.53). The interpreter did not translate Lola's question, but Habermas asked him to do so. After listening to it, Habermas said: 'This is a brilliant and very critical question.'

This example shows us how the 'other women' are able to engage in dialogue with intellectuals who are prepared to promote a public discussion with civil society. This example illustrates not only the way in which 'other women' are able to make their voices heard in different spaces, including academic ones, but also how they enrich the academic discussion. Lola's question pushed the speaker, and the discussion, to connect its high academic discourses to real problems that affect the majority of women's everyday lives. The behavior of the interpreter and of the whole situation is described because this kind of elitist derision is not unique, and it is not just confined to academic lectures. Similar cases have been documented by court interpreters in domestic violence cases (Lemon, 2006), ever more so when the victims are women belonging to vulnerable groups (Menjíbar and Salcido, 2008). The example of Lola brings an awareness of the ways in which marginalized voices are heard, erased, or ignored, and the implications of this for social justice, and for the development of research and theories that might better help the public.

Lola's story illustrates the kind of personal and social transformation that public sociology can inform. Lola is an active participant in the Dialogic Literary Gatherings, an internationally recognized and successful action group in the overcoming of inequalities. In the Dialogic Literary Gatherings, people who have never read a book before enjoy reading works of classical literature by writers such as James Joyce, Virginia Woolf, Shakespeare, or Cervantes. In many cases, these people, who have learned to read through the literary gatherings, start becoming very active in cultural and social movements aimed at extending democratic and egalitarian values. Participants in the Dialogic Literary Gatherings have considerably increased their self-confidence, they participate in academic forums through their involvement with this successful action, overcoming their fears and fighting against different forms of discrimination. This is what occurred with Lola at that academic event.

This empowerment of the 'other women' is breaking many cultural and educational stereotypes. On one occasion, Pierre Bourdieu went to Barcelona and said: 'When people without university degrees look at the Goya's painting *La Maja Desnuda* [The Nude Maja], they cannot see art, they just see pornography' (Flecha, 2009, p. 335). The 'other women' movement in Barcelona strongly protested; they considered this statement to be both classist and sexist. They disapproved of how Bourdieu spoke on their behalf, and that he did not ask them about it. Not only did he speak without taking into account the voices of those he was speaking for, but he also dismissed their capacity to understand and enjoy artistic works. He denied and ignored their agency, reproducing cultural stereotypes linked to social class. It is from their sense of agency that these women reacted against such cultural injustice.

Thanks to their participation in cultural activities, such as the Dialogic Literary Gatherings, people like Lola know about art and classical literature, far more than many of the academics who cast aspersions. As Lola remarked, while she was reading and enjoying Kafka and Sappho, the scholars who laughed at her were probably reading *Millennium* by Stieg Larson, or *Perfume* by Patrick Süskind. Because of these literary gatherings, created by a public sociologist in permanent dialogue with participants, Lola could go beyond the structural limitations put upon her. Today, the Dialogic Literary Gatherings are implemented in different countries around the world, from Australia and Brazil, to China. This cultural program brings about important social changes: it fells elitist walls, and makes high culture, which had before been only for the elites, available to all publics. In addition, through the Dialogic Literary Gatherings, participants with working-class backgrounds can come to participate in social and cultural spaces that are thought to be for upper classes, such as opera, museums, and theater, an act of empowerment that leads some of them to become grassroots leaders for the good of their communities.

History has shown that a relationship between the concepts and ideas found in civil society and those of experts can be developed in different fields. Participants of the literary gatherings, like Lola, are aware of this. They know very well that García Lorca was one of the intellectuals who knew how to praise folk-creativity through his poetry, using metaphors, obtained from the people, to name things. For example, *heaven fat* to designate a type of candy. Another artist and intellectual, Gaudi, was able to create his unique architecture by understanding the global dimensions and integrating different manual arts into his design (e.g. pottery, glass works, the forge). He would use these folk-crafts, recreating his works in scaled models.

The Roma people, like Carmen, also appreciate how García Lorca was able to express the Roma experience of prosecution and exclusion through his Gypsy Ballads. He was able to communicate the deep feelings of passion and sorrow, because he had dialogued with them, and shared their concerns. Artists and intellectuals, like Lorca and Gaudi, to name a few, did not understand why traditional academic sociology did not work in close contact with civil society as they did. Because this level of dialogue and collaboration has been rare, however, it is all the more celebrated when the orientation of public sociology includes local voices and relates to local needs.

Roma women from the cooperative in La Milagrosa barrio were well aware that their project had been made possible because public sociologists had shared with them the information about actions that had been successful in other contexts, creating sustainable employment and ground to compete in the market. Together, through dialogue, they had recreated these actions in relation to their own lifeworlds and life experiences. This has been the knowledge base for the transformation of their barrio, and the creation of their cooperative. This shift in knowledge production is aligned with a de-monopolization of expert knowledge (Beck et al., 1994), in which authority is gained through dialogue and argumentation with all agents involved.

Sociologists like Alfred Schütz have tried to lend their contributions to this area. Opposing Parsons, and other functionalist and structuralist theorists, Schütz et al. (1967) defined the close relationship that must be developed between scientific concepts and the meaningful acts of citizens: 'It is to this already meaningful data that his scientific concepts must ultimately refer: to the meaningful acts to individual men and women' (1967, p. 10). Habermas (1984), also, has made relevant contributions along these lines, basing comprehension in the social sciences upon validity claims (which can be made by every human being) rather than power claims (made only by experts). More recently still, Beck et al. (1994), discuss the need for a de-monopolization of expert knowledge through a process of reflexive modernization in current societies, in which citizens question traditional authorities in the scientific, economic, and political spheres.

Public sociology, however, goes one step beyond this. The 'other women', non-academic women traditionally excluded from academic feminist debates, are producing scientific knowledge jointly with academics. This is being done through a dialogic process where the validity of the arguments being presented depends upon how they contribute to a solution, rather than the privileged position of the speaker. According to this communicative paradigm, both the 'other women' and feminist sociologists are implementing and recreating sociological knowledge in civil society in order to improve the living conditions of all people.

Dialogic Knowledge and the Prevention of Gender Violence

The dialogic relationship between academic and non-academic people, in the creation of knowledge, has a clear impact on social transformation. In 2004, the Spanish Act Against Gender Violence was an important step forward in the fight against violence affecting women. However, there was a mistake when violence against women was understood as being only when it is perpetrated by a partner or ex-partner. When this violence occurs on a date, the legislation does not consider it to be gender violence (BOE, 2004). This can happen even in cases where the woman is murdered. Additionally, most people considered the victims of gender violence to be primarily older women with low educational backgrounds and weak economic independence. These older women were perceived as being more likely to be victims of gender violence, while younger and highly educated women were assumed to have overcome this problem.

Research done by public sociology clarified these mistakes, and these contributions have been taken into account by new legislations, like the Catalan Act Against Sexist Violence in 2008. Researching through dialogue with several different social actors makes it impossible to ignore the folk-assumptions that the victims of gender violence are only non-academic and excluded women, or that violence against women is only domestic. For instance, in studies done on violence while dating, many young female university students were identified as either having friends who had or had themselves been victims of such violence. In this way, research conducted *with* the people, rather than *on* the people, has indicated that violence against women does not always come from partners or ex-partners, but also from men on occasional dates, or whom a woman may have just met (Flecha et al., 2011). Feminist public sociologists engage with all these women, old and young, mothers and sisters, connecting with the experiences from their lives in order to change their previous theoretical frameworks through fresh dialogue and new analysis.

Without having listened to these many voices, the academic sociologists who advised the first Act were unable to interpret the media when it reported cases that had victims who were young, educated women, or when the violence occurred in the course of a date. Part of the academic sociology is so isolated in its academic spaces that it cannot comprehend when reality deviates from theory. Objectivity, understood just as distance, does not guarantee scientific knowledge. Fortunately, the process was different in the second Act, and its new legislations. The 'other women' movements, in collaboration with academic women working on public sociology, have already made important contributions to these.

Lola participates on the Women's Council in her district. This council provides information to the women in her community and represents them in the municipality. They organized a performance in her neighborhood with the slogan, 'Let's break the silence'. Their goal is to raise awareness that violence against women is not a private issue, and that both denouncing and preventing it needs to involve everyone. They promote women's solidarity by saying, 'If you see or hear something next door, talk to your neighbor, let her know you care, that you are ready to listen and to help'. In a corresponding gesture, Carmen, and The Roma Association of Women, became involved in denouncing a case of gender violence against a young Romaní woman. They have also included this issue as a new topic in their regular meetings.

Today, the number of mothers reporting their own daughters' gender violence cases has doubled in only one year. Many of the 'other women', whom the traditional academic sociology considers to be the ones who have 'accepted' violence from their husbands, are, in fact, the ones denouncing it. Local associations, such as the Women's Council, in which Lola participates, have created solidarity and support networks among women to help each other face these difficult situations. They have become the main actors in the fight for social justice and dignity, at the grassroots level.

The prejudice of the traditional academic sociology about gender violence was finally overcome, both scientifically and socially, when public sociologists published a study about gender-based violence in Spanish universities. The study was funded by the Spanish Women Institute (CREA, 2006–2008). The media released the results: 60% of female students reported having experienced gender-based violence, or knew of a case. 98% also reported they did not know any place at the university they could go and get support for these issues. The results from this research pushed the Act for Equality to include a stipulation requiring all Spanish universities to have an equality unit and protocols against sexual harassment. This legal step was key in the defense of human rights for all women at the university. Women's struggles in this area have not yet been resolved, however, and solidarity among these women is still crucial within an institutional context.

Thanks to the contributions of public sociology, we know that successful actions against gender violence have to be focused on preventive socialization, as they are the ones that obtain successful results (Valls et al., 2008). These actions must include all women's voices, not only the expert ones (Oliver et al., 2009). Variables relating to age, academic level, and economic independence do not guarantee that one will be free from gender-based violence. Consequently, new fields of research and action have been opening, looking at ways to prevent violence against women. These have focused on affective and sexual socialization, and developing research through the conversations between non-academic and academic women who are deeply engaged in social transformation.

Interactions and conversations with women from different cultures, and from both low socio-economic and academic backgrounds, are informing an understanding of the existence of additional external barriers. Those with less privilege can often seem like victims in comparison to women from more mainstream social and cultural groups (Abraham, 2000). It is essential to take this into account, and to develop more effective policies on this topic. Additionally, analyses on the causes and prevention of gender violence, which emerge from the public engagement of feminist public sociologists, tend to be less simplistic, and are able to overcome stereotypes around these 'other women' that are built upon racist, classist, and sexist ideas (Sokoloff and Dupont, 2005). Overall, having dialogue between feminist scholars and marginalized women is a part of the social justice struggle, both locally and globally.

One Example of a Public Institute Doing Public Sociology

Every other Monday, in the evening, around 40 members of the research institute CREA meet in a theoretical discussion group called 'With the book on hand' (Soler-Gallart, 2017). The same researchers who dialogued with Carmen, Lola, and their various women's groups do public sociology in the framework of this Institute. In this 'book on hand' seminar, we have discussed the most important works in the social sciences: Weber's *Economy and Society*; Smith's *Wealth of Nations*; Marx's *Capital*; Habermas' *Theory of Communicative Action*; Sen's *Development and Freedom*; Searle's *Speech Acts*; Beauvoir's *The Second Sex*; Freire's *Pedagogy of the Oppressed*; and Freud's *Totem and Taboo*. Our theoretical developments are thus built on our direct reading and debating of major scientific contributions. This is very different to what mainstream sociology does in our country. For instance, still today, in some Spanish universities professors teach the theory of Marx through what Althusser and Balibar (1977) wrote about in *Reading Capital*. Many have never read *Capital*, and unfortunately, they do not know that Althusser recognized that he had not read *Capital* himself when he wrote *Reading Capital*, and that he considered his Marxism to be an imaginary one (Althusser, 1992, pp. 196–197).

The 'Book on hand' seminar is grounded in dialogic democracy. All participants note which page they are referring to when they speak, no matter if they are full professors, young scholars, or students. This is a way to avoid the common practice in the social sciences of talking and writing about that which one has not read (as Althusser did). This same democratic procedure helps the Institute's public sociology gain consistency between its social justice aims and the scholarly process of knowledge creation, which gives voice to everyone on equal terms, regardless of their academic status. In the seminar, a first-year undergraduate sociology student has the same right to contribute to the theoretical dialogue as does a full professor. Likewise, the first-hand reading of the classical works makes everyone ready to denounce false interpretations and anti-intellectual postures like those of Althusser.

The kind of egalitarian dialogue that is established in this academic setting, between full professors, students, practitioners, and other people, would not have been possible without the experience of the multiple exchanges that researchers have had with non-academic people. This is especially important for the case of CREA Women's Group SAFO, named after the Greek female poet Sappho de Lesbos. As was exemplified with the stories of Carmen and Lola, SAPHO researchers have been engaging in dialogue with 'other women' about what are the significant and important questions for feminism. These precedents have been crucial to developing a seminar that provides solid and rich theoretical training for the Institute researchers, and an effective model to expose junior researchers to sociological theory, economy, anthropology, and the like.

The seminar has also created new types of relationships at the university, which are much more democratic and egalitarian.

As an example, in 1998 we invited Ulrich Beck to come to the Institute and lead a seminar. At that time, the feudal structure of Spanish universities dictated that when an important author came, only full professors could talk to him or her. In this case, the condition to participate in the seminar was to have read all the books written by the invited speaker, regardless of one's academic position. A young undergraduate, who spent the whole summer reading Beck's books and was a participant in the 'Book on hand' seminar, raised her hand during the debate. She had found a contradiction between something the author had just said and something he had written on one of the pages in his book, *Risk Society*. She could prove, with the book in her hands, that she was right. Beck exclaimed, 'Where's the miracle?' (meaning, 'How extraordinary!'). From this moment onward, he has valued in a very special way the theoretical training of these young researchers.

The Institute was born in 1991, after a long time and through close collaboration between a few professors and various social movements. They were all doing grassroots work and theorizing about social change. It was partially inspired by the successful actions of the libertarian socialist athenaeums, and the 'Free Institution for Education' in Spain. In the first part of the 20th century, in the libertarian athenaeums, after a ten-hour working day, workers used to debate the books by Dostoyevsky, Zola, Cervantes, and Kropotkin. The 'Free Institution' made possible the flourishing of a Spanish intellectualism during the first half of the 20th century, contributing to the works of García Lorca, Picasso, Buñuel, and Machado, at a moment when Spain was considered to be an underdeveloped country.

Grounded in an analysis of these historic successes, the founder of the Institute engaged with the civil society of a working-class barrio in Barcelona and provided the social analyses needed for its transformation. His analyses allowed the neighbors, and especially the women, to organize a 'dream' of their barrio[1] and to undertake the social actions needed to make it a reality. Some years later, they had accomplished their dream, and the barrio needed to dream again in order to continue its transformation. The idea of creating a public institute to conduct public sociology was oriented toward making these kinds of social transformations and theories available to other barrios, and in other contexts.

The Institute includes roughly 83 members, scholars who work in academia, and researchers who are professionals in private companies, members of public administrations, NGOs, schools, etc. This opens up academic spaces to people who would otherwise never get an opportunity to engage in such dialogues. Different than any other research center in Spain, the Institute is a highly pluralistic and diverse institute, which includes a study group for inter-faith dialogues formed by Muslims, Christians, Jews, and Agnostics, as well as a Roma studies group, created by Roma and non-Roma scholars, an Arab and Muslim studies group, 'Alhiwar', a group for the study of non-capitalist economy, and the SAFO Women's Group. These groups are unique within the Spanish academia, and they were all created to address situations of inequality and marginalization. For all of these groups, the objective is the same: to develop theories and shed light on practices that are already advancing social justice. Among these groups, the SAFO women's group represents one of the main areas of research with the greatest amount of influence at the Institute. It is also a source of meaning making for many of the Institute's activities.

The Institute's plurality allows researchers to achieve deeper understandings of social phenomena. At the Institute there are sociologists, anthropologists, economists, educators, psychologists, social workers, linguists, engineers, and biologists. They all come from different ideologies and cultural backgrounds, and are of different ages, genders, sexual orientations, and types of family. All of this diversity makes the debates and dialogues richer and closer to real society, which is plural.

When we read Habermas' (1984) *Theory of Communicative Action*, we had a very rich discussion in relation to the 'Intermediate reflections' (p. 273), where the author discusses speech acts theory. We noticed he did not incorporate Searle's understanding of locutionary, illocutionary, and perlocutionary speech acts in his revision of Austin's concepts (Searle, 1969). Habermas thus quotes Searle wrongly. Habermas did all of his impressive work alone. In a pluralistic, interdisciplinary group he would have discussed with many different people, perhaps including some who had read all the works of Austin and Searle. We consider Habermas' *Theory of Communicative Action* to be extraordinarily relevant for sociology; however, we think that this contribution would have been improved had it been developed under the orientation of public sociology.

Besides their dedication to studying theory, most of the Institute's members are also active participants in different kinds of social movements. For example, SAFO's involvement with the 'other women' movement, and its struggle against gender-based violence. This engagement helps researchers escape from the old positioning of sociologists as experts, isolated in their ivory towers, disconnected from the needs and hopes of socially excluded groups. By participating with real people, academic activity is tightly connected to everyday life and social action, something which enriches the scientific community and its production of knowledge, making the research center more socially useful. The dialogic approach of the Institute as it participates in public sociology contributes to the advancement of various social improvements locally, and also furthers the global agenda of social justice.

The public sociology research institute works well because, along with its diversity, its members share a common goal: a focus on the theories and practices that reduce inequalities and advance social justice. For instance, in the debate about Sen's *Development as Freedom*, there were many diverse contributions. An economist who thinks that many economists have ignored Smith's discussion of inequalities in *Wealth of Nations* explained that Sen had said, in his Adam Smith course at Harvard, that almost all of the quotes from Smith's book are taken from the first pages. A sociologist noticed that the same happens with Weber's *Economy and Society*. Yet another member, engaged in ecological movements, criticized Sen for not taking into account the negative side of development. A feminist appreciated the role that Sen gives to women in the development and in the reduction of poverty. Members who were educators explained how Sen was educated in the school founded by Rabindranath Tagore, connecting this experience to the importance that the author gives to education in society.

These kinds of debates and contributions go back and forth among members and are influenced by the social movements they are working with. This everyday connection gets mixed in with the public sociology of the Institute, making its results more useful for civil society. In turn, the debates with citizens are crucial for the theoretical creation that arises from the Institute. The research is not limited to the analysis of inequalities; it also aims at providing the elements that contribute to reduce them. These citizens and social movements support this kind of sociology.

Some sociologists in Spain complain about the lack of motivation young people have for sociology and for society in general. It is a lack of motivation which they attribute to structural reasons or to generational causes. The activity described in this example, and which also takes place in other groups doing public sociology, demonstrates that the lack of motivation is probably related to the kind of sociology that those scholars are doing.

Public sociology is already improving society and there are many young scholars who are ever more enthusiastic about studying and implementing the contributions of social science. They know that this will make a difference in the lives of real people, in real places, within our society. They know this because they have the evidence showing that when sociology is developed together with the public, rather than on the public, the social sciences contribute to further social justice goals and open up new horizons of possibilities for those in the most vulnerable situations. The words and actions of people like Lola and Carmen, ready to engage with public sociologists who share with them dreams of a better and more just world, become a driving force of the exciting agenda for sociology in the 21st century.

Note

1 The 'Dream' or 'Sueño de Barrio' is a process based on assemblies and direct participation in which the community set goals for the future and ways to achieve them.

References

Abraham, M. (2000) *Speaking the Unspeakable: Marital Violence among South Asians in the US*. New Brunswick, NJ: Rutgers University Press.

Althusser, L. (1992) *El porvenir es largo*. Barcelona: Destino.

Althusser, L. and Balibar, E. (1977) *Reading Capital*. London: NLB.

Beck, U., Giddens, A., and Lash, C. (1994) *Reflexive Modernization: Politics, Tradition and Aesthetics in the Modern Social Order*. Stanford, CA: Stanford University Press.

Beck-Gernsheim, E., Butler, J., and Puigvert, L. (2003) *Women and Social Transformation*. New York, NY: Peter Lang.

BOE (2004) Ley orgánica 1/2004, 28 de diciembre, de Medidas de Protección Integral Contra la Violencia de Género, BOE, 29 December, p. 42166.

Burawoy, M. (2005) For public sociology. *American Sociological Review*, *70*(1), 4–25.

Butler, J. (2006) *Precarious Life: The Powers of Mourning and Violence*. New York, NY: Verso.

Collins, P.H. (1998) *Fighting Words: Black Women and the Search for Justice*. Minneapolis, MN: University of Minnesota.

CREA (2006–2008) *Violencia de género en las universidades españolas* [Gender Violence at the Spanish Universities], National R&D Plan, Ministry of Labor & Social Affairs.

De Botton, L., Puigvert, L., and Sánchez, M. (2005) *The Inclusion of Other Women: Breaking the Silence through Dialogic Learning*. Dordrecht: Springer.

Flecha, A. Pulido, C., and Christou, M. (2011) Transforming violent selves through reflection in critical communicative research. *Qualitative Inquiry*, *17*(3), 246–255.

Flecha, R. (2000) *Sharing Words: Theory and Practice of Dialogic Learning*. Lanham, MD: Rowman & Littlefield.

Flecha, R. (2009) The educative city and critical education. In M. Apple, W. Au, and L.A. Gandin (eds), *The Routledge International Handbook of Critical Education*. New York, NY: Routledge.

Gopal, M. (2012) Caste, sexuality and labour: The troubled connection. *Current Sociology*, *60*(2), 222–238.

Habermas, J. (1984) *The Theory of Communicative Action: Reason and the Rationalization of Society*. Boston, MA: Beacon Press.

Hancock, I. (2002). *We are the Romani People*. Hatfield: University of Hertfordshire Press.

Lemon, N.K. (2006) Access to justice: Can domestic violence courts better address the need of non-English speaking victims of domestic violence. *Berkeley Journal of Gender, Law & Justice*, *21*(1), 38–58.

Menjíbar, C. and Salcido, O. (2008) Immigrant women and domestic violence. Common experiences in different countries. *Gender & Society*, *16*(6), 898–920.

Oliver, E., Soler, M., and Flecha, R. (2009) Opening schools to all (women): Efforts to overcome gender violence in Spain. *British Journal of Sociology of Education*, *30*(2), 207–218.

Schütz, A., Walsh, G., and Lehnert, F. (1967) *The Phenomenology of the Social World*. Chicago, IL: Northwestern Universities.

Searle, J. (1969) *Speech Acts: An Essay in the Philosophy of Language*. Cambridge: Cambridge University Press.

Sen, A. (1999) *Development as Freedom*. New York, NY: Oxford University Press.

Sokoloff, N.J. and Dupont, I. (2005) Domestic violence at the intersections of race, class and gender: Challenges and contributions to understanding violence against marginalized women in diverse communities. *Violence Against Women*, *11*(1), 38–64.

Soler-Gallart, M. (2017) *Achieving Social Impact. Sociology in the Public Sphere*. Cham: Springer-Nature.

Valls, R., Puigvert, L., and Duque, E. (2008) Gender violence amongst teenagers: Socialization and prevention. *Violence Against Women*, *14*(7), 759–785.

11

Struggles for Social Justice in the 21st Century

The Breakdown of Normality and the Practice of Citizenship

Evangelia Tastsoglou and Maria Kontos

Introduction

The Online Forum

On 14 October 2011, an online editorial comment entitled 'Let us stop the downward slide' was published on the website of a Greek, broad-cir-culation, conservative, daily newspaper called *Kathimerini.* It sparked a lengthy and animated online discussion by readers, which lasted for three days and involved 174 responses. The majority of these responses were substantial opinion pieces. Although many of the readers were responding to the original editorial comment, or to one another, the majority of them were in dialogue with the first respondent to the editorial, a 'Paris2', who boldly and eloquently introduced a new theme, that of leaving the country permanently. This theme, however, was not directly related to the edi-tor's plea to the public to help put an end to the 'violence' and increasing 'irrationality' of public life in Greece, following the attacks against newly elected mayors that had just taken place.[1]

While the editor had claimed that the anger and frustration of the pro-testers, resulting from the broken promises of politicians to their clientele, were justified, and that the protesters were victims, Paris2 opened up a rad-ical criticism of current social relations and argued in favour of emigration as the only appropriate strategy for individuals to tackle the Greek crisis. Paris2's response struck a chord with many readers who expanded into an assessment of emigration as a strategy for themselves, as well as its impli-cations for society and the country under the current circumstances. The assessment of emigration as a strategy was intertwined with the respond-ents' own perceptions and interpretations of the economic and social crisis, its causes and culprits, and other suggestions as to possible solutions and routes for individuals and the country to take. As the respondents offered their comments, they interjected their own biographical experience.

A Snapshot of the Crisis

Since the publication of its high public debt, and the involvement of IMF, the EU, and ECB, in the process of lending to the Greek state under the pre-condition of a fiscal and structural adjustment program of a massive scale and within an unprecedented time frame, there has been a rapid deterioration in the living conditions of the population. This includes a decrease in individual incomes, pensions, and social benefits. This is occurring even while the social security contributions in Greece are among the highest in Europe (Malkoutzis, 2011), and the cost of living remains high. To make matters worse, there has also been a dramatic increase in taxation, as well as the unemployment rate, along with a radical labour market restructuring and dismantling of labor institutions and loss of social and trade union rights.[2] According to IMF data, the gross national product in Greece fell in 2009 by 3.14%, in 2010 by 4.94%, in 2011 by 7.11%, and in 2012 by 6.38%. This can be compared to the unemployment rate in 2009, which was 9.41%, and increased in 2013 to 26.99%.[3] The youth are especially affected. In Greece roughly a tenth of the population (1.1 million people) is under the age of 25, and another 1.5 million are aged between 25 and 34. Youth unemployment rose to 57% in the third quarter of 2013, and 49% in the third quarter of 2015 (Eurostat, n.d.).

These developments have led to a series of mass protest actions, including general strikes and other forms of political mobilization, which have, however, had little effect on the austerity measures being imposed on the country. At the same time, a media campaign against the Greek state, calling it a 'failed state' (e.g. Schrader et al., 2013), and labelling the Greek people as 'lazy' and 'incapable', has begun in northern European countries, especially Germany, and has subsequently been reflected in the Greek media. This transfer of a negative identity is severely damaging for both the people of Greece and its diaspora.[4]

Aims of Research

In the present chapter we investigate how and why emigration and other options are constructed in the online forum as strategies out of the current crisis. In the process of doing so, we analyze the participants' assessments and constructions of the crisis and its causes. We view all the strategies discussed, encapsulated as negotiation, resistance, and exit, as instances of citizenship in practice. This is viewed through the lens of a 21st-century venue: cyberspace. It is also considered within a context of ongoing protest and contestation of socioeconomic injustice and the lack of political transparency and accountability. Since one of the solutions is the emigration proposal, we consider the various social constructions of migration in this exchange, and we examine the social processes and social conditions generating them. The emigration proposal is the backbone of this exchange, giving rise to the discussion of other options as counter-proposals.

Conceptual and Theoretical Framework

The Public Sphere and Cyberspace

We consider the online exchange as being a public debate on the crisis. Through the readers' responses and exchanges a transnational mini-public emerges. This is a-synchronic, mostly anonymous, and disconnected from physical space. Online fora may be considered part of the emerging electronic public space with much easier and immediate, even transnational, trans-global, participation for citizens and non-citizens alike. It is far more accessible than the public space of the traditional communication media, such as print media, radio, and television.

In contrast to Habermas' pessimistic view (1989) of the contemporary structural transformation of the public sphere – that capitalism had originally enabled from the 1700s onward – into an arena of consumerism and manipulation of a depoliticized population, cyberspace appears to enable the development of a new transnational and even global public sphere (Dahlgren, 2001; Olesen, 2005; Thörn, 2007). It has become a space where common concerns are being discussed, and it holds a great potential for the democratic project in the 21st century – what some scholars have called cyberspace democracy (Kellner, 2007). From this point of view, the analysis of the online forum affords us an opportunity to gain substantial insight into the discursive constructions emerging from the deep economic and social crisis currently unfolding in Greece, and people's responses to this crisis.

Social Justice

We argue that respondents' responses derive from contestation and protest against the political and economic injustice people experience, and, as such, constitute struggles for social justice and participatory democratic politics. Social justice is a concept greatly discussed in philosophy, as well as in political and social theory. Over the course of centuries, scholars and writers have attempted to come to terms with the notion of social justice, and to identify concrete ways to advance it (Sen, 2009). More recently, social scientists and philosophers have analyzed social justice across a number of dimensions, such as distribution, recognition, and representation (Lister, 2007; Fraser, 2003, 2005; Sayer, 2005; Young, 1990), and on a number of levels, such as national, subnational and supranational, or in other words, domestic and global (Lister, 2007).

The electronic exchange that we look at vividly illustrates struggles for redistribution, recognition, and representation, mostly at the national level, as the majority of responders locate the injustice as being within the formal state, its politics, and its class struggles historically. Only a few responders view the socioeconomic crisis in Greece as part of a broader EU socioeconomic and political crisis, which is in turn part of a global neoliberal socioeconomic order and process. Their claims for redistribution of resources, though analytically distinct, are inseparable from claims for recognition and representation. The latter emerge from the critique respondents launch of civil servants and trade unions as being opaque, partial, self-interested, and outright corrupt in carrying out their duties. It then proceeds to a critique of the state and government, which, though democratically elected, are being perceived as directly contributing to, or, at best, being unresponsive to, the suffering of the marginalized. Redressing the misrecognition, where large groups of the population are increasingly ignored and their needs not seen, and redressing the misrepresentation – where these groups do not have a say – will directly result in improving misdistribution. All three are constituted as social justice violations and thus provide the basis for justice claims. Raising such claims constitutes the practice of democratic freedoms by politically engaged citizens, in order 'to enhance social justice and [ensure] a better and fairer politics' (Sen, 2009, p. 351).

Citizenship Practice

The present chapter discusses this online exchange as being a 'practice of citizenship' (Abraham et al., 2010) under, or despite, conditions of a breakdown of normality, which the crisis in Greece has generated. Citizenship in practice refers to a range of diverse citizen activities, by which individuals express their commitment and belonging to a state, fulfill lawful obligations and implement their legal, civic, political, social, and economic rights, as well as engage in an ongoing process to safeguard and expand them, struggling for more inclusion and social justice. Our particular lens offers a micro-level glimpse into the experience of the crisis, on the ground, from the inside, through the everyday theories of a self-selected sample of individuals expressing themselves through a 21st-century medium, based on electronic technology and cyberspace. Citizenship practice, in the case of an electronic forum, is limited as a result of certain features of the forum: anonymity, non-locality, informality, unaccountability, no face-to-face exchange, lack of repercussions of opinion-voicing even the general ones of a vote, and non-permanence. We argue that this form of citizenship practice is of significant value, however, in terms of revealing the spontaneous, 'in-formation', discursive constructions of the crisis, and a spectrum of strategies and options based thereupon, as well as pointing to the potential of the latter to strengthen citizens' voices to mobilize for social justice. More specifically, our chapter focuses on the negotiations, resistance, and 'exit' strategies that responders discuss, and we consider them as citizenship in practice.

Emigration/Exit

In contrast to current understandings of emigration at the micro level, as an individualistic choice, based on utilitarian considerations that pertain mostly to one's self and broader family, we suggest in this chapter that even the physical 'exit' option, i.e. the emigration proposition, is also an instance of citizenship in practice. The ongoing ethical questioning, the need for discursive historical contextualizing in the effort to understand the present situation, and, above all, the engagement with others in the electronic forum that accompanies this option tend to construct it more as a strategic tactic to accomplish broader goals rather than an individual exit. Furthermore, the threat or possibility of an exit strengthens the 'voice' mechanism (i.e. negotiation or resistance) of others to effect social change.

According to Hirschman's (1970, p. 83) classic treatise of the relationship of exit, voice, and loyalty, voice and exit are recuperative mechanisms restoring lapses or correcting errors. The underlying assumption is that both voice and exit, through the intervening mechanism of loyalty, operate on a systemic and collective level, beyond the individual one, and the consequences of their operation applies to an entire collectivity and is not necessarily incurred to individuals alone.

Breakdown of Normality

A breakdown of normality refers to the conditions of life generated by a number of radical breaks, which have produced new and heightened levels of social and economic injustice. These are characterized by extensive precariousness in the labour market, broad marginalization of large segments of society, a severe strain on social cohesion, and wider gender inequalities. Thus, we refer by this term to the breakdown of, until then taken for granted, social expectations for a stable social order and for chances of improving living conditions. 'Normality' refers to a self-positioning toward the social, which refers to imagined or normative standards about prevailing conditions for the general population (Link, 2006). In sum, the normality of life in Greece, as it had been lived until the austerity policies started in 2010, has broken down.[5]

Methodological Considerations: Toward a Critical Sociology

In the *Kathimerini* online exchange several participants are migrants themselves, settled in other countries and recounting their experiences and assessments. Some are former migrants who have returned to Greece and feel the need to re-evaluate their decisions of returning. Finally, others are in various stages of 'back-and-forth'. In this sense, the readers and participants reflect both the strong relationships between the Greek society in Greece, and the broader Greek diaspora, and the diasporic experience of the Greek population overall. Ultimately, the *Kathimerini* online public is a truly transnational public. According to Kissau's findings (2012), migrants with a focus on events in their country of origin mostly use the internet in exactly the way in which the *Kathimerini* responders did (i.e. by commenting on newspaper articles) and prefer this kind of political activity above other offline possibilities. Although this particular online newspaper is not part of alternative media, its online public presents itself as a 'subaltern counter-public' (Fraser, 1992; Thörn, 2007), speaking out against the official state.

We consider the participants' comments as social constructions themselves, not illuminating social processes but rather being products of social processes. They are responding mainly to a broad scale economic squeeze, and marginalization process of large segments of the Greek middle and lower-middle class, in the context of a rising socioeconomic inequality perceived by 'lay normativity' (Sayer, 2005, pp. 5–12) as being injustice. To the extent that the participants' analyses are limited by their understandings, we can say that they produce social critique and engage in 'folk sociologies' (Sayer, 2005, p. 4).

As sociologists we see our role as moving beyond 'folk sociologies', toward a 'sociology of critique', questioning where participants' attitudes and practices may come from (Boltanski, 2010). Beyond this, we hope to adopt a 'critical sociology' perspective (Lessenich, 2013), identifying the inherent tensions, contradictions, and fault lines in positions and practices, where the potential for change may be located. For example, such fault lines may refer to how the staying vs. leaving dynamic is going to play out, not only among this electronic public but more generally as well. What is likely to be the impact of this tension on the government in terms of social change and the democratic project in Greece? What is likely to be the impact of the transnational electronic counter-public in creating a more global movement in the EU, especially in its southern states, for social justice? Ultimately, what are the limits of a counter-public, which is, in addition, transnational and Internet-based?

Assessing the Legitimacy and Morality of Emigration as a Strategy in Systemic Crisis

Beginning the online responses, the reader signing as 'Paris2', in response to the journalist's exhortation to 'stop the downward slide' to chaos, eloquently articulates an argument for the necessity of 'exit' and emigration as the only solution. Paris2 brings a different exhortation altogether: '*My proposition: let us leave ... don't search further ... Leave!!!.. Leave, go far away.*'

Historically, emigration has been part of the Greek culture. Large migratory waves have taken place several times in the course of the late 19th and the 20th century, under economic crises, war and civil war conditions, and because of immigration and employment policies in other countries.

This has led to large Greek diasporic communities becoming established in several countries (Tsoukalas, 1999). It was only in the late 1970s and 1980s that emigration came to a standstill, and even reversed in some cases (Sotiropoulos, 2012), under conditions of economic prosperity, and particularly with Greece becoming a full-fledged EU member in 1981. What is remarkable in the present context is that individuals from all walks of life, in particular well-educated youth, are opting for migration again in response to the crisis. According to Bank of Greece data (2016, p. 75), from 2008 to 2013 roughly 223,000 youth (between ages 25–39) emigrated from Greece, while the gross figure of those moving permanently out of Greece, from 2008 to 2014, is 427,000.

Paris2 locates his/her exhortation in a specific perspective on the actual situation of Greek society. Instead of referring to an obscure threat that is coming and that we cannot name – as the author of the editorial does – Paris2 characterizes the present situation in Greece as having already deteriorated beyond control, as a latent 'civil war'. One side of the conflicting parties are those who want to continue with the old regime, of 'bribes, clientelism and nepotism'. In this context, Paris2 identifies powerful 'unionists' and 'public servants' as being those who hold the rest of the population hostage by their strikes and their fight to defend their privileges. The other side is then composed of those with talents, abilities, values, qualifications, and the desire to work hard and the ambition to go far. Paris2 considers themself a representative of this side, this 'other Greece', and wants to move away in search of a social environment that will recognize and reward them for who they are and what they can do.

The concept of clientelism has been developed by social scientists to analyze a system of exchange of favours for political support, observed in several political and cultural regimes and sometimes attributed to social and political underdevelopment. Clientelism has been used to study the European South by several scholars (Farelo Lopes, 1997; Fukuyama, 2012; Hopkin, 2001; Katz, 1986; Lyrintzis, 1984; Mouzelis, 1978; Piattoni, 2001). The concept has been central in the public debates that emerged within the Greek crisis. It is currently being used by politicians from almost all political parties, in order to denote the pathology of the current sociopolitical order, and as a counterpoint for a much-needed new democratic social reality. The participants of this forum utilize this very discourse in order to understand the crisis and articulate a critique of the social and political order from a social justice perspective, as well as put forth a plea for democratization.

The uncanny ability of Paris2 to connect his own individual solution to a broader structural problem, a national problem, coupled with a youthful-sounding enthusiasm 'to work productively', appealed to many readers who responded personally, as if the dilemmas Paris2 presented were also their own. Furthermore, Paris2 attempts to justify – and thus legitimate – emigration at the present time on a number of grounds.

The reason for these efforts is a historic lack of legitimacy for emigration in Greek society, despite, or perhaps because of, the long history of emigration. Both its necessity, and the lack of legitimacy for emigration, is reflected in popular music, art and proverbial sayings.[6] Much of this is grounded in the trauma of separation through emigration (Grinberg and Grinberg, 1990), as well as the betrayed norms of familial and communal solidarity. Breaking these norms is negotiated and countered by other normative structures, inherent to modern individualized societies. This includes the norm of responsibility of the individual to be active in devising strategies for survival and improvement for his or her own life conditions, and the legitimacy of the right to seek recognition when wronged.

The first argument – to counter the non-legitimacy of emigration as a strategy out of the crisis – refers to the 'incapacity' and 'inability' of the 'army of public servants' who will not allow the population with whom Paris2 identifies as 'us' to be 'rescued'. The 'way of thinking' of the public servants is shaped by their social position, vested interests, and socialization. They are 'not able to understand' and thus to accept the necessary reforms and social change that might encroach on their privileges. Hence, Paris2's argument is related to a perception of the situation in Greece as entirely hopeless, and of public servants as being a powerful social group within the status quo.

The second argument – to counter the non-legitimacy of emigration as a solution to the crisis – is related to the notion of personal responsibility for one's survival. In this argument Paris2 contrasts the personal responsibility for survival with the responsibility of the state to contribute to the survival of the people, by offering services and support when needed. The Greek state is presented as caring only for the public servants and leaving the rest without support, which is an important component of the perception of social injustice.

A third argument counters the perception that emigration is a 'non-patriotic act' by arguing that considering to leave or leaving, is, under certain circumstances, more patriotic. It would be more 'patriotic' to see the 'problem' as a 'national problem', like being in 'war', rather than remaining complacent as 'they' do not recognize the situation in this way. 'They' are most probably the 'public servants' who defend their privileges, as Paris2 maintains in the previous lines. The argument thus considers that leaving may be understood as a protest against those in privileged positions within Greece.

A fourth argument refers to Paris2's 'dignity' being damaged by current state policy, and by the actions of the public servants and union leaders. At this point we might hypothesize that Paris2 has experienced rejection in his efforts to get a suitable job, or in his interaction with the public sector in general. He feels cast aside, overlooked, and has had his perception of his own self-worth and dignity wounded. It is this dignity that hopes to be restored through emigration.

Finally, a fifth argument revolves around the 'shame' that is piled upon Greeks because of the bankruptcy of their public finances, and by the media abroad. On this argument Paris2 presents his personal experience of being ashamed when travelling abroad because people condemn 'the Greek way of living', which has led to the high state debt. Paris2 refers to the media campaigns in European countries, which attribute the fiscal and economic crisis to the 'laziness' of Greek people and to their many alleged privileges that cannot be paid for and maintained by the state. While accepting and internalizing this criticism as a result of the 'controlling images' of the media (Collins, 2008), Paris2 seems to expect that once he has left the country, he will no longer be identified with the 'Greeks in Greece', and thus he will not be blamed.

The passionate plea of Paris2 for exit from a chaotic and extremely hurtful social context, which he feels he cannot influence, triggered a wide range and number of responses. In particular, the argument for emigration as an individual response, conditioned, and perhaps directly dictated by the logic of the crisis, is cogently countered by a number of commentators on various grounds, mainly the need to stay and fight (Hirschman, 1970). This view expresses the opinion that there is the need to fight by voicing one's own positions and not by voting with one's feet. For example, DM claims that the solution to the crisis of corruption is to stay and fight, not to help the corrupt ones by leaving and creating more space for them.

Other readers and commenters jump in to strengthen the arguments around the need to stay and fight. Their arguments fall into three categories:

1. Pointing to the norm of loyalty to the collective: leaving is an individualistic, self-serving solution that contributes nothing to the broader Greek society (Alzheimer Macht Frei; Patridamouglykia[7]). KN writes a clear and succinct

statement about the obligations they feel as a citizen to contribute to social change and social justice: '*About 10 years ago I was thinking as you do [responding to Paris2]. I managed to leave Greece and to live for several years abroad. I returned making a conscious choice when the crisis was starting – two and a half years ago. I do not regret it at all. I want to be here to help out as much as I can this country. If I cannot do it here, I cannot do it anywhere.*'

2. Arguing that leaving one's country at a time of 'war', as the present situation is, is tantamount to cowardice and treason. The metaphor of war in relation to the 'country' and in relation to the 'ravens of our country' points to severe conflicts on two levels: the level of the 'war' with the intervening actors from outside, like the EU, IWF, ECB, and Germany, and the level of the war between social groups within Greek society, those working in the public sector and those working in the private sector.

3. Pointing to the need for a deconstructing of the anti-Greek media campaigns in European countries. These responders criticize the unquestioned acceptance and identification of the 'Greek' as these media campaigns present it. '*There is nothing to be ashamed of in being Greek. Germans and Japanese had much more to be ashamed of after WWII and yet they went ahead and re-built their societies*' (Paratirisi).

Assessing the Necessity of Emigration: The Dialectics of 'Push' and 'Pull'

The arguments for emigrating are presented by the participants who support emigration as a solution (the 'leavers') in a twofold manner: (i) through factors pushing away from Greece, under conditions of crisis, including a detailed criticism of the 'wrongs' done by the country; and (ii) through factors attracting immigrants to other destinations, mostly in the West but also globally. This two-fold line of reasoning is also strengthened by the voices of people who have already emigrated and live abroad, and by some who have returned to Greece after living abroad and have regretted it. These arguments are countered, in turn, by the perspectives of immigrants already settled abroad, other returnees, and those who do not support leaving ('stayers').

'Push' Factors

Push factors are reasons to leave. They are constructed through a complex, discursive, and ideological field of evaluating the social specificities in Greece. There is a long list of 'wrongs' that are generally shared by most respondents. The list may weigh differently for different individuals, but there is an overall agreement on certain points. The list of 'wrongs' amounts to a popular analysis of the current political system, public life, and accompanying cultural ethos. Readers make connections between these broader structural factors and their own personal lives, tracing their experiences to them. By doing so, they resist and reject the government by personalizing their problems, yet this is compounded by the official view of events that somehow the crisis is a 'given' over which individual citizens have little control.

The political system is identified by many as the main 'push' factor, through being a system based on atomism and social mobility dependent upon political party affiliation: '*the principle of party rule in all social levels is, in my opinion, our problem, not the civil servant, the taxi driver or the garbage collector. This party rule has completely eroded everything worth valuing there ever was in the Greek people and in every institution*' (N). Participants in many cases connect the political system with a 'corrupt trade unionism' and 'economic corporatism', which have been favoured by the socialist PASOK governments ascending to power since 1981.

A main construction in the reasons given for the Greek crisis necessitating emigration is a reference to the 'privileges of the civil servants'. Much of the anger being expressed is directed against civil servants who are seen as parasitic and protesting in order to keep what others see as their privileges. GZ, who has lost his job in the private sector, writes: '*What can the civil servants say with special bonuses ... whom we pay, for the 800,000 private sector employees who have been laid off without a nose getting bloody.*' Less frequently, the civil servants are being defended, often by individuals who admit, though timidly or with bitterness, that they are of that class yet have never accepted bribes or idled in their posts (Tsi). Occasionally they are defended by a few respondents who are capable of a more differentiated analysis of the historical context that produced the present circumstances in Greece, including the 'little dictators' that civil servants appear to be (Alzheimer Macht Free).

Another frequent construction around the problems of the Greek economy and society that legitimizes emigration refers to a specific way of thinking of the Greek people, the Greek 'mentality'. There is a range of expressions around what is thought to be the 'Greek mentality', which is named as the culprit by many respondents: '*If one asks the average Greek if s/he preferred to be French or German ... they would respond positively. We are a nation of people "extremely hungry for Europe" instead of focusing on what is good for the whole, we care only what our b[ehind] will catch'* (Yianna Z).

The pejoratively framed colloquialism 'hunger to be part of Europe' is a reference to the individualistic desire for self-improvement, for further-ing one's own private interests. This 'Europe-hungry' Greek has no sense of the common interest and wellbeing of society as a whole. It is obvious that the 'extreme hunger for Europe' is related to a denial of one's own national identity and a wish for a 'metamorphosis', to become a member of a different nationality, or a wish to escape the country. At the same time, Greek people are placed outside of Europe, and Greece is constructed as the opposite of Europe. We see here the construction of a polar-ity between an essentialized Europe and Occidentalism, and an equally essentialized Greek 'collectivist' tradition, which is being hurt by the atomism of Occidentalism. But, as Herzfeld (2003) argues, Occidentalism was imposed from the west as an ideology and national identity on the 19th century's newly independent nations, and on the basis of Greece's ancestral heritage, to the point where in Greece it became widely adopted and identified as 'the Hellenic tradition'. The line between individualism and collectivism in 'the Hellenic tradition' is much more blurred than ste-reotypically presented.

A particular expression of this supposed 'Greek mentality' is an attitude of not being able to take responsibility for one's own faults. Apostolos, a medical doctor and academic living overseas, writes: *'For some reason ... Greece preferred a strange way to move ahead. She thought ... and still thinks that always and still it is everybody else's fault, it is the others who have to work and not speak. She is here to scream loudly and call out "wooden" mottos and nonsense.'* It is note-worthy that some respondents see 'mentality' as being an outcome of institutions. In systemic terms: *'the good, mild-mannered Greeks from abroad whom I knew within a [short] period of time upon returning to Greece changed behaviour and followed the system'* (Evan, self-identified as a Greek living abroad).

Participants construct, in a self-hating manner, the overwhelming caricature of the 'bad Greek mentality' and the 'bad Greek'. The latter, existing inside Greece, is constructed in contrast to the 'good Greek', liv-ing outside of Greece. Some others use stronger demeaning expressions for outlining what they think the Greek 'mentality' is. These are com-bined with racist language referring to the 'hated other'. For instance, in the dominant ideology, the Turks are prototypes of the uncivilized 'other' living outside Greece, while the Vlachs and gypsies act as prototypes of uncivilized ethnic minorities within Greece. The self-hating expression 'Psorokostena'[8] is also used to give emphasis to the condemnation of the Greek 'mentality'. Other regions, which are considered by this dominant ideology as being prototypes of the uncivilized, are the Middle East and the Balkans. George, who has already left Greece, is advising others to do the same. He is bitter, angry, palpably hurting. He writes, '*This is Greece! Younanistan! Poor Kostas' wife! ... The land of Vlachs, of "manges"* [9] *and of ancient ancestors! Geographically in Europe, but in terms of culture between the Middle East and the Balkans, ... poor fools!*'

A further construction of the Greek 'mentality' has to do with the attraction of the public sector and the significance attributed to it: '*Is it not the dream of every parent to place his child somewhere in the public sector? ... Is it not the dominant philosophy of a job in the public sector (for relaxation) and work in the evening (in the private and 'black' economy)?*' (EB). There follows a long list of criticisms by many readers against particular categories of privileged professions (e.g. civil servants, teachers, doctors who demand money from their patients on top of their salaries) and less privileged occupations within the public sector (e.g. garbage collectors, and those in contractually limited positions who expect a permanent position) as well as state organizations in Greece (e.g. electricity company), and public employee unionism.

Most readers who pick up the journalist's editorial disagree with the assessment of those 'who attack the mayors' as 'victims' of the politicians who had promised them tenure in their positions and failed to come through. Instead, they see the particular categories of employees as parasitic and certainly not victims. DG argues from a standpoint of social justice and democracy, against the protesters who, presumably, feel betrayed by the mayors because the latter did not fulfill their promise to secure them stable jobs: '*I do not understand in which way those who sold their vote to a politician in order to receive a position in the public service or to secure privileges for their trade, now feel betrayed. Using one's vote toward one's own benefit is a deeply anti-democratic act, an act that erodes ethics and hurts society's interests, an act responsible to a large extent for today's suffering of the Greek people. ... The least consequence for those who used their vote this way in order to secure jobs, is now to lose them.*'

Another important factor 'pushing' individuals to exit the country is the sense that the country is already in a state of civil war, that any control of the situation is no longer possible, at least not by individuals. AD writes: '*This country can no longer avoid a second Civil War.*' While at this point there is no liberation army 'in the mountains' or in the poor neighbourhoods, this is the direction in which the country is heading. Tseligkas sees the 'civil war' as having started in the newspapers and their forms. This civil war is thus between the 'underprivileged' of the 1980s, a category including the prime minister and PASOK president Andreas Papandreou, those who are now privileged and fight to preserve their privileges, and those who were privileged at the time, the old middle class, the bourgeoisie, the small business people, all those who are now called upon to save the country.

'Pull' Factors

The social representation of life abroad is appealing to many. In the present context, 'abroad' is where there are prospects of getting a job, receiving recognition for one's qualifications and experience, having less stress about everyday life, making a good salary, leading a more predictable life, and enjoying a civilized urban infrastructure. 'Abroad' becomes 'the Promised Land'. These arguments come from the perspective of those who agree with exit as a strategy but also get reinforced by those who have already left. Kostas, a Greek living abroad, in summarizing his own experience speaks for many: '*In a country where there are fewer educated people from those that its economy requires, there are hopes for the individual. Here there is infrastructure as well. Most of the time there is a logic to the system. ... Living and working conditions, the ability to plan your life, the green in the cities – all simple things and many others – make the difference.*'

George A. tries to moderate the expectations expressed in the forum, by speaking a voice of caution from his own experience: '*First of all, I hear many people who say they want to emigrate. I do not really understand why they believe that things here are so rosy. Does anyone think that there is work here waiting for us? On a daily basis, millions [sic] of resumes are getting sent from people from around the world – this means that competition is very high. Unemployment is high. I had been applying for over a year (having completed a post-graduate degree in a very good university, with very good marks) and I did not get more than five responses from employers who asked me to an interview. Eventually, I got a good job, because their first choice rejected the offer.'* Others on the forum try to deconstruct the notion of 'abroad' being the 'good place'. EAG, another immigrant, is blunt: *'If you see a "nice" reality about life in a different country on television, or you have heard about "awesome" opportunities about a "good life" from second or third hand ... you are being fooled, with all due respect [in response to Paris2].'*

Another 'pull' argument from the point of view of Greeks settled abroad involves a re-conceptualization of their role in the diaspora as contributing members to the Greek society in times of need, and contextualizing this into the perspective of historical contributions of Greek diasporas to the Greek nation-state. These individuals de-couple the migration decision from any moral assessment of being a 'patriot' or having to contribute their dues to Greece. The online persona One More writes: *'living abroad does not mean resignation from one's obligations and rights as a Greek citizen. I personally continue to pay income taxes for the last five years that I do no longer live in Greece (although I do not use any public service during this time)but I have also voted in every election that has taken place.'*

Systemic Crisis, Social Inequality, and the Practice of Citizenship

The analysis of the online forum illustrates the desperate situation of the participants, the 'breakdown of normality' in the context of the current systemic crisis in Greece. They feel socially and economically excluded, morally deceived and wronged by the state, and in particular by privileged groups. Yet, at the same time, they are not immobilized by the enormity of the situation. They seek to understand the crisis in systemic terms and make connections that reach beyond their individual lives into the higher echelons of power and politics. They are motivated to do so not only by the desire to identify culprits and see fair punishment meted out, but also in order to take appropriate action and correct the direction of greater social justice, increasing the democratization of Greek society. Thus, despite their overgeneralizations and the self-hating stereotype of 'the Greek mentality', they do act as citizens, assessing options and taking positions vis-à-vis social issues.

By initiating the exchange, responding to one another, reinforcing each other's views or raising objections, the participants, above all, engage in citizenship practice, despite the generalized social and economic crisis that seems to be signalling the end of democratic political practice. Such citizenship practice demonstrates their agency but also attachment and sense of belonging to their country, their 'loyalty' (Hirschman, 1970). This loyalty is evident even as it translates into leaving, or planning to leave, the country as a last resort. More specifically, citizenship in practice involves three interrelated processes.

The first of these processes is that participants as citizens *negotiate options*, both for themselves and for the Greek society in crisis, by assessing rationally and thoroughly the advantages and disadvantages of each option. They do so via cyberspace, through engaging directly with one another in public, and are motivated not only by their own private interests but also by social justice and social responsibility toward the whole, as they explain.

Secondly, the participants demonstrate their resistance to the institutional and state breakdown that seems to be unfolding. This is demonstrated in that they are not accepting events as they come; they question particular groups; they condemn some groups; they propose various types of action; they have recommendations; and they are trying to build something new, for themselves and also for others.

Thirdly, participants contemplate, debate, plan, and have even tried exiting the situation through emigration. We have argued that it is too simplistic to say that such an exit is an individualistic solution furthering narrow-minded interests. The ongoing ethical questioning and historical contextualizing of the current situation, the public discursive engagement of every option with fellow citizens before any exit is attempted, and the intention to use the exit as a strategy to help those behind, all provide the grounds to consider the exit decision, not as an individualistic decision to remove oneself from the crisis but, above all, as a strategic choice and a tactic to deal with the systemic crisis at the present time.

In addition to this, the threat, possibility, or reality of exit by some strengthens the negotiation and resistance strategies of the rest. As such, exit may provide the ideal potential (with the 'voice' of the rest) for real recuperation from the economic and institutional crisis. This is 'threat of exit made by the loyalist – who leaves no stone unturned before he resigns himself to the painful decision to withdraw or switch' (Hirschman, 1970, p. 82). Under conditions of systemic crisis and a breakdown of normality, it is ultimately a form of citizenship in practice in the struggle for social justice and democratization.

Notes

1   See: www.tovima.gr/society/article/?aid=425259. Such instances had already started and continued after the October attacks for several months, marking an increasing violence in Greek political life.

2   This is the classic IMG 'shock therapy' proven, time and again, to trap economies into a vicious circle in which austerity generates recession, followed by more austerity, new taxes, and deeper recession (Lanara, 2012).

3   See: http://de.statista.com/statistik/daten/studie/14538/umfrage/wachstum-des-brutto inlandsprodukts-in-griechenland/.

4   Malkoutzis (2011), Lanara (2012), and Sotiropoulos (2012), among others, debunk the major misrepresentations perpetuated by the media.

5   An indicator for the social disintegration is the rapid rise of suicides in the last years. Economou et al. (2011) reported an increase of 36% in the numbers of those who reported having attempted suicide from 2009 to 2011.

6   'Την ξενιτιά, την ορφανιά, την πίκρα, την αγάπη, τα τέσσαρα τα ζύγιασαν, βαρύτερα είν' τα ξένα', proverbial saying, demotic song, taken from: http://diasporic. org/2011/01/batsikanis-nikos/%CE%AD%CE%BB%CE%BB%CE%B7%CE%BD%CE %B5%CF%82-%E2%80%93-%CE%BE%CE%B5%CE%BD%CE%B9%CF%84%CE% B9%CE%AC/ ('Emigration, becoming an orphan, sorrow and love, all four were weighed, and the heaviest was emigration', authors' translation).

7   Respondents have been anonymized. Where the anonymity seemed to be protected through an obvious pseudonym or abbreviation of name we kept the pseudonym or abbreviation.

8   It means literally 'poor Kostas' wife', alluding to the country, and denoting someone who is worth little but not aware of this.

9   Manges: popular types of the early 20th century, poor men and boys of low education, street-smart, living on the border of legality and illegality.

References

Abraham, M., Ngan-ling Chow, E., Maratou-Alipranti, L., and Tastsoglou, E. (eds) (2010) *Contours of Citizenship: Women, Diversity and Practices of Citizenship*. Farnham: Ashgate.

Bank of Greece (2016) *Executive Director's Report for the Year 2015*. Athens: Bank of Greece.

Boltanski, L. (2010) *Soziologie und sozialkritik (Frankfurter Adorno-Vorlesungen 2008)*. Berlin: Suhrkamp.

Collins, P.H. (2008) Mammies, matriarchs, and other controlling images. In: P.H. Collins, *Black Feminist Thought* (pp. 69–96). New York, NY: Routledge (originally published in 1990).

Dahlgren, P. (2001) The public sphere and the net: Structure, space and communication. In: W.L. Bennett and R.M. Entman (eds), *Mediated Politics: Communication in the Future of Democracy* (pp. 33–55). Cambridge: Cambridge University Press.

Economou, M., Modianos, M., Theleritis, C., Peppou, L., and Stefanis, C.N. (2011) Increased suicidality amid economic crisis in Greece. *The Lancet*, *378*(9801), 1459.

Eurostat, Employment and Unemployment (Labour Force Survey) (n.d.) *Harmonized Unemployment by Sex-Age Group 15–25*. Available at: http://ec.europa.eu/eurostat/web/lfs/data/main-tables (accessed 18 August 2016).

Farelo Lopes, F. (1997) Partisanship and political clientelism in Portugal (1983–1993). *South European Society and Politics*, *2*(3), 27–51.

Fraser, N. (1992) Rethinking the public sphere: A contribution to the critique of actually existing democracy. In: C. Calhoun (ed.), *Habermas and the Public Space* (pp. 109–142). Cambridge, MA: MIT Press. The article was originally published in 1990 (*Social Text*, 25(26), 56–80).

Fraser, N. (2003) Social justice in the age of identity politics: Redistribution, recognition, and participation. In: N. Fraser and A. Honneth (eds), *Redistribution or Recognition? A Political–Philosophical Exchange* (pp. 7–109). London: Verso.

Fraser, N. (2005) Reframing justice in a globalizing world. *New Left Review*, *36*, 69–88.

Fukuyama, F. (2012) The Two Europes. *The American Interest* [Online]. Available at: http://blogs.the-american-interest.com/fukuyama/2012/05/08/the-two-europes/ (accessed 8 May 2012).

Grinberg, L. and Grinberg, R. (1990) *Psychoanalyse der migration und des exils*. Munich and Vienna: Verlag Internationale Psychoanalyse.

Habermas, J. (1989[1962]) *The Structural Transformation of the Public Sphere: An Inquiry into a Category of Bourgeois Society* (T. Burger and F. Lawrence, trans.). Cambridge, MA: MIT Press.

Herzfeld, M. (2003) Hellenism and occidentalism: The permutations of performance in Greek bourgeois identity. In: J.G. Carrier (ed.), *Occidentalism. Images of the West* (pp. 218–233). Oxford: Oxford University Press.

Hirschman, A.O. (1970) *Exit, Voice and Loyalty. Responses to Decline in Firms, Organizations and States*. Cambridge, MA: Harvard University Press.

Hopkin, J. (2001) A 'southern model' of electoral mobilization? Clientelism and electoral politics in post-Franco Spain. *West European Politics*, *24*(1), 115–136.

Katz, R. (1986) Preference voting in Italy: Votes of opinion, belonging or exchange. *Comparative Political Studies*, *18*, 229–249.

Kellner, D. (2000) Habermas, the public sphere, and democracy: A critical intervention. In: L.E. Hahn (ed.), *Perspectives on Habermas* (pp. 259–287). Chicago, IL: Open Court.

Kissau, K. (2012) Structuring migrants' political activities on the internet: A two-dimensional approach. *Journal of Ethnic and Migration Studies*, *38*(9) (November), 1381–1403.

Lanara, Z. (2012) Trade unions in Greece and the crisis: A key actor under pressure. *Occasional Paper, International Policy Analysis Unit (IPA), Friedrich Ebert Stiftung*, April. Available at: http://library.fes.de/pdf-files/id/ipa/09012.pdf (accessed 19 April 2018).

Lessenich, S. (2013) What's critique got to do with it? Crisis, sociology and change. Plenary Session presentation, 11th European Sociological Association Conference, Turin, Italy, 28–31 August.

Link, J. (2006) *Versuch über den normalismus: Wie normalität produziert wird*. Göttingen: Vandenhoeck & Ruprecht.

Lister, R. (2007) Social justice: Meanings and politics. *Benefits*, *15*(2), 113–125.

Lyrintzis, C. (1984) Political parties in post-junta Greece: A case of 'bureaucratic clientelism'? *West European Politics*, *7*, 99–118.

Malkoutzis, N. (2011) Greece – a year in crisis: Examining the social and political impact of an unprecedented austerity programme. *Occasional Paper, International Policy Analysis Unit (IPA), Friedrich Ebert Stiftung*, June. Available at: http://library.fes.de/pdf-files/id/ipa/08208.pdf (accessed 19 April 2018).

Mouzelis, N. (1978) Class and clientelistic politics: The case of Greece. *The Sociological Review*, *26*, 471–497.

Olesen, T. (2005) Transnational publics: New spaces of social movement activism and the problem of global long-sightedness. *Current Sociology*, *53*(3), 419–440.

Piattoni, S. (ed.) (2001) *Clientelism, Interests, and Democratic Representation*. Cambridge: Cambridge University Press.

Sayer, A. (2005) *The Moral Significance of Class*. Cambridge: Cambridge University Press.

Schrader, K., Bencek, D., and Laaser, C.F. (2013) IFW-Krisencheck: Alles wieder gut in Griechenland? *Kieler Diskussionsbeiträge*. Available at: www.ifw-kiel.de/pub/kd/2013/kd522_523.pdf (accessed 19 April 2018).

Sen, A. (2009) *The Idea of Justice*. Cambridge, MA: Belknap Press.

Sotiropoulos, D. (2012) The social situation in Greece under the crisis. *Basic socioeconomic data for Greece*, 2011. *Occasional Paper, Friedrich Ebert Stiftung*, September. Available at: http://library.fes.de/pdf-files/id/09330.pdf (accessed 19 April 2018).

Thörn, H. (2007) Social movements, the media and the emergence of a global public sphere: From anti-apartheid to global justice. *Current Sociology*, *55*, 896–918.

Tsoukalas, K. (1999) *Social Development and the State: The Setup of Public Space in Greece*. Athens: Themelio (in Greek).

Young, I.M. (1990) *Justice and the Politics of Difference*. Princeton, NJ: Princeton University Press.

12

Social Justice Perceptions, Class, and Institutions in the Contemporary Russian Context

Mikhail F. Chernysh

Theoretical Debate

References to culture have been increasingly frequent in the polemics on the Russian reforms of the 1990s. There are several reasons why the 'cultural turn' is regarded by some social scientists as being more desirable than structural logic. Firstly, it has become a convenient way to enter the current global discourse on the role of culture and its impact on mass behavior. Post-structuralism opened the gates of the structural 'iron cage' and empowered sociology to address issues that had so far been regarded as less important than the patterns of domination and ownership. The post-structural arguments in sociology had a limited impact but they obviously paved the way for cultural logic and its usage to explain social outcomes. It has now become possible to portray an actor as being a carrier of age-long cultural models, rather than just a member of a class, or a subject of domination. Power relations have dwindled to a lower status, considered to be the result of an interaction between the macro patterns, norms of daily behavior, and legitimation procedures.

Secondly, the strengthening of the cultural trend owed a lot to the revitalization of the civilization theory. This theory proposed to regard many of the tendencies of the contemporary world as being an outcome of perennial cultural differences. Civilizations were portrayed as stable entities capable of raising social tensions and igniting social conflicts. In the course of the debate the concept of civilization revealed its inherent ambiguity. On the one hand, it referred to a hierarchical reality that marked a distance between endogenous life and the standards set by the developed countries of the West. On the other hand, it described the cultural proximity characteristics of nations living next to each other. The two definitions merged and gave birth to the critique of culture and calls to submit to the imperative of 'civilization and modernization' – the change of cultural codes in order to bring nations closer to the desired standards of modernity. The empowerment of the civilization argument with a short-time political agenda became one of the novelties of the Russian debate. The new discourse combined the concept of civilization, the critique of culture, and appellation of the political. In this context culture ostensibly arose as a new perspective of the social world, and a tool with which the authorities must operate if they had plans for modernization (Yakovenko, 2012).

Thirdly, the renaissance of the cultural argument resulted from the desire of the architects of the Russian reforms to look for the causes of Russian failure elsewhere than in their own decisions and inept implementations. They viewed culture as a convenient explanatory strategy in which policy effects were mitigated by the domination of stable, age-old models.

The cultural trend could not avoid obvious contradictions and lacunae. If culture was the main determinant of social outcomes then the theory of rational choice, even in its moderated version, broke down into unimportant smithereens. After all, what is rational about a choice if on the micro-level an individual is reduced to reproducing stable cultural patterns. In a way, the strong cultural program morphed into a new (old) grand theory with a ready explanation for all observable phenomena. The Russian society came to be regarded, solely, as an epiphenomenon of its history.

It is precisely in this way that the theory of institutional matrices proposed to analyze the present situation. Svetlana Kirdina (2000) followed in the track of Wittfogel (1976), by dividing societies into two basic institutional types: X and Y, Western and Asiatic. The Russian society naturally fell into the Asiatic category, characterized by redistributive practices – the dominance of the state in the economy and politics. A similar tack was proposed by Simon Kordonsky (Kordonsky et al., 2012), who claimed that the current Russian crisis was provoked by a set of stable attitudes to equality and social justice that determined the structure of society by reviving estates. The estates were abolished in the Russian Federation in 1918 by one of the first laws adopted by the Bolsheviks. The Russian society lived through a long period of dramatic cultural transformation through which estates were condemned as pre-revolutionary and backwater, the relics of the past. Kordonsky, however, insisted that while abolishing some status differences, the Soviet authorities legitimized a new set of inequalities of the same nature. The estates persisted in a specific situation, with the authorities establishing full control of vital resources and the population revealing readiness to tolerate the dominance of the distribution principle. The scheme proposed by Kordonsky could only be possible if: a) public consciousness held uniform perceptions of social justice and ways of its enforcement; and b) the social justice values became immune to social change and could successfully survive revolutions, wars, periods of modernization, and social collapse. Though flimsy and unconvincing, Kordonsky's theoretical claims had a positive silver lining. Social justice as a distinct social phenomenon became the object of a heated discussion in the milieu of Russian social scientists.

The debate around what constitutes justice is not a new one. The issue of justice has been endemic to social thought since early philosophy started reflecting on the nature of good and evil. Plato's *Republic* explored the problematic of justice via questions that Socrates had to handle while traveling a road to a remote place in the company of other philosophers (Plato, 2003). Cephalus claimed that justice was tantamount to 'giving every man his real due' (Plato, 2003, p. 6). This definition sounds akin to the principles of socialist justice: from each according to his ability, to each according to his or her labor. Both versions of the equity principles, ancient and Soviet, appeared rather vague. In both cases, it required a counting agency capable of gauging his or her due, ability, or the amount of work done. In other words, the equity principle implied the existence of a strong institutional setup with its own measurement program. Thrasymachus stated brazenly that justice was what was appropriate for the powerful (Plato, 2003, p. 20). In his interpretation, the relations of domination constituted the real source of justice and its perception: the authorities not only practiced the relations of distribution, but also defined the principles in which the relations were grounded. Polemarchus defined justice as being tit for tat – a way to grant good things to friends and punish enemies (Plato, 2003, p. 9). The principle became a favorite strategy for dictators and tyrants aiming to abduct the state: close friends earn the right to be beneficiaries, while others must face the law, often repressive.

Socrates dealt with all of these definitions through logic. Justice cannot be regarded as the whim of a ruler, because the ruler, whatever his merits, can err on the side of justice. Justice cannot be privatized by a small clique of chosen elites, it cannot be used to do evil things and apply violence on the basis of 'us and them'. The debate made it clear that justice is a public good and depends on the nature of society in which it is practiced. It also emphasized that the matter of justice cannot be downsized to the level of an individual. The implementation of justice is dependent on social institutions, procedures, and, in Ludwig Fleck's definition, to 'thought styles' in a society during each period of its history (Fleck, 1981). The perception of justice is also very likely to be dependent on group membership.

Modern sociology and philosophy addressed the above arguments by seeking a better internal conceptual structure for the justice principle. John Rawls proposed a classical understanding of justice in a country with effective institutions (Rawls, 1990). Following the Kantian logic of exploring reason as the starting point towards moral necessity, he claimed that the understanding of justice comes in a natural way if someone imagines themself in an ideal state of ignorance with zero resources accumulated by the previous generation. In this case, an individual would want justice to include freedom to perform. In a modern society it might be tantamount to free enterprise. It is also paramount that justice incorporates the removal of all barriers that might hinder social mobility. It was also desirable for justice to be based on the principle of societal support for those who did not succeed, for various reasons, in the exploitation of the two previous principles. Any decision in society affecting distribution might be legitimate from the justice point of view if it benefits the underdog of society. Rawls' theory followed in the footsteps of political moves to accept social rights as an important prerequisite of life in a modern society. Amartya Sen claimed that the general theory is unlikely to provide practical guidance in such matters as social justice. Justice or fairness, even if accepted as a general principle of life, requires concrete policy choice, and action on a policy level. Practical moves to amend injustice might be a better way to enforce justice than attempts to theorize it into an ideal state.

Michael Sandel explores justice in the intermediary zones of ambiguity (Sandel, 2010). Is it fair if the rich substitute donations to the state budget for actual service in the army in times of war? Is it fair to sacrifice the life of an individual in order to save the lives of many more individuals? New developments in science contribute to the ambiguity of many issues on the justice agenda. Who has more rights to a child – a biological mother or the woman caring for it? The answer to all these questions is never straightforward. There is always a variance in the ways that a problem can be handled. These and other issues emerge as decisions taken by individuals in their interaction with institutions. They are always a response to state policies and situations defined by social structure, class, and other social group relations.

Survey Hypotheses

The Russian case is a good illustration of the practicalities involved in the implementation of justice principles. Issues of justice became the focal point for a large survey based on a representative sample.[1] There were several key hypotheses that were tested in the survey. The first hypothesis explored the class nature of the contemporary Russian society. If Russian society qualifies as class-based, then resources might be unevenly distributed between social groups and access to resources dependent on one's social position. The second hypothesis focused on the role of institutions. If society is class-based, then institutions might display unusual flexibility in allocating resources. Thirdly, it was deemed necessary to test the attitude of society toward individual action versus collective action to restore justice.

The procedure used to test the hypotheses was based on situation-bound vignettes. A vignette was used to describe a concrete situation that could be regarded by the respondent as common. It specifically focused on technical descriptive aspects of the situation, leaving the respondent to build his or her explanatory logic of the event in question. In each case the respondent was provided with a set of possible answers but could also add his or her own version of events and offer his or her explanations of why and how they happened.

The First Vignette: 'Salesman-thief'

The first of the vignettes introduced the respondent to the following situation. A salesman holds a job in a large trade network, possibly in one of its grocery store outlets. His salary is low and in addition the administration of the store often delays paying him. He responds to mistreatment by stealing some of the products that are entrusted to him, he sells it elsewhere and thereby compensates for the losses in income. A respondent might view this situation as being quite common, given the publicity that some thefts acquired in the Russian media:

programmers fired from an enterprise without fair compensation took their database with them and sold it to the company's competitors; or there was a salesman who used the company resources to boost his own business in order to compensate for wage arrears. In all of these cases a criminal act had been preceded by an act or a sequence of acts that portended injustice. The salesman in question was maltreated by his employers and seemingly had the right to get his compensation, even if his actions violated the existing institutional rules. If the salesman could stay invisible by acquiring the Gyges ring, then he could act with impunity and deal only with his conscience, which would probably not bother him much. In this particular case, however, the respondent has discovered the salesman's activities and must decide how to react to this knowledge.

In the survey there were several options that the respondent can contemplate. Firstly, he or she could inform the law-enforcement agencies, let them know about the theft and thereby stop the law violation. In most societies with developed institutional systems justice is tantamount to law enforcement, and this line of action would be regarded by a large part of the population as being appropriate and morally desirable. This assumption is based on cases where class or gender injuries are accounted for and remedied through court decisions. An illustration of such a possibility is the *Lilly Ledbetter vs. Goodyear* case, which set a precedent on institutional and state interference on behalf of a worker whose quest for equality received great publicity. Lilly had a long record working in the company, received numerous commendations, and in 1996 received a special award from the employer. In 1998 when she was already retired she learned that her equal pay rights had been violated. She appealed to the court against her former employer. A trial by jury pronounced a verdict in her favor and entitled her to compensation for all the losses she had borne while working. The company appealed, and in 2007 the Supreme Court rescinded the court verdict claiming the law can only be used in respect to current violations. The Congress reviewed the case and in 2008 when the Democrats got the majority in the Senate, it adopted a special law that granted overall victory in the case and compensation. If Lilly tried to restore justice privately, and used illegal practices, she would hardly be able to claim public support and become popular in the media.

There are cases, however, when the institutions regulating matters of distribution are either absent or inaccessible. Mary Douglas illustrates this case by Fuller's fictional case of the 'Speluncean Explorers' (Douglas, 1986, p. 4). The case builds around five researchers who are exploring the earth's crust and become blocked in a deep cave. The rescue team is working to help them but is moving too slowly to reach them in time. There are food reserves, but they have run out and it has become obvious that the explorers cannot last on what they have. They are still able to get messages from those who are outside, and when the pressure on them mounts they pose a question: what would the attitude of 'external society' be if they resorted to cannibalism, and sacrificed one of their comrades in order to save the rest? None of the outsiders – a doctor, a philosopher, or a priest – can tackle the question. The result is that the explorers act on their plan and save four of the team by sacrificing one. When they finally are rescued, however, they have to face the Supreme Court, but the judges cannot come to a common verdict. One of the judges claims the men deserve to be exonerated; they were at a distance from societal institutions and had the right to follow their own agreement. The matter of justice was therefore relegated to the level of a small collective that received the privilege to generate their own norms and follow them. The second judge refuses to pronounce a verdict, since the accused were away from society at the time and thus society does not have the right to address their moral problems. The third judge voices a more conventional position by insisting that the accused are guilty of murder. The fourth judge demands an acquittal on the basis that 'human beings should submit to other human beings rather than written laws'. The treatment of the case thus forces upon society a moral and practical dilemma: what happens if formal rules do not work, and what is just is determined by a group of people in their own milieu? It is obvious that the weaker the institutions that enforce the principles of justice, the more leeway individuals will have to agree on their own forms of justice. In this case their judgment depends on contingency and procedure that they adopt to make their decisions acceptable to others.

The respondent whose task was to pronounce his or her own verdict for the 'salesman case' had to use his own judgment to measure distance between the institutions and the individual, assess the possibility of restoring justice through procedure rather than individual action. The respondent had to choose between several models of amending the worker's injuries – institutional, corporate, and compensatory – and, through individual action, had to distance him or herself away from the situation thus avoiding any moral dilemmas.

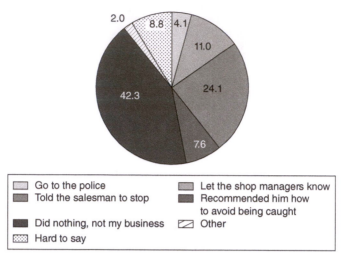

Figure 12.1   Choice of justice models

    The majority of respondents in the first case claimed that they would
do nothing to change the situation and would stay away from any involvement. Close to one quarter would give preference to a private talk with the
respondent in the hopes of convincing him to stop thieving. This group
recognized the case of injustice but disapproved of the way the salesman
chose to amend it. They assumed the role of a judge, but appealed only
to one side of the conflict, displaying sympathy for the salesman but no
understanding of the store management's perspective, and no reliance on
law enforcement. One in ten respondents did not find any justification in
the salesman's actions and would side with the management letting them
know about the salesman's misdeeds. A small, but sizable group came
firmly on the side of the salesman, and became not only his ally, but also
an indirect participant in the crime. The institutional option came out as
the weakest one, supported only by 4.1% of respondents.
    Multiple regression models singled out two variables with significant
influence of the above distribution. The younger cohort appeared to be
less disposed to resort to institutions than the older one, and less inclined
to support the thieving salesman: in the younger cohort only 3.5% chose
the option of going to the police, while in the older cohort the proportion
was twice as high at 6.9%. The younger generation seemed to have less
trust in law enforcement and its ability to restore justice than the 'Soviet'
generation that still harbored belief in relatively unbiased police judgment.

The second factor of importance was the sector of employment. In the state sector a position of non-interference was chosen by 35.5% of respondents, in the private sector an indifferent attitude was assumed by almost half of those questioned (46.4%). The state sector employees appeared to be more inclined to moralize on the consequences of actions, and counsel the sales-man on how to cope with circumstances in a very unpleasant situation (28.4% and 21.7% correspondingly). The position of the state employees is shaped by their specific stance of 'watching it at a distance', because they are less likely to face similar problems of justice in their own places of employment.

The second question concerning the case asked that the respondent des-ignate the salesman's behavior as being either acceptable or unacceptable. The respondent was given three options: full justification of the crime, a divided option, and its full condemnation.

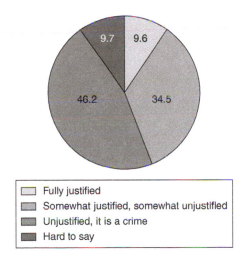

Figure 12.2 Justification of theft

It turned out that 10% were ready to support individual action, at vari-ance with the established way of restoring justice. Close to one third related to the position of partial justification with elements of condemnation, and 46.2% claimed that no considerations could justify the behavior that was running counter to the law. The respondents' judgment was followed by a question on what they would do if they found themselves in a similar situation – seek justice through an institutional setup, act in the same way as the salesman, or make an exit. The choice was shaped as a dilemma of 'voice' or 'exit', a decision to openly challenge management and fight for one's rights or leave the company that violated the justice principles. The 'voice' decision assumed an institutional network that would contribute to the solution of the critical conflict, while the 'exit' option proposed an individual strategy of solving the problem. Expectedly, the largest number of respondents chose an 'exit' option (37%). They would choose to quit the company and try to find another job. One fifth of respondents claimed they would attempt a direct talk with the management. However, it was obvious that in the absence of a developed institutional network (only 6% felt the presence of trade unions at their workplace) this option could hardly bring about amendment for injustice. It is the usual practice of employers in Russia to rid themselves of those who display a proclivity for mooting unpleasant questions. Close to 10% might go to court over injustice, though their hopes of achieving a positive solution did not look very convincing. In contemporary Russia employment practices quite often admit an informal 'envelope' salary payment so that the employer will have a chance at tax evasion. The state statistics allow one to speculate that almost half of all workers get their salary in this way.[2] In court, 'envelope' underpayments would not stand up to scrutiny and could not be a basis for the restoration of justice. 7.5% would appeal to a trade union or a human rights civil organization. A similar proportion would opt for theft, or, in other words, follow in the salesman's footsteps.

Though the 'exit' option is the most popular one, it has structural limitations. Under certain circumstances, for instance, in a small city with undeveloped industries and infrastructure, the 'exit' option looked problematic. Anyone in need of a new job would have to leave the place and migrate to where getting a job might be easier. Hence another hypothesis: the strategy of 'voice' was more popular in small cities or villages, and least popular in capitals – Moscow or St. Petersburg. The hypothesis was tested in a binary logistic regression equation where 'voice' and 'exit' were represented as two alternatives.

There is convincing proof in the data that the first hypothesis on the dependency of the 'exit' on types of settlement is a factor that contributes to the decision-making process of how to handle injustice if it occurs. It also flows from the data that in a crisis situation, when the rights of workers are violated, the 'exit' option becomes problematic. In conditions of crisis, workers are becoming increasingly insistent that the state must interfere to help them correct possible injustices. The federal authorities

Table 12.1 Factors that might contribute to restoration of justice (logistic regression)

Factor	Score	DF	Sig	Exp(B)
Type of enterprise	0.11	1.00	0.74	0.98
Sex	1.56	1.00	0.21	2.08
Age	0.75	1.00	0.39	1.04
Living standards	0.03	1.00	0.86	1.00
Education	0.37	1.00	0.54	0.98
Type of settlement	10.30	1.00	0.00	0.78

usually oblige and hurry to assist with a special set of laws that prevent salary arrears, or the closure of the factory, which is vital for the survival of employees belonging to certain urban communities.

The practice of emergency state intervention is illustrated by the case of the Far Eastern fish-processing factory located on the Shikotan Island. The owners of the company stopped paying salaries and treated workers as though they were prison inmates: 'They made them work for 12 hours, and forced them to live in the hostel where conditions resembled more a prison than decent housing.'[3] A worker wrote in his diary: 'I do not have a mobile phone. They took our mobile phones from us. Only two of us could hide their phones. We called the police, but they did nothing. Food is bad. We are all sick. Each morning they push us to work. After three months they throw workers out without anything. I do not know what to do.'[4] The workers managed to reach President Putin during a direct question and answer line: 'Meet the President'. He ordered Procurator General and other officials to immediately go to the place and start an investigation. When the officials arrived on the island they discovered that there was not one but several enterprises where workers were exploited and kept without payment. When faced with possible harsh prison terms, the factory managers delivered an apology and immediately started to compensate workers for their losses. The authorities promised to keep a close watch on the management so that workers would continue to get their salaries and live in decent conditions. It is symptomatic that the state institutions started to work only when mass violations of workers' rights became public and local officials got a kick from the president himself.

The malfunctioning of institutions, collusion between local authorities and local businesses, and absence of functioning trade unions is conducive to creating a situation where workers appeal to the central authorities. If no assistance is forthcoming from any other quarter, then the state, as a macro institution, comes under fire. The reason is not that the Russian workers or the Russian population regard social justice as being the pre-requisite of the state. In a situation of weak equalizing institutions, they choose the only institution that is effective.

There is one more question that is pertinent for the 'salesman' case. Can the personal circumstances of the salesman's life change the structure of attitudes towards his or her misdemeanor? To test the hypothesis, that a personal portrait matters, a few details were added to the situation. The respondent was made to know that the salesman was also responding to a personal problem. His child was in need of expensive medical treatment, and he was trying to save money to help him. It appeared that the 'personal touch' had very little impact on the evaluation of the salesman's deeds. The proportion of those who justified his actions went up from 9.6% to 14.2%. The change occurred at the expense of those who endorsed his actions any-way, though only partially. As for those who condemned his thieving, their number remained almost unchanged (43.9% and 46.3% respectively). The majority endorsed a view that the perception of justice should be compart-mentalized into a personal and normative agenda. Normative variance is more important in justice perception than personal circumstances.

Institutions and Classes: The 'Doctor's Choice' Case

There was another vignette that was administered to the respondents in the course of the survey: icy roads in the Moscow countryside become the cause of a traffic accident, in which five cars collide. As a result, three peo-ple suffer bad injuries and are in need of an emergency operation. The first of the victims is a highly placed federal bureaucrat, the second the owner of a large trade company, and the third is a local worker. The ambulance takes all three of them to the local hospital. The hospital, like many local hospitals in Russia, does not have facilities that allow three operations to be performed at once. Local surgeons can do only one operation at a time. This implies that only one of the victims can be saved. Respondents were called upon to decide which of the victims were likely to be operated on first, and what would be the reasons that they, and not the others, would get that chance to survive.

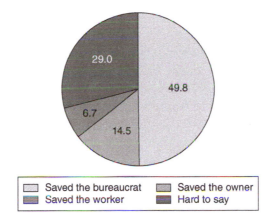

Figure 12.3   The probability of surgeons' choice

Almost half of all respondents decided that the bureaucrat had the best chances of being saved. Close to 30.0% opted for the rich owner. Only 6.7% of all respondents put their chances with the worker. In the public consciousness bureaucrats are regarded as being a group endowed with special privileges that even money cannot beat. In the present system their life is more valuable that the life of any other citizen, and the doctors would have to take this fact into account when making their decision. But what about the institutions? The doctors as professionals have their own code that applies to such situations. If institutional norms that ensure justice are valid, then it is impossible to make the decision prior to know-ing other details. The doctors would have to examine each of the victims, estimate the chances of survival for each of them, follow the instructions that regulate the procedures of choice. In other words, if the principles of justice embodied in the workings of institutions had been relevant, the respondents en masse would have chosen to abstain from answering the question. However, the number of respondents who preferred this option turned out to be much smaller than the number of those who were certain that the choice would be made on other grounds than formal instructions.

It seems that the formal institutions, whose rules are clearly stated, are replaced by a different informal system in which the hierarchy of impor-tance is determined on the basis of social stratification realities. It is worth noting that the special position of the Russian bureaucrats has consistently been accentuated by the Russian respondents as one of the main causes of injustice. In another survey based on the representative sample of the

Saint Petersburg population of 1,500 (a Russo-Chinese study comparing Saint Petersburg and Shanghai), 62% of respondents named the conflict between bureaucracy and the population as being the most dangerous one, a conflict that might possibly threaten the social stability of contemporary Russia. It is also symptomatic that the distribution of judgments did not change in any of the social dimensions against which it was tested – sex, age, education, or participation in decision-making.

The respondents were asked to explain their point of view and mark reasons that contributed to their decision.

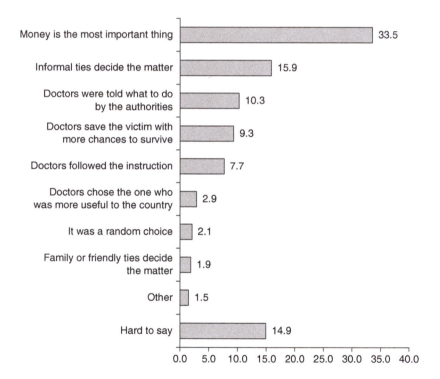

Figure 12.4   The case of 'doctor's choice': motivation of decision

Opinion on how the matter was decided differed. The largest number of respondents chose money as being the most important factor in the doctor's decision. It appears that money works better in the case of a bureaucrat than in the case of a wealthy asset owner. The asset owner is likely to pay for the service done by the surgeons and that would be the end of the story. A Russian bureaucrat, however, has the power to change the way money in the region is distributed. He can allocate government resources to the clinic and benefit the staff of the clinic and the entire region. The second choice is expectedly the informal ties. The doctors would be making their choice because a bureaucrat or an asset owner has an opportunity to influence the local authorities. It is also possible that the doctors might get a direct cue from their higher-ups as to the victim they should save. Only one in ten respondents speculated that the doctors might save the victim whose chances to live were better than those of the others. The number of respondents who believe that the doctors would follow formal instructions was even smaller.

This is the resource of domination explicitly described by Kordonsky as being a cultural predisposition. This would be the case if the inherent values of the Russian culture regarded this situation as natural. However, available data shows that culture and structure moved apart in the judgments that were expressed around this question. The respondents were given a chance to step in and decide who would be saved, based on their own judgment. Almost four out of ten respondents (37.6%) insisted that they would act according to the existing formal instructions. About one quarter of respondents said they would choose the victim with more chances of survival. One in ten respondents said they would take into account the family situation of each victim: a respondent with a large family, a breadwinner for many kids, should be given a greater chance. For the sake of comparison, only 2.4% of respondents would save the victim with more money than the others while 2.9% believed that preference should be given to a person more useful for the country than the others. Regional identity was even less important: only 1.9% said they would favor a neighbor, or a person living near to them.

Discussion

The 'doctor's choice' case proves that a just order recedes when a concrete situation arises and difficult decisions have to be taken. The rules that are imposed by the macro institutions, an embodiment of just decisions, are replaced by another set of institutions that guide matters of choice in concrete situations. The matters of class and status enter the equation when decisions concern concrete individuals belonging to different social groups and classes. It is not that the institutional order is absent. Formal institutions do exist and exert an influence on social life, but in most cases they are ineffective and cede place to institutions that operate on a lower, informal level.

In public consciousness wage arrears or salary cutbacks are regarded as cases of injustice. The 'thieving salesman' does not get public support. His strategies of amending injustice are viewed as basically flawed. Justice turns into legitimate entitlements when it assumes the form of an open procedure – a court procedure or civil action taken on the basis of existing law. However, the majority of Russians are aware of the class bias in the existing law-enforcement and legal system. They know all too well that the system delivers goods for the one who can master resources – wealth or power. The weaknesses of civil society or trade union movements, specifically targeted by the ruling class, empower informal institutions. These are private interactions in which a precarious contract, or an oral contract, can become the basis of decision-making. The classes with more say in the decision-making process, or asset owners (which are often the same people) often use this opportunity to their advantage. Millions of Russians get salaries in the 'envelope', which diminishes their input into pension funds and reduces their future pensions.

No court, or any other formal procedure, can protect a worker from being victimized by an employer who decides to arbitrarily cut down on their wages. Favorite strategies of employers in the 2008 crisis were to fire women who had legitimate child-care leaves, or the handicapped, those who were formally protected by the law. When the situation was not critical, however, most employers tended to stick to their informal agreements with the workers. They knew quite well that the institutional system that favors one class over the other can only be sustained through a regular application of its norms. If informal institutions fail, the workers resort to the strategy of 'exit'. The standard reaction of 'exit' is then extended beyond a concrete relation between an employer and an employee, to a macro context.

If the principles of justice expounded by Rawls as freedom, equality of access to public resources, and social support for the underdog are grossly violated, if policies deviate from the course outlined by Sen (Sen, 2011) as correction of injustice, a minority would opt for direct action and thereby would boost the crime rate statistics. The majority would 'exit' the macro contract of support for the existing system. This ultimate strategy might be quite effective since it weakens the existing informal institutions and deprives macro institutions of their legitimacy. The upshot of the situation is paradoxically the increase of social mobility, including mobility of labor and a boost for emigration from the country. Michael Sandel illustrates this point with conclusions drawn from the 19th-century American Civil War (Sandel, 2009, p. 44). If the wealthy get a chance at draft evasion through bribery, then the poor cease trusting the law and increasingly engage in criminal activity, finding their own ways of draft evasion. The poor regarded the policy of buying up substitutes for army service as a violation of the justice principles.

The case of 'doctor's choice' shows that the weakness of formal institutions capable of ensuring procedural justice is regarded by the respondents as creating policy with the potential to benefit the Russian bureaucracy and primarily the stratum of bureaucracy placed high enough to dispose of state resources. The privileges of the bureaucrats, however, can hardly be qualified as characterizing an estate. Estates are a legitimized form of inequality. In contemporary Russia these privileges are regarded as illegitimate, corrupt, and applied in violation of the principles of justice. If the respondents had been given a chance to regulate the distributional practices, he or she would give a priority to formal rules that regulate the behavior of professional groups and those in power. It is likely they would opt for informal institutions to be relegated to the dark zone of illegal wheeling and dealing. The study showed that the perception of justice is an important basis for the functioning of key institutions with a capability to moderate the effects of the class structure. The Russian society problem does not consist in the prevalence of egalitarian thinking, it lies in the contradiction between the principles of justice embedded in public consciousness and regular informal practices that favor privileged groups. This contradiction breeds social tension and leads many Russian citizens to become skeptical about the level of justice in contemporary Russian society.

Notes

1   The survey was held in 2013 and was based on a probability sample of 2,003 respondents. The PPS principle was applied in order to proportionally represent all six Federal districts. Inside every district six strata were formed on the basis of settlement type. In each stratum, three to six rayons (local regions) were chosen (depending on the number of units) on a random basis. Households were selected randomly in accordance with an itinerary issued to every respondent. Inside households, respondents were chosen on the basis of the Kisch table. The refusal rate was equal to 21% of all households. Some regions in the Northern part of Russia were qualified as inaccessible. On the whole the inaccessible regions constituted no more than 3.4% of the entire population of Russia.

The data processing and analysis was supported by the Russian Science Foundation grant number 14-28-00217 'Intergenerational social mobility from 20th to 21st century: Four generations of Russian history'.

2   *38 zanimautskya nepontyanto chem* [38 million working age Russians are not accounted for in the labor statistics]. Available at: www.vesti.ru/doc.html?id= 1071317&cid=5 (accessed 23 April 2018).

3   *Остров, где не платят зарплату* [An Island where they do not pay salary]. Available at: http://sovsakh.ru/ostrov-gde-ne-platyat-zarplatu/ (accessed 23 April 2018).

4   *Остров, где не платят зарплату* [An Island where they do not pay salary]. Available at: http://sovsakh.ru/ostrov-gde-ne-platyat-zarplatu/ (accessed 23 April 2018).

References

Douglas, M. (1986) *How Institutions Think*. Syracuse, NY: Syracuse University Press.

Fleck, L. (1981) *Genesis and Development of a Scientific Fact*. Chicago, IL: Chicago University Press.

Kirdina, S. (2000) *Institutsionalnie matritsi I razvitie Rossii* [Institutional matrices and the development of Russia]. Moscow: Teis.

Kordonsky, S., Dekhant, D., and Molyarenko, O. (2012) *Soslvnie kompenenti sotsialnoi strukturi Rossii: hipotetiko-deduktivni analiz I popitka modelirovania* [The estate components of social structure in Russia: Hypothetical deductive analysis and attempts at modelling]. Universe of Russia (Mir Rossii), No. 2, 62–112.

Plato (2003) *The Republic* (B. Jowett, trans.). Sharebooks. Available at: www.spiritual-minds.com/philosophy/plato/Plato–The%20Republic%20-%20Rationalist%20Philosophy.pdf (accessed 20 April 2018).

Rawls, J. (1990) *A Theory of Social Justice and its Critics*. Stanford, CA: Stanford University Press.

Sandel, M. (2010) *Justice: What is the Right Thing to Do?* New York, NY: Farrar, Strauss and Giroux.

Sen, A. (2011) *The Idea of Justice*. Boston, MA: Harvard University Press.

Wittfogel, K.A. (1976) *Oriental Despotism*. Hartford, CT: Yale University Press.

Yakovenko, I. (2012) Chto Delat' [What is to be done]. *Novaya Gaseta* [*New Gazette*], 16 March.

13

Re-Discovering Justice

Some Insights from Research on Societal Development and Care in Contemporary Capitalism[1]

Brigitte Aulenbacher and Birgit Riegraf

Justice has always had a bearing on modernity and capitalism, sometimes carrying more weight, sometimes less, in society and sociology. Its precise nature has been defined by the vagaries of contemporary and scientific history, and social geography (see Fraser, 2003; Nussbaum, 2010; Rawls, 1979; Sen, 2010). Since the financial crisis of 2008, and in the wake of austerity policies that have been regaining significance in societies of the Global North, and their respective sociologies, the idea of justice has become increasingly important in the public discourse as well as in labour disputes (Aulenbacher et al., 2017). This societal and sociological re-discovering and resurgence of the justice theme is prompted by increasing experiences of injustice, arising from changes in working and living conditions, which entail social vulnerabilities and existential insecurities (Castel, 2000).

Existential insecurity is indivisibly linked with capitalism, although in the first half of the 20th century the capitalist idea of growth and progress – referring to economy and technology – has been associated with a promise of universal prosperity (Siegel, 1993). What is more, the promise came true, in the second half of the 20th century, when considerable parts of the population in the societies of the Global North enjoyed a brief phase of prosperity. Especially in Western Europe, poverty, scarcity and deprivation gave way to a relative prosperity that seemed to be stable. This applied particularly to the middle classes, which were becoming established, although with the concomitant privileging of men over women, nationals over migrant populations, whites over minorities, etc. (Castel, 2000; Kohlmorgen, 2004; Streeck, 2013). In contrast, infringements of justice remained the normal throughout the Global South, which experienced widespread instances of deprivation (Nussbaum, 2010; Sen, 2010). The Global South has historically represented, and partially continues to represent, the flipside of what Ulrich Brand and Markus Wissen (2011) analyse as the growth-based 'imperial mode of living', which mainly, though not exclusively, proceeds from the capitalist policies and lifestyles of the Global North.

This book's principal line of inquiry – how far justice is a significant societal and sociological issue for the 21st century – is pursued in this essay in three steps. In the first step we discuss how far society's heightened attention to justice issues needs to be seen within the context of developments in contemporary capitalism, which we discuss with reference to sociological studies on Europe. The second step illustrates how such issues surface in the field of care and care work, citing examples from Austria and Germany, but also addressing phenomena that are not limited to these countries. The third and final step is to discuss how far societal developments challenge us to reflect on the connection between a critique of everyday life, a societal critique, and on a more robust cross-correlation of local and global perspectives in sociology, and how far justice constitutes a key issue for both.

Issues of Justice in Contemporary Capitalism

Modern societies see themselves as being meritocratic societies, which have transitioned historically from the aristocracy to the principle of meritocracy. The modern understanding of autonomy and individualism, the promise of equality, as well as what is seen as being just or unjust, cannot be separated from this principle of merit and performance-orientation. Social mobility, and the corresponding status of certain members of society, is enabled by the view of the modern subject as being: an autonomous individual; free and with agency; adult citizens capable of self-care rather than needing care. Thus, status is considered to be based, according to this idea of the modern subject, upon performance (Aulenbacher et al., 2017). In capitalism this is specified and narrowed down insofar as the definition of what counts as performance is based on paid work or is income-based or fixated.

This has been discussed by Regina Becker-Schmidt (2014) in connection with the societal organisation of work and social reproduction. Capitalist conditions of property ownership, and exploitation, the relations of economic and social reproduction are founded on the relations of gender, race and class, and connected with a more or less stable as well as flexible reorganisation of inequalities. Once incorporated into the merit principle, performance-orientation and other patterns of modern thought, however, these social inequalities often become invisible and their injustice goes unrecognised (Klinger, 2003). They may also appear justified or even legitimised by the performance-oriented, merit-based promise of equality. This can occur, for example, when causal assumptions are made about lack of effort or performance, or when the efforts that are made go unrecognised or unappreciated by society (Fraser, 2003). While justice issues touch upon basic principles of modernity, and the foundations of capitalist society, they often are not framed in that way (Aulenbacher et al., 2017).

In the Western European capitalisms, controversies over merit, performance and justice from the second half of the last century referred essentially to the configuration of the triad of employment system, modes of living and welfare state. How it is configured is defined substantially in terms of access to the goods of these societies, and hence in terms of economic, social, cultural and political participation chances. The formulation and assertion of ideas and criteria not only of merit-based and performance-oriented justice (*Leistungsgerechtigkeit*) but also of concepts of justice referring to individual needs (need-based justice, *Bedarfsgerechtigkeit*) and participation (participatory justice, *Teilhabegerechtigkeit*) can be grasped as the outcome of labour policy and socio-political struggles and negotiations in the context of economic prosperity and of expansion of the welfare state in the second half of the last century; how Christoph Butterwegge (2007) has shown with regard to the question of justice and Robert Castel (2000) to the question of redistribution.

In line with Nancy Fraser's (2003, p. 58) norm of 'participatory parity' and referring to the various dimensions of justice mentioned above the question has always been who is entitled to what and why. Here social inequalities can become an issue in many different ways, for both modernity and capitalism. The ideas of merit, performance and justice, handed down historically, are constantly up for renegotiation, they can be criticised and fought, watered down, abolished or legitimised, toughened up. There are historically, intra-societally and internationally, many disparate understandings of what merit, performance and justice and even equality actually mean. What counts as merit or performance, what is seen as being just, which forms of inequality are acceptable, is up for endless debate. It has to be contextualised historically and locally to understand how diverse

concepts of justice and equality as well as the justification and the legit-
imisation of inequality are embedded in the relations of economic and
social reproduction and of gender, race and class in different societies
at different times (Abraham and Tastsoglou, 2016; Aulenbacher et al.,
2017; Fraser, 2007; Riegraf, 2013; Sauer, 2013). This is not, however, the
place to go into such distinctions and to reconstruct how ideas of justice
are developed and embedded. Our emphasis is instead upon the particular developments that are giving rise to new issues of justice through the
societal organisation of work, social reproduction and (social) statehood
in Western Europe.

In the societies of Western Europe, a break has to be mentioned: the
economic crisis in the mid-1970s, precipitated by the opening of the
global economy following the collapse of state socialism (Streeck, 2013)
and complete upheaval of employment systems, modes of living and state
paternalism under those regimes (Österle, 2014) and subsequently under
the auspices of financial market capitalism. After the 2008 financial crisis,
this development – further amplified in the wake of austerity policies –
brought issues of social justice onto the societal agenda in new ways.
Drawing on various strands of research, these can be assigned to the various dimensions of justice depending on the focus of the studies on paid
work, social reproduction or statehood.

Studies in precarity, gender and inequality research, show that in regard
to the employment system, modes of living and the welfare state, previously stable historical compromises – class compromises as well as gender
contracts – have lost their validity; these include the regulation of work
and employment (particularly permanent contractual employment), the
gender-hierarchic division of labour hitherto practised in the nuclear family (the male breadwinner model), and 'social property' (Castel, 2000) in
the sense of an entitlement to benefits of the welfare state. Precarious work
and employment arrangements, more versatile, sometimes more emanci-
pated modes of living, and activation policies of the social state have taken
their place. They are linked to a new primacy of merit-based or performance-oriented over need-based, and participatory principles of justice
(adult worker model, workfare state), and are accompanied by existential
insecurities and social vulnerabilities (i.e. precariousness and precarity).
These vary in scale and impact, however, in the context of intra-and inter-
societal inequalities and polarisations (Castel and Dörre, 2009; Standing,
2011; Therborn, 2013; Völker and Amacker, 2015). Issues of social justice and legitimate expectations of effort and performance, divisions of

work and labour, and social protection entitlements, are being newly debated and contested, both individually and collectively, in the fields of paid work (e.g. performance-oriented policies), with regard to modes of living, and within the social state (e.g. in the context of social investment), as research on the social state, work and gender shows (Aulenbacher et al., 2017; Butterwegge, 2007; Kratzer et al., 2015; Lessenich, 2009; Riegraf, 2013; Sauer, 2013; Völker and Amacker, 2015).

Issues of merit-based and performance-oriented, need-based and participatory justice, transected by the intergenerational and gender aspects, are touched upon in varying ways. As one example of the combination of performance-orientation and gender justice, social investment policies may discover women as a target group in the sense of desirable human capital in the Northern and Western European welfare states that is worthy of support, hence the association of these with equality policies (Sauer, 2013). As a contrasting example, the dramatic dismantling of state benefits in the Mediterranean countries has induced families, and largely women, to compensate public care provision by unpaid work – to the detriment of their own participation in paid employment (Picchi and Simonazzi, 2014). Justice issues surface in society in two ways: on the one hand, social protests are ignited by experiences of injustice; on the other hand, as the understanding of justice is reformulated particularly within the frame of performance-orientation as the new priority, it is paralleled by the legitimation of inequalities going along with the crises of capitalism. The situation in Greece is one, especially stark, example; discourses about austerity are interconnected with discourses about justice, justifying and legitimising the decline of the Greek welfare state by assumptions about (wilfully) inadequate effort of the population to work for their money and welfare (cf. Kentikelenis et al., 2014; Streeck, 2013) Another example is the so-called new underclass debate (*Unterschichtendebatte*, Dörre et al., 2013) or debate about the working class as a 'dangerous class' (Standing, 2011) in Western Europe painting a picture of people's unwillingness to work and justifying the decline of the welfare state or the new line of politics of activation; how Klaus Dörre et al. (2013) criticise the turn in employment and social policies legitimising precarity and inequality.

While these examples are showing how the discussion about inequality and justice is related to performance-orientation and referring to paid work and income-fixation, the organisation of care – meaning all activities to face the contingency of life and to save livelihood in society and everyday life – is another instructive case, because paid and unpaid labour as well as different forms of justice are touched. Therefore it usefully illustrates various dimensions upon which justice issues emerge to instigate societal debate and challenge sociology. This is because care and care work are organised around the functional separation of spheres and sectors and the division of labour. It is carried out in the private sector, provided by the state, and also in the third sector and in domestic households. The societal organisation of care and care work, therefore, affects all pillars of the triad of employment system, modes of living and social state. It goes along with and touches the idea and concepts of merit-based and performance-orientated, need-based, participatory, intergenerational and gender justice. And the societal organisation of care and care work is connected to questions of inequality particularly with regard to the questions of who receives what amount of care, who should provide it under what conditions and who receives care at the cost of whom. We will illustrate this by a few empirical reflections.

Care, Care Work and Justice: The Cases of 24-hour Care and Residential Care Communities

Building on current knowledge from the international sociology of care, three interlocking developments in the societal organisation of care and care work can be discerned. First, care and care work are undergoing a precipitous marketisation and economisation, which subjects them to new patterns of commodification and de-commodification in the private sector, in the state, and in the third sector and private household. Second, worker recruitment and the regulation of job and employment formalities become linked to the trans-nationalisation of labour and politics. Third, new forms of governance and the re-conceptualisation of social statehood influence and change the care regimes. In all these developments, supranational, international, and national influences are observable; for instance in the presence, or absence, of any normalising, steering and/or regulating of these activities (Anderson and Shutes, 2014; Aulenbacher et al., 2014b; Kofman and Raghuram, 2015; Klenk and Pavolini, 2015).

To explore the question of how justice becomes an issue, we select two care arrangements as examples; both of these concern care for relatives. The first case is 24-hour care and its intermediation by home-care agencies, which represent an example of the precipitous transnational commodification of care and care work. The second case, in some ways the complete antithesis of the first, deals with the search for new care arrangements when the desired quality of care provision is not available through the market, the family or the social state. In these cases we are witnessing inter- and transnational tendencies in the marketisation of care and/or the reconfiguration of the welfare state as well as the historical and local contexts in which they are embedded – challenging sociology to consider and analyse both (Abraham and Tastsoglou, 2016).

24-hour Care: Care as a Business and Issues of Justice

The fact that care and care work are done as paid domestic work, and that labour and employment relations are characterised by divisions of labour according to gender, ethnicity and class, is neither historically new nor socio-geographically localised. It is a long-standing and global phenomenon (Anderson and Shutes, 2014). It is nothing fundamentally new for domestic workers to live in the households in which they work. What can be seen as a relatively new phenomenon, are forms of live-in care work based on shuttle migration. Proximity to a border goes along with new transnational care arrangements, first of all in the case of 24-hour care for relatives in, for example, Germany, Austria and Switzerland. This care is often provided by Eastern European women who commute between their countries of origin and employment. They generally reside, for several weeks at a time, in the household where they are paid to supply that care, without giving up their obligations to the family members left behind in their households back home (Haidinger, 2013; Lutz, 2007; Schilliger, 2014).

What is striking is that this form of 24-hour care was legalised around 10 years ago, in Austria, in response to a public outcry. It is now not only tacitly accepted but legally legitimised, a socio-politically subsidised arrangement, which relieves the middle classes, particularly, of care-giving to relatives without forcing them into public, or expensive private-sector, care establishments, which are often considered inadequate (Weicht and Österle, 2016). At the same time, it eases the welfare state's financial burden, since alternatives such as investing in the public sector would be costly. On this basis, for some time and in growing numbers, home-care agencies have been offering intermediary care services in the Austrian market. There is a broad spectrum of intermediary operations, from one-person companies, third-sector providers like Caritas or Volkshilfe, and regional, national and transnational private-sector companies of different sizes. Some of these operate legally, and some operate in the grey area

between legal and illegal practices as regards the nature of worker recruitment, service packages and working conditions (Österle et al., 2013).

How justice issues become significant here, may be highlighted with
reference to three aspects: intergenerational justice; the conservative
Austrian welfare state's expectation of family care-giving for relatives;
and changing modes of living. Issues of justice are particularly relevant
regarding the paid work of female migrants, which replaces the previously
unpaid availability of care-giving from wives, daughters and daughters-in-
law. This transfer of labour responsibility makes it possible to then avoid
answering questions about a gender-equitable division of labour between
men and women, because it redistributes the work among other women
(Aulenbacher et al., 2014a).

From the perspective of merit-based or performance-oriented justice,
which touch on two basic principles of modernity – autonomy and equality –
work and employment relationships arise that operate below the standards otherwise valid in Austria (Weicht and Österle, 2016). Accordingly,
people view 24-hour care critically, yet make use of it for their own con-
venience and thereby condone it. A typical example of this is the notion
of 'slave labour', where migrants accept live-in contracts that Austrian
care workers would not accept. The 24-hour care practice is criticised, yet
becoming a care-giver for relatives is not something these critics would
consider doing themselves (Bachinger, 2015). Besides just this, there are
also powerful ideologemes at work, particularly the 'win–win situation'
discourse. It obscures the relations of dominance and inequalities and
is part of the global pitting of precarities we are witnessing in the field
of care as well as in other fields of work, labour and living conditions.
Arising from judgements made based upon the employment opportunities
in their countries of origin, the female migrants in 24-hour home care are
considered to be winners, while the women (there is no talk of men) as
employers or clients in the receiving countries are also winners who are
relieved of their care-giving tasks (Aulenbacher et al., 2014a).

In Switzerland, a network of domestic care workers has taken court
action against poor labour conditions and has fought for their time on-call
to be recognised as working hours. Such issues speak to the heart of these
work relationships in the light of around-the-clock availability (Schilliger,
2014, 2015). Finally, a complete survey of the websites of care agencies
in Vienna, conducted in July 2016, shows that within the service packages
being offered, need-based and intergenerational justice are being reorganised along market lines. Because of this, accountability is then reassigned

to household purchasing power. As an example: while care services are offered at varying professional, sometimes certified, standards, the familiar atmosphere of being cared for in one's own home is emphasised, and services can be bought like commodities, singly, combined, or in modular fashion by households, care recipients and/or relatives (Aulenbacher and Dammayr, 2016/2017).

If the transnational set-up of such care arrangements is traced, it will be recognised that not only in Austria, and much of Western and Eastern Europe, but also in other regions of the world, new inequality divides are being brought forth. Criticising the metaphor of a global care chain, Helma Lutz and Ewa Palenga-Möllenbeck (2011, 2015) show how new transnational spaces are emerging. Scenarios of being cared for in one region, and in certain parts of the population, go hand-in-hand with being uncared for in other regions or parts of the population. Thus, obtaining justice and suffering injustice stand in regard to the position being held in these care arrangements. In this way, the organisation of care and care work affects the modern principles of merit and performance, autonomy and equality. It is an empirically evident area for critique of everyday life, as the 'slave labour' appellation reveals, but can also be a theme of social protest and a critique of capitalism as we are witnessing in many new forms of care protests (Bachinger, 2015; Schilliger, 2015; Winker, 2015).

Residential Care Communities: A New Pathway of Care Provision?

The curtailment of social protection in Western European welfare states, the emphasis on meritocracy and performance, and policies aligned with the adult worker model are obliging every member of society to take paid employment. Without provision to ease the burden of care and care work, these policies leave households with care gaps, which, as outlined above, are filled by resorting to the labour of predominantly female migrants. In recent years alternative care arrangements like residential care communities (RCCs) have developed and infiltrated these constellations. In reorganising care work by a combination of innovation and reform, these have partially disrupted the previous societal allocation of responsibility and service provision to the 'private' domain, whilst simultaneously aiming to overcome the deficiencies of public service provision. The latter arise because care services offered under competitive market conditions, while often being more professional than those in the domestic sector, do not fulfil the particular demands of care and care work. Care arrangements like RCCs are increasingly attracting socio-political attention, especially when considering how care and care work can be managed in the future. RCCs are being eyed as a possible pathway in solving the care crisis of Western and Northern European welfare states (Reimer and Riegraf, 2016).

The question raised around these care arrangements is whether they will lend any insights into how society might be fundamentally reorganised, as was considered over 20 years ago by Nancy Fraser (1994) in the 'universal caregiver' model. It is an issue that is currently being debated in the context of protest movements and sociological critiques of capitalism, if, and how, there is to be a more (gender) equitable redistribution of care and care work and how the care sector could and should be reorganised in the sense of a new orientation on individual as well as societal needs (Völker and Amacker, 2015; Winker, 2015).

In Germany, RCCs arose predominantly at the initiative of care-giving relatives, because of the inadequacy of public care provision, given the excessive burdens and care gaps that occur when 24-hour care is needed. RCCs are organised in a way that seek to make caring responsibility compatible with the demands of paid employment and other dimensions of life. Depending on time, and the physical and mental resources at their disposal, relatives should be able to get involved in RCCs. RCCs generally rely on a 'mixed provision' of voluntary, semi-professional and professional care and support services, providing flexible care in keeping with a resident's individual needs. RCCs are partly based on the self-organisation of caring relatives to solve the care demands that arise. This means a greater time commitment from relatives than would be required in public establishments. At the same time, staff ratios for semi-professional and professional care in these communities are also higher than in the usual public establishments, which is financed by these same relatives via surcharges. Since care arrangements are organised in line with the individual needs of clients and care receivers, the higher staff ratio and participation of relatives is aimed at meeting care requirements as flexibly and need-appropriately as possible, without neglecting the welfare needs of the relatives as well. Family and public contributions go hand in hand with voluntary involvement and services organised according to market-economic principles. Semi-professionals and professionals team up in the RCCs with relatives. This 'mixed provision' of care touches the dichotomies of modernity and demarcations between the domestic and public sphere. Privacy and professional work become interrelated. This also touches the relation between need-based justice, performance and merit-based justice. The question in such a 'mix' is: what counts as performance and what is considered to be adequate to meet the care receivers' and care givers' needs and interests in terms of intimacy, professionality and justice. The care arrangements in these communities offer a range of care potentials. They can lead to a more equitable distribution of societal care requirements between genders, and within one gender. They are organised in line with the needs of both clients and care-receivers, and what is more, they give recognition to societally necessary care that was previously provided in domestic contexts and remained invisible. The care requirements that are consigned to the domestic sphere in modern societies, along with relevant behavioural requirements like nurturing and emotionality, are now key characteristics of care arrangements in the RCCs. These characteristics are an essential component of the RCCs and should be emphasized within public social services and professional care.

Requirements and behavioural orientations like nurturing, emotionality and approachability are contrary to the societally dominant logic of profit maximisation, self-involvement and assertiveness. By promising – in the sense of the 'mixed provision' of care – decent, high-quality care arrangements in domestic surroundings, designed wholly and flexibly to address care-client needs, particularly emotional needs, these communities provide a professional framework for requirements and behavioural orientations that were previously assigned to the prevue of the family alone. The employees working professionally and semi-professionally within these RCCs also feel considerably more satisfaction with their work situation. These care arrangements are more congruent with their professional self-concept than employment situations in the more mainstream establishments organised under market-competitive conditions, which are subject to the usual rationalisation and new marketisation processes in that sector. RCCs promise better quality and more personalised care of the dependent clients than the mainstream care establishments, and, less visible, are combined with more gender equity, because women's unpaid work and care for relatives in the traditional core family partially is substituted by paid work and combined with better working and employment conditions compared with parts of the care sector. They seek to guarantee this care quality not least by applying more appropriate staff ratios, which they secure by surcharging the relatives financially, and hence in accordance with family resources and attitudes. Some community facilities have approximately twice as many staff available, as do in-home care services, although similar numbers of professionals are employed in both arrangements (Kremer-Preiß and Narten, 2004; Reimer and Riegraf, 2016). Nevertheless, there is no reason to 'romanticise' RCCs; given the declining engagement of the welfare state and restricted budgets, precarious work belongs to their realities, too. Alongside the question of financing and responsibility for tasks, what seems to matter – at least in the care communities involving high personal involvement in self administration – is the sociocultural capital of the caring relatives. In the present circumstances, the time and additional financial costs that this care arrangement means for relatives can only be met by a well-situated middle class.

Thus, this high-quality care is reserved only for a small group and it is based on a welfare state framing the family's engagement by established institutions, rules and professions in the provision of care. These are conditions in the Global North and West that do not mean that civil society's engagement can be found in these countries exclusively. All over the world, initiatives – of the families, the neighbourhood, social networks – are bridging care gaps. The question of how far they are able to initiate and stimulate alternative arrangements and pathways in and of the welfare state only can be answered by analysing them in regard to their specific historical, national and local contexts (Abraham and Tastsoglou, 2016; Aulenbacher et al., 2014b).

Justice as a Key Issue of Society and Sociology

In both cases – the 24-hour care and the RCCs – we are witnessing new forms of commodification and de-commodification of care and care work as a result and going along with labour disputes, the declining welfare states in Western Europe and re-thinking justice in terms of who gives and receives care. Societies in crisis as well as care in crisis is a fundamental problem of the majority of the world population and, as described above, a phenomenon coming back to Western Europe after a period of prosperity. Let us ask two questions: What is the task of sociology? What do we have to think about if the empirically analysed tendencies and development are part of the societal change in the Global North?

Sociology reflects on societal developments, but also mirrors and represents them. The gaps between national sociologies show how hegemony in society goes along with hegemony in sociology, in our field and in others. Feminist scholars, like Regina Becker-Schmidt (2014) or Silvia Federici (2012), are criticising the genuine Andro- and Euro-centrism of capitalism and of sociological and other theories and strands of research reflecting on this mode of economic and social reproduction without considering the inherent relations of gender and race or paying them scant attention (Aulenbacher et al., 2015). In the context of a global sociology Michael Burawoy (2015) criticises the international divide, pointing out that the hegemony of the sociologies of the Global North (particularly the USA) is not only to reflect in terms of the professional standards but also the agendas of the discipline. The Western European sociology and the sociologies of the German-speaking countries are – compared with the Anglo-American sociology – far away from being hegemonial in the scientific discourse, but nevertheless the pattern of agenda setting is the same: the heightened attention towards issues such as precarity, care and justice mirrors and represents developments in these societies. Indeed, such themes had and have been issues already for decades, with strong traditions in women's and gender studies, development sociology and some more strands. But, in general, they have been climbing the sociological agenda, since existential insecurities, social vulnerabilities, care crises and new injustices have escalated to new dimensions affecting not least the formerly privileged, natives, male, high-skilled workers of the Global North or Western Europe. Conversely, and expressed with the requisite sociological self-reflection in mind, the new sociological openness to these issues reflects the discipline's orientation, which is primarily Andro-centric and middle class and Euro-centric or related to the Global North. This prompts the question of what sociology can and should do to pursue these questions of social justice, and to reflect on its own agenda in the sense of a contextualization of empirical findings as well as sociological perspectives (Abraham and Tastsoglou, 2016). Let us address this by looking at the relation between everyday life criticism (*Alltagskritik*) and critiques of society, first, and with the question of local and global perspectives, second. Justice can be discussed as a key issue in both contexts.

First, experiences of injustice and issues of justice are, as François Dubet (2008) described, a momentum within everyday life criticism. They point beyond it by touching on fundamental principles of modernity, such as the entitlement to autonomy, meritocracy and equality. Everyday life criticism refers to justice as a, however contested, promise of modernity and therefore can be seen as a point of departure for criticism of capitalism, too. Our two examples – care as a business case, and the alternative idea of decent care in RCCs – show that justice is a contested terrain in capitalism in all dimensions of merit-based and performance-oriented, need-based, participatory, intergenerational and gender justice

(Aulenbacher et al., 2017). Needs of clients and care receivers in the case of 24-hour care are served at a cost of the working and living conditions and needs of female migrants. The alternative mode of caring in RCCs is middle-class based, therefore exclusive pathway in the reconfiguration of the performance-oriented welfare state. If everyday life criticism refers to experiences of injustice, then the challenge is to place them into a larger context by facilitating awareness of the contexts in which unequal working and living conditions are rooting, the causes and the relations of dominance reproducing them. From an analytical or a theoretical standpoint, we can reflect on capitalism as a system that for inherent reasons is not able to safeguard livelihood and to guarantee a good life for all; on the contrary, its 'structural carelessness' (Aulenbacher and Dammayr, 2014, pp. 69,74) and the forces of destruction are predominant. Nevertheless, what is visible from such a perspective must not be visible in everyday life. Our thesis – inspired by insights from our empirical research as well as research like that of François Dubet (2008) – is that justice can be conceived of as a key issue that helps build a bridge between everyday life experience, and criticism and critiques of a modern society that promises equality and justice, but only provides them for the minority of the world population in contemporary capitalism. Sociology with its wide range of elaborated knowledge about societal relations can contribute to bridging the gap between everyday life criticism and a profound understanding of the societal structures, dynamics and development in which injustice and inequality are rooting.

Second, experiences of injustice and expectations of justice cannot be thought about separately from the various interrelated intersectional inequalities that exist within and between societies. What becomes visible here in the microcosm of care arrangements – the direct gain in quality of life for the cared-for clients at a cost of the uncared-for relatives in the case of 24-hour care or the middle class and the welfare- and middle-class-based pathway of alternative arrangements like RCCs – is also the case in the global macrocosm. This can be seen in the global disparity in working and living conditions and care regimes as well as the care gaps in and between societies (Aulenbacher et al., 2014b). Therefore, when it comes to linking up local and global perspectives, there is another challenge: concepts, ideas, visions of justice and, not less prominent, solidarity in the field of care often are discussed based on analyses of societal developments and criticism of capitalism on the national level without neglecting the transnational and international relations (Winker, 2015), but also without referring to them systematically. Concepts such as the 'imperial mode of living' (Brand and Wissen, 2011) or critiques of the global pitting of precarities are going beyond and are reflecting on the relations between the Global North and South, West and East and the forms of dominance and oppression in contemporary capitalisms prohibiting a good life for all. However, neither society nor sociology can sidestep viewing and studying the societal developments locally and globally (Abraham and Tastsoglou, 2016; Burawoy, 2015), described in the frame of this essay: experience of injustice is a local phenomenon. But injustice itself is a global phenomenon. Thus, justice issues cannot be discussed either societally or sociologically without cross-correlating perspectives, both the local and the global, and without contextualising theories, approaches and findings societally as well as scientifically. This is especially the case when dealing with critical perspectives on society and with the question of how dominance can successfully be replaced with solidarity, embracing a liveable coexistence for all. If justice today is re-discovered in society and sociology and constitutes a key issue for the analysis and critique of contemporary capitalism in the Global North and Western Europe, then the responsibility of the discipline is to be aware of its Andro- and Euro-centric, middle-class orientations. This means to contextualise societal developments – and with them their own sociological agenda – and to bridge the gap between local experiences of injustice and the global tendencies with which they are more or less visibly interconnected.

Note

1   We would like to acknowledge Margaret Abraham and the anonymous reviewers for their worthy and helpful comments.

References

Abraham, M. and Tastsoglou, E. (2016) Interrogating gender, violence, and the state in national and transnational contexts: Framing the issues. *Current Sociology Monograph*, *64*(4), 517–553.

Anderson, B. and Shutes, I. (eds) (2014) *Migration and Care Labour. Theory, Policy and Politics*. Basingstoke: Palgrave Macmillan.

Aulenbacher, B. and Dammayr, M. (2014) Krisen des Sorgens, Zur herrschaftsförmigen und widerständigen Rationalisierung und Neuverteilung von Sorgearbeit. In: B. Aulenbacher and M. Dammayr (eds), *Für sich und andere sorgen, Krise und Zukunft von Care in der modernen Gesellschaft* (pp. 65–76). Weinheim and Basel: Beltz Juventa.

Aulenbacher, B. and Dammayr, M. (2016/17) *Care als Geschäft. Transnationale Arbeitsvermittlung in der 24-Stunden-Betreuung.* Research project, March 2016–February 2017, at the Johannes Kepler University of Linz, Austria.

Aulenbacher, B., Dammayr, M. and Décieux, F. (2014a) Herrschaft, Arbeitsteilung, Ungleichheit – Das Beispiel der Sorgearbeit und des Sorgeregimes im Gegenwartskapitalismus. *Prokla 175, Zeitschrift für kritische Sozialwissenschaft, Schwerpunktheft: Klassentheorien, 44*(2), 209–224.

Aulenbacher, B., Riegraf, B. and Theobald, H. (eds) (2014b) *Sorge: Arbeit, Verhältnisse, Regime – Care: Work, Relations, Regimes.* Soziale Welt, Sonderband 20. Baden-Baden: Nomos.

Aulenbacher, B., Riegraf, B. and Völker, S. (2015) *Feministische Kapitalismuskritik: Einstiege in bedeutende Forschungsfelder mit einem Interview mit Ariel Salleh.* Münster: Verlag Westfälisches Dampfboot.

Aulenbacher, B., Dammayr, M., Dörre, K., Menz, W., Riegraf, B. and Wolf, H. (eds) (2017) *Leistung und Gerechtigkeit: Das umstrittene Versprechen des Kapitalismus.* Weinheim and Basel: Beltz Juventa.

Bachinger, A. (2015) 24-Stunden-Betreuung als Praxis. Identitätskonstruktionen, Arbeitsteilungen und Ungleichheiten – eine Intersektionalitätsanalyse. *SWS-Rundschau, 55*(4), 476–495.

Becker-Schmidt, R. (2014) Abstraktionsprozesse in der kapitalistischen Ökonomie – Ausblendung in der Selbstpräsentation von Männlichkeit. Theoretische Dunkelfelder in der Kritik herrschender Care-Ökonomie. In: B. Aulenbacher, B. Riegraf and H. Theobald (eds), *Sorge: Arbeit, Verhältnisse, Regime [Care: Work, Relations, Regimes]* (pp. 89–105). Soziale Welt. Sonderband 20. Baden-Baden: Nomos.

Brand, U. and Wissen, M. (2011) Sozial-ökologische Krise und imperiale Lebensweise. Zu Krise und Kontinuität kapitalistischer Naturverhältnisse. In: A. Demirović, J. Dück, F. Becker and P. Bader (eds), *Vielfachkrise im finanzmarktdominierten Kapitalismus* (pp. 79–94). Hamburg: VSA Verlag.

Burawoy, M. (2015) *Public Sociology: Öffentliche Soziologie gegen Marktfundamentalismus und globale Ungleichheit.* Reihe Arbeitsgesellschaft im Wandel. Weinheim and Basel: Beltz Juventa.

Butterwegge, C. (2007) Rechtfertigung, Maßnahmen und Folgen einer neoliberalen (Sozial-)Politik. In: C. Butterwegge, B. Lösch and R. Ptak (eds), *Kritik des Neoliberalismus* (pp. 135–219). Wiesbaden: VS Verlag für Sozialwissenschaften.

Castel, R. (2000) *Die Metamorphosen der sozialen Frage: Eine Chronik der Lohnarbeit.* Konstanz: UVK Verlag.

Castel, R. and Dörre, K. (eds) (2009) *Prekarität, Abstieg, Ausgrenzung: Die soziale Frage am Beginn des 21. Jahrhunderts.* Frankfurt am Main: Campus.

Dörre, K., Scherschel, K., Booth, M., Haubner, T., Marquardsen, K. and Schierhorn, K. (2013) *Bewährungsproben für die Unterschicht? Soziale Folgen aktivierender Arbeitsmarktpolitik.* Frankfurt am Main: Campus.

Dubet, F. (2008) *Ungerechtigkeiten: Zum subjektiven Ungerechtigkeitsempfinden am Arbeitsplatz.* Hamburg: Hamburger Edition.

Federici, S. (2012) *Caliban und die Hexe: Frauen, der Körper und die ursprüngliche Akkumulation.* Wien: Mandelbaum.

Fraser, N. (1994) After the family wage: Gender equity and the welfare state. *Political Theory, 22*(4), 591–618.

Fraser, N. (2003) Soziale Gerechtigkeit im Zeitalter der Identitätspolitik: Umverteilung, Anerkennung und Beteiligung. In: N. Fraser and A. Honneth (eds), *Umverteilung oder Anerkennung? Eine politisch-philosophische Kontroverse* (pp. 13–128). Frankfurt am Main: Suhrkamp.

Fraser, N. (2007) Zur Neubestimmung von Gerechtigkeit in einer globalisierten Welt. In: L. Heidbrink and A. Hirsch (eds), *Staat ohne Verantwortung? Zum Wandel der Aufgaben von Staat und Politik* (pp. 343–372). Frankfurt am Main: Campus Verlag.

Haidinger, B. (2013) *Hausfrau für zwei Länder sein: Zur Reproduktion des transnationalen Haushalts.* Münster: Verlag Westfälisches Dampfboot.

Kentikelenis, A., Karanikolos, M., Reeves A., McKee, M. and Stuckler, D. (2014) Greece's health crisis: From austerity to denialism. *The Lancet, 383,* 748–753.

Klenk, T. and Pavolini, E. (eds) (2015) *Restructuring Welfare Governance: Marketisation, Managerialism and Welfare State Professionalism.* Aldershot: Edward Elgar.

Klinger, C. (2003) Ungleichheit in den Verhältnissen von Klasse, Rasse und Geschlecht. In: G.A. Knapp and A. Wetterer (eds), *Achsen der Differenz. Gesellschaftstheorie und feministische Kritik II* (pp. 14–48). Münster: Verlag Westfälisches Dampfboot.

Kofman, E. and Raghuram, P. (2015) *Gendered Migrations and Global Social Reproduction.* Basingstoke: Palgrave Macmillan.

Kohlmorgen, L. (2004) *Regulation, Klasse, Geschlecht: Die Konstituierung der Sozialstruktur im Fordismus und Postfordismus.* Münster: Verlag Westfälisches Dampfboot.

Kratzer, N., Menz, W., Tullius, K. and Wolf, H. (2015) *Legitimationsprobleme in der Erwerbsarbeit: Gerechtigkeitsansprüche und Handlungsorientierungen in Arbeit und Betrieb.* Baden-Baden: Nomos.

Kremer-Preiß, U. and Narten, R. (2004) *Betreute Wohngruppen: Struktur des Angebotes und Aspekte der Leistungsqualität.* Pilotstudie. Köln: Bertelsmann Stiftung.

Lessenich, S. (2009) Mobilität und Kontrolle: Zur Dialektik der Aktivgesellschaft. In: K. Dörre, S. Lessenich and H. Rosa (eds), *Soziologie – Kapitalismus – Kritik: Eine Debatte* (pp. 126–177). Frankfurt am Main: Suhrkamp.

Lutz, H. (2007) *Vom Weltmarkt in den Privathaushalt: Die neuen Dienstmädchen im Zeitalter der Globalisierung.* Opladen: Verlag Barbara Budrich.

Lutz, H. and Palenga-Möllenbeck, E. (2011) Das Care-Chain-Konzept auf dem Prüfstand: Eine Fallstudie der transnationalen Care-Arrangements polnischer und ukrainischer Migrantinnen. *GENDER. Zeitschrift für Geschlecht, Kultur und Gesellschaft, 3*(1), 9–27.

Lutz, H. and Palenga-Möllenbeck, E. (2015) Care-Arbeit, Gender und Migration: Überlegungen zu einer Theorie der transnationalen Migration im Haushaltsarbeitssektor in Europa. In: U. Meier-Gräwe (ed.), *Die Arbeit des Alltags: Gesellschaftliche Organisation und Umverteilung* (pp. 181–199). Wiesbaden: Springer VS.

Nussbaum, M.C. (2010) *Die Grenzen der Gerechtigkeit: Behinderung, Nationalität und Spezieszugehörigkeit.* Frankfurt am Main: Suhrkamp.

Österle, A. (2014) Care-Regime in den neuen EU-Mitgliedsstaaten. In: B. Aulenbacher, B. Riegraf and H. Theobald (eds), *Sorge: Arbeit, Verhältnisse, Regime – Care: Work,*

Relations, Regimes (pp. 363–378). Soziale Welt. Sonderband 20. Baden-Baden: Nomos.

Österle, A., Hasl, A. and Bauer, G. (2013) Vermittlungsagenturen in der 24-h-Betreuung'. *WISO – Wirtschafts- und sozialpolitische Zeitschrift, 36*(1), 159–172.

Picchi, S. and Simonazzi, A. (2014) The Mediterranean care model in times of austerity. The case of Italy and Spain. In: B. Aulenbacher, B. Riegraf and H. Theobald (eds), *Sorge: Arbeit, Verhältnisse, Regime. Care: Work, Relations, Regimes* (pp. 379–395). Soziale Welt. Sonderband 20. Baden-Baden: Nomos.

Rawls, J. (1979) *Eine Theorie der Gerechtigkeit* [English original: *A Theory of Justice*, 1971; Übersetzung: Hermann Vetter]. Frankfurt am Main: Suhrkamp.

Reimer, R. and Riegraf, B. (2016) *Geschlechtergerechte Care-Arrangements? Zur Neuverteilung von Pflegeaufgaben in Wohn-Pflege-Gemeinschaften.* Weinheim and Basel: Beltz Juventa.

Riegraf, B. (2013) New Public Management, die Ökonomisierung des Sozialen und (Geschlechter) Gerechtigkeit. Entwicklungen in der Fürsorge im internationalen Vergleich. In: E. Appelt, B. Aulenbacher and A. Wetterer (eds), *Gesellschaft: Feministische Krisendiagnosen* (pp. 127–143). Münster: Verlag Westfälisches Dampfboot.

Sauer, B. (2013) Komplexe soziale Ungleichheiten, Citizenship und die Krise der Demokratie. In: E. Appelt, B. Aulenbacher and A. Wetterer (eds), *Gesellschaft: Feministische Krisendiagnosen* (pp. 167–185). Münster: Verlag Dampfboot Verlag.

Schilliger, S. (2014) *Pflegen ohne Grenzen? Polnische Pendelmigrantinnen in der 24h-Betreuung. Eine Ethnographie des Privathaushalts als globalisiertem Arbeitsplatz.* PhD dissertation. Basel: University of Basel.

Schilliger, S. (2015) 'Wir sind doch keine Sklavinnen!' – (Selbst-) Organisierung von polnischen Care-Arbeiterinnen in der Schweiz. Available at: www.zeitschrift-luxemburg.de/wir-sind-doch-keine-sklavinnen (accessed 23 April 2018).

Sen, A.K. (2010) *Die Idee der Gerechtigkeit.* München: C.H. Beck Verlag.

Siegel, T. (1993) Das ist nur rational, ein Essay zur Logik der sozialen Rationalisierung. In: D. Reese, E. Rosenhaft and C. Sachse (eds), *Rationale Beziehungen? Geschlechterverhältnisse im Rationalisierungsprozeß* (pp. 363–396). Frankfurt am Main: Suhrkamp.

Standing, G. (2011) *The Precariat: The New Dangerous Class.* New York, NY: Bloomsbury.

Streeck, W. (2013) *Gekaufte Zeit: Die vertagte Krise des demokratischen Kapitalismus,* Frankfurter Adorno-Vorlesungen 2012. Berlin: Suhrkamp.

Therborn, G. (2013) *The Killing Fields of Inequality.* Cambridge: Polity Press.

Völker, S. and Amacker, M. (eds) (2015) *Prekarisierungen: Arbeit, Sorge und Politik.* Reihe Arbeitsgesellschaft im Wandel. Weinheim and Basel: Beltz Juventa.

Weicht, B. and Österle, A. (eds) (2016) *Im Ausland zu Hause pflegen: Die Beschäftigung von MigrantInnen in der 24-Stunden-Pflege.* Wien: Lit-Verlag.

Winker, G. (2015) *Care Revolution: Schritte in eine solidarische Gesellschaft.* Bielefeld: Transcript.

Index